The Complete Alkaline Diet Cookbook for Beginners

A Complete Acid-Base Balance Healthy Guideline with 600 Healthy and Easy-to-Follow Recipes to Get More Energy and Live Better

By Edward Taylor

Copyright© 2022 By Edward Taylor

All Rights Reserved.

No part of this guide may be reproduced, transmitted, or distributed in any form or by any means without permission in writing from the publisher except in the case of brief quotations embodied in critical articles or reviews.

Legal & Disclaimer

The content and information in this book is consistent and truthful, and it has been provided for informational, educational and business purposes only.

The content and information contained in this book has been compiled from reliable sources, which are accurate based on the knowledge, belief, expertise and information of the Author. The author cannot be held liable for any omissions and/or errors.

Content

Introduction ... 1

Chapter 1: Understanding the Alkaline Diet 101 — 2

What is the Alkaline Diet? ... 2
Understanding PH Balance in the Body ... 2
The Benefits of Alkaline Diet and Alkaline-Forming Foods ... 3
Following the 80/20 Rule ... 4
Alkaline-Forming Foods to Enjoy ... 5
Acid-Forming Foods to Avoid ... 6
Neutral Foods to Limit ... 7
Tips and Techniques for Adhering to the Alkaline Diet ... 7
Alkaline Diet FAQs ... 8

Chapter 2: Breakfast — 11

Kale Sweet Potato and Onion Breakfast Hash ... 11
Baked Squash and Apples ... 11
Garlicky Spaghetti Squash Hash Browns ... 11
Overnight Mango Banana Oats ... 12
Maple Oat Coconut Flax Granola ... 12
Margherita Pizza with Veggies ... 12
Chilled Vanilla Granola Bars ... 13
Chilled Pumpkin Seed-Protein Oats Balls ... 13
Breakfast Mixed Vegetable Fajitas ... 13
Sushi Avocado Hand Roll ... 14
Banana Alkaline Breakfast Bars ... 14
Creamy Vegan Mayonnaise Deviled Eggs ... 14
Baked Apples with Walnuts ... 15
Banana Date Muffins ... 15
Carrot Fruit Breakfast Porridge ... 15
Chickpea Salad Burritos ... 17
Carrot, Hemp Seed and Oat Muffins ... 17
Blueberry Flax Oats Muffins ... 17
Herbed Breakfast Bean Sausage ... 18
Homemade Nutty Amaranth ... 18
Mushroom Pepper Fajitas ... 18
Spelt Banana Walnut Bread ... 19
Nori Avocado Zucchini Burritos ... 19
Walnut Kamut Porridge ... 19
Healthy Kamut Porridge with Dates ... 19
Amaranth Porridge with Walnuts ... 20
Sweet Oatmeal Porridge with Mango-Chia Fruit Jam ... 20
Amaranth Walnut Polenta ... 20
Amaranth and Black Quinoa Porridge ... 20
Vegan Baked Portobello with Avocado ... 21

Zucchini Hummus and Lettuce Wrap 21

Chapter 3: Vegetable — 23

Cucumber Asparagus Hummus Sandwiches 23
Barbecued Mango Zucchini Stuffed Mushroom Sliders 23
Brussels Sprouts with Ginger Sauce 23
Sautéed Eggplant and Spinach with Quinoa 24
Spicy Eggplant and Bell Pepper Stir-Fry 24
Baked Cheesy Potato and Onion 24
Carrot Fennel Slaw with Dijon Vinaigrette 25
Stuffed Mushroom Mini-Pizzas 25
Jalapeño, Cilantro and Lentil "Burgers" 25
Almond Spiced Baked Onion Rings 26
Baby Potato Fries with Mushroom 26
Avocado Toast with Spinach Basil Walnut Pesto 26
Roasted Garlic 27
Garlic Broccoli Bites 27
Stuffed Sweet Potato with Broccoli-Almond Pesto 27
Tomato Zoodles with Avocado Sauce 28
Sweet Potato "Toast" with Spicy Garlic Avocado Topping 28
Red Pepper Tapenade Eggplant Rollups 28
Spiced Tomato Okra Curry 29
Healthy Stir-Fry Mixed Vegetables 29
Zucchini and Kale Pesto with Spaghetti Squash 29
Homemade Roated Garlic Cabbage 30
Root Vegetable Chips 30
Garlic Almond Breadsticks 30
Zucchini Linguine with Avocado Sauce 31
Rosemary, Carrot and Sweet Potato Medallions 31
Potato, Cauliflower and Broccoli Mash 31
Easy Baked Sweet Potato and Apple 32
Garlic Mushroom Pâté 32
Garlic Bell Pepper-Stuffed Portobello Mushrooms 32

Cauliflower Popcorn 34
Garlic Lentil and Sweet Potato Taco Wraps 34
Cauliflower, Almond and Date Porridge 34
Cheesy Baked Kale Chips 35
Roasted Zucchini Lasagna 35
Nori Vegetable Rolls with Avocado-Jalapeño Spread 35
Vanilla Spiced Quinoa Pumpkin Casserole 36
Nutty Spinach, Artichoke and Tomato Dip 36
Tomato Mushroom Stuffed Eggplant 36
Quinoa Vegetable Stuffed Peppers 37
Baked Buffalo Cauliflowers 37
Lettuce, Zucchini and Hummus Wrap 37
Grilled Vegetable Stuffed Mushrooms 38
Mixed Vegetable Pancakes 38
Garlic Cashew Cream–Stuffed Mushrooms 38
Baked Sweet Potato Fries 39
Mixed Vegetable Potpie 39
Lentil Tacos with Onions and Bell Peppers 39
Squash "Noodles" with Tomato Spaghetti Sauce 40
Onion Sautéed Kale 40
Sweet Potato Slices with Garlic Artichoke Spread 40
Jamaican Jerk Vegetable Patties 41
Fresh Vegetable Pizza with Garlic Tahini-Beet Spread 41
Homemade Easy Roasted Vegetables 42
Avocado Tomato Guacamole 42
Garlic Broccoli Carrot Bake 42
Hummus, Carrots and Pesto Lettuce Wraps 42
Spiced Zucchini Dish 43
Morning Mixed Vegetables 43
Pasta with Alkaline Sauce and Veggies 43

Chapter 4: Grains and Rice — 45

- Alkaline Veggies Fried Rice 45
- Avocado Tomato and Basil Pasta 45
- Baked Nutty Macaroni 45
- Vanilla Rice Treats 46
- Easy Spelt Pasta 46
- Date Cashew Oat Bites with Raisins 46
- Walnut, Spinach and Basil Pesto with Pasta 47
- Baked Vanilla Bean and Cinnamon Granola 47
- Wild Rice, Mushroom Leek and Miso Soup 47
- Cinnamon Mango Quinoa Porridge 49
- Mixed Vegetable Fried Rice 49
- Stir Fried Kale Mushroom Wild Rice 49
- Stir Fried Mushroom Wild Rice 49
- Brown Rice Stevia Porridge 50
- Quinoa and Wild Rice with Cherries 50

Chapter 5: Bean and Legume — 52

- Ginger Green Beans Almondine 52
- Chickpea Falafel 52
- Black Bean Pumpkin Chili 52
- Homemade Easy Chickpea Quinoa Burgers 53
- Alkaline Chickpeas Hot Dogs 53
- Broiled Chinese-Style Green Beans 53
- Quinoa Vegetable Casserole 54
- Black Bean Vegetable Tostada with Avocado 54
- Vegetable and Garbanzo Bean Burger 54
- Garlicky Parsley and Tahini Hummus 55
- Tahini Fennel-Seasoned Falafel with Hummus Dressing 55
- Chickpea Mushroom Loaf 55
- Easy Homemade PB Frosting 57
- Roasted Chickpea and Kale 57
- Healthy Eggplant Hummus 57
- Tahini Hummus with Crudités 57
- Whipped Aquafaba Cream 58
- Teff Chickpea Sausage 58
- Easy Healthy Hummus 58
- Chickpea Sloppy Joe 58
- Mashed Chickpeas 59
- Revitalizing Onion and Chickpea Dish 59
- Delicious Onion Chickpea Nuggets 59

Chapter 6: Salads — 61

- Fresh Salsa Fresca 61
- Apple Grape Dates Waldorf Salad 61
- Curried Almond and Raisin Tofu Salad with Greens 61
- Lime Summer Fruit Salad 62
- Garlicky Green Olive Pasta Salad 62
- Date and Watermelon Tofu "Feta" Salad 62
- Hawaiian Fruit Veggie Salsa 63
- Chickpea Rainbow Salad with Mango-Lemon Salsa 63
- Chopped Veggie Salad with Garlic-Avocado Dressing 63
- Peach Basil Salad with Sweet Orange Dressing 64
- Tofu Salad 64
- Peach Cilantro Salsa Salad with Sweet Lemon Tahini Dressing 64
- Avocado and Orange Salad 65
- Pineapple Cabbage Salad with Garlic-Lime Vinaigrette 65
- Lemon and Red Lentil Pasta Salad with Sautéed Vegetables 65

Mixed Melon Salad 66

Vegetable and Blueberry Salad with Roasted Garlic and Miso Dressing 66

Warm Garlic Asparagus Salad with Lemon-Cashew Dressing 66

Avocado, Cucumber and Quinoa Salad 67

Strawberry Spinach Salad with Mustard Dressing 67

Warm Garlic Sweet Potato Salad with Spicy Cashew Cilantro Dressing 67

Garlicky Orange Broccoli Salad 68

Asian-Style Vegetable Salad 68

Garlic Mushroom and Lentil Salad with Lime Tahini Dressing 68

Russian Style Beet Salad 69

Roasted Vegetable Salad 69

Roasted Artichoke Salad with Sesame Seed Dressing 69

Zucchini, Radish and Spring Greens Salad 70

Amaranth Bowl with Butternut Squash and Collard Greens 70

Roasted Carrot and Onion Salad with Cashew-Miso Dressing 70

Baby Tomato and Kale Salad 72

Roasted Broccoli Salad with Spicy Cashew Dressing 72

Lime Dandelion and Strawberry Salad 72

Warm Spinach Mushroom Salad 73

Sautéed Onion and Strawberry Dandelion Salad 73

Fresh Herb Potato Salad with Lime Garlic Dressing . 73

Over-Night Marinated Beans Carrot Salad 74

Broccoli, Asparagus and Quinoa Salad 74

Thai-Style Vegetable Salad 74

Mango and Mixed Veggies Salad 75

Roasted Beet and Kale Salad with Lemon-Garlic Dressing 75

Roasted Chickpea and Avocado Salad 75

Vegetable Salad Lettuce Wrap 76

Summer Veggies Salad 76

Cranberry, Brussel Sprouts and Quinoa Salad 76

Stick Salad 76

Spinach and Strawberry Avocado Salad 77

Romaine Lettuce and Onion Salad 77

Spring Salad with Walnuts 77

Spicy Wakame Pepper Salad with Sesame Seeds 77

Cabbage Almond Slaw 78

Sea Vegetables Salad 78

Kale Tomato and Avocado Salad 78

Wakame Lime Salad 78

Amaranth Chickpea Salad 79

Fonio and Mixed Veggies Salad 79

Olive and Mixed Vegetable Salad 79

South of the Border Chopped Salad 79

Cucumber Arugula Detox Salad 80

Healthy Watercress Cucumber Salad 80

Orange Arugula Salad 80

Avocado, Kale and Sprouts Salad 80

Watercress Avocado and Onion Salad 81

Grilled Romaine Lettuce with Lime Dressing 81

Spicy Vegetable and Squash "Noodle" Salad 81

Chapter 7: Soup and Stew 83

Squash and Onion Soup 83

Avocado, Zucchini and Basil Soup with Pumpkin Seeds 83

Creamy Roasted Carrot and Tomato Soup 83

Garlic Coconut and Jalapeño Soup 84

Garlic Ginger and Pear Soup 84

Garlic Onion and Kale Soup 84

Chilled Zucchini Cucumber and Lime Soup 85

Artichoke, Potato and Asparagus Soup 85

Creamy Mushroom Coconut Soup 85

Zucchini Chickpea and Kale Soup 86	Vegan "Beef" Stew 92
Creamy Coconut Squash Soup 86	Kamut Squash and Chickpeas Soup 92
Creamy Mushroom Clams Chowder 86	Spiced Mixed Vegetable Soup 92
Chayote Mushroom Chickpea Stew 87	Creamy Onion Mushroom Soup 93
Chilled Berry Lemon and Mint Soup 87	Lemon Cashew Tarragon Soup 93
Creamy Spinach Zucchini Soup 87	Vegan Mushroom Chowder 93
Garlic Parsnip Leek Soup 88	Cucumber Avocado Gazpacho 94
Garlicky Broccoli and Potato Soup 88	Creamy Cucumber Avocado Gazpacho 94
Lentil, Carrot and Potato Stew 88	Onion and Butternut Squash Soup 94
Watermelon Jalapeño Gazpacho 89	Spicy Soursop and Kale Squash Soup 94
Pumpkin Apple and Date Soup with Raisins 89	Alkaline Zucchini Green Soup 95
Squash and Mushroom Soup 89	Vegetable Spelt Noodles Soup 95
Mushroom Gravy with Walnuts 91	Broccolini, Bok Choy and Rice Soup 96
Easy Roasted Garlic Cauliflower Soup 91	Roasted Carrot Soup 96
Spiced Tomato Bean and Bell Pepper Soup 91	

Chapter 8: Dessert and Snack   98

Ginger Date Spice Pudding 98	Vanilla Bean, Coconut and Cashew Truffles 104
Dates, Spelt and Raisin Cookies 98	Peach Banana Muffin with Walnuts 104
Almond and Sweet Potato Waffles 98	Vanilla Almond and Quinoa Muffins 104
Nondairy Sour Cashew Cream 99	Easy Roasted Okra Bites 105
Spiced Flatbread 99	Ginger Rhubarb Pumpkin Pie 105
Sesame and Hemp Seed Oatmeal Cookies 99	Baked Onion Rings 105
Onion Rye Crackers 100	Amaranth and Chickpea Pancakes 106
Santa's Ginger Coconut Snaps 100	Thanksgiving Pumpkin Pudding 106
Spiced Chickpea French Fries 100	Chia Seed – Cashew Cookies 106
Strawberry Spelt Sorbet 101	No Baking Fig Almond Balls 108
Garlic-Jicama Fries with Scallion Cashew Dip .. 101	Nut Cheesecake with Strawberry and Mango . 108
Easy Homemade Tortillas 101	Self-Frosting Pineapple Carrot Cake 108
Healthy Blueberry Muffins 102	Burro Banana Walnut Muffin 109
Frozen Cashew Butter Fudge 102	Vegan Mushroom Chickpea Fritters 109
Butternut Squash Pie 102	Flourless Cashew and Pumpkin Seed Cookies . 109
Baked Spelt Biscuits 103	Coconut Cashew Almond and Date Bars 110
Easy Homemade Cashew and Almond Butters . 103	Herbed Almond Crackers 110
Vanilla Snickerdoodle Cookies 103	Almond Tarragon Crackers 110

Walnut Date Balls with Sesame Seeds 111
Basic Pie Crust 111
Black Sapote and Nuts Pudding 111
Spelt Banana Walnut Pancakes 111
Date Carrot Cake Cookies with Cashew Cream Frosting 112
Avocado Lime and Tomato Toast 112
Spicy Garlic Almonds 112
Coconut Chocolate and Date Cookies 113
Blueberry Banana Sea Moss Pudding 113
Blueberry Coconut Spelt Pancakes 113
Vanilla Orange Apple Pie 114
Zucchini Banana Bread Pancakes with Walnuts 114
Coconut and Date Energy Balls with Walnuts 114
Vegetarian Chickpea Mushroom Sausage Links 114
Homemade Ravioli 115
Zucchini Kale and Amaranth Patties 115
Chickpea Flour Vegetable Quiche 116
Healthy Crackers with Sesame Seeds 116

Chapter 9: Smoothies 118

Fruit and Veggie Smoothie 118
Apple and Dandelion Green Smoothie 118
Pineapple Spinach Smoothie 118
Cherry and Watermelon Smoothie 118
Kale, Avocado and Banana Smoothie 119
Ginger Kale and Lemon Green Smoothie 119
Pineapple Banana and Kale Smoothie 119
Spinach Cucumber Liquid Guacamole 119
Blackberry, Banana and Avocado Smoothie 120
Lettuce, Kale and Peach Protein Smoothie 120
Date Almond Raspberry Smoothie 120
Nutty Coconut Sea Moss Smoothie 120
Ginger Pear Green Sparkling Smoothie 121
Avocado Blueberry Green Smoothie 121
Homemade Chocolate Cherry Smoothie 121
Mango Kiwi and Cashew Smoothie 121
Tropical Piña Smoothie 122
Vanilla Coconut Ice Cream Sundae with Fruit 122
Avocado Cucumber Smoothie 122
Homemade Gazpacho Smoothie 122
Mixed Berry Banana Smoothie 123
Spinach, Blueberry and Mango Smoothie 123
Apple, Avocado and Pear Smoothie 123
Vegan Dandelion Detox Smoothie 123
Peach, Orange and Kale Smoothie 125
Banana, Raspberry and Lime Smoothie 125
Papaya, Mango and Raspberry Smoothie 125
Healthy Orange Banana Smoothie 125
Kale Detox Smoothie 126
Hemp Seed and Banana Chard Smoothie 126
Berry Peach Sea Moss Smoothie 126
Kiwi, Blueberry and Hemp Seed Smoothie 126
Sunshine Fruit Smoothie 127
Spinach Peach Green Smoothie 127
Recovery Strawberry and Watermelon Smoothie 127
Nutty Mixed Berry Smoothie 127
Triple Berry Protein Coconut Smoothie 127
Sweet Peach Smoothie 128
Breakfast Quinoa Melon Smoothie 128
Banana Mango Smoothie 128
Apple and Berries Smoothie 128
Apple Pie Sea Moss Smoothie 128
Nutty Vanilla Banana Smoothie 129
Irish Walnuts Moss Milkshake 129
Zucchini, Avocado and Dandelion Green Smoothie 129
Nutty Strawberry Shake 130

Apple Banana Sea Moss Delight 130

Warm Garlic Ginger and Lemon Smoothie 130

Chapter 10: Fruit — 132

Apple Slices with Peanut Butter and Granola 132

Baked Garlicky Almond Avocado Fries 132

Nutty Banana Berry Chia Pudding 132

Baked Raisins Stuffed Apples 133

Baked Peach Coconut Cobbler 133

Baked Vanilla Fruit Granola 133

Watermelon Greens Salad with Basil Vinaigrette 134

Homemade Apple Butter 134

Sweet Blueberry and Chia Seed Vanilla Cobbler 134

Almond and Coconut Stuffed Dates 135

Sweet Thumbprint Cookies with Blueberry–Chia Seed Jam 135

Baked Oatmeal Stuffed Apple Crumble 135

Baked Grapefruit and Coconut 136

Vanilla Apple Pie Crumble 136

Chia Seed and Strawberry Overnight Oats Parfait 136

Mixed Berry Chia Seed Coconut Pudding 137

Banana Walnut Muffins 137

Pear Nachos and Almond Butter Drizzle with Almond 137

Winter Warm Fruit Compote 139

Blackberry Lime Jam 139

Fresh Fruit with Vanilla Cashew and Lemon Cream 139

Chilled Mango Lime Pepper Slaw 140

Banana Almond Spilts with Cherry 140

Sweet Chia Seed Fruit Jam 140

Vanilla Banana and Cashew Cream 140

Quick Blueberry-Banana Ice Cream 141

Summer Fruit Vanilla Pops 141

Banana Veggies Fries 141

Coconut Banana Candy Coins 141

Kale and Almond Stuffed Avocados 142

Spiced Party Mix 142

Blackberry Banana Bars 142

Avocado, Banana and Strawberry Ice Cream 143

Cream Berry Peach Parfait 143

Lemon Blueberry and Banana Soft Serve 143

Chapter 11: Bowl — 145

Barbecued Broccoli Rice and Pineapple Bowl 145

Arugula, Zucchini and Pesto Grain Bowl 145

Chickpea, Mushroom and Zucchini Bowl 145

Bell Pepper, Zucchini and Mushroom Bowl 146

Black Bean Quinoa and Vegetable Bowl 146

Indian Curried Quinoa Vegetable Bowl 146

Creamy Banana Bowl with Strawberry and Almond 147

Coconut, Raspberry and Avocado Smoothie Bowl 147

Lentil and Pasta Bowl with Basil Cider Dressing 147

Quick Frozen Banana and Protein Breakfast Bowl 148

Quinoa Eggplant and Tomato Bowl 148

Southern Collard Green and Okra Bowl 148

Healthy Spiced Mushroom Bowl 150

Pineapple and Coconut Oatmeal Bowl with Pumpkin Seeds 150

Wild Rice and Broccoli Bowl with Roasted Garlic Cashew Sauce 150

Sautéed Broccoli Carrot Bowl 151

Red Quinoa Cherry Bowl 151

Shredded Squash Tomato Bowl 151

Mashed Potato Bowl with Green Peas 151

Berry Smoothie Bowl with Mango 152

Super Kale Quinoa Bowl 152

Hearty Tomato Quinoa Bowl...............152	Apple Potato Rice Bowl...............153
The Hollywood Fruit Bowl...............152	Mexican Style Black Bean Avocado Bowl...............153

Chapter 12: Drinks — 155

Avocado and Apple Juice Mix...............155	Respiratory and Elderberry Syrup...............160
Avocado, Raspberry and Dates Moss Drink...............155	Prodigiosa Kidney Cleansing Tea...............160
Berry Mix Sea Moss Milk...............155	Peach and Raspberry Moss Drink...............160
Breakfast Tamarind, Arugula and Cucumber Drink 155	Respiratory Mullein and Guaco Cleansing Tea...............160
Dandelion Liver Cleansing Tea...............156	Irish Sea Moss Gel...............160
Gallbladder Rhubarb Cleansing Tea...............156	Banana Herbal Drink...............161
Dandelion and Bromide Plus Cleansing Drink...............156	Banana Sea Moss Green Drink...............161
Date and Banana Moss Drink...............156	Sweet Dates Green Drink...............161
Healthy Walnut Milk...............156	Chamomile and Bromide Plus Revitalizing Tea...............161
Linden Immune Boosting Tea...............157	Watermelon Lime Refresher...............161
Key Lime Dill Tea...............157	Date Sea Moss Drink...............162
Liver-Kidney Dandelion Cleansing Tea...............157	Easy Almond and Coconut Milks...............162
Sweet Hempseed Milk...............157	Kale Apple Green Sea Moss Drink...............162
Strawberry Sea Moss Drink...............157	Watermelon, Strawberries and Coconut Drink...............162
Fragrant Chamomile Tea...............158	Raspberry Sea Moss Coconut Drink...............163
Gallbladder Cleansing Tea...............158	Homemade Aquafaba...............163
Orange and Banana Bromide Drink...............158	Creamy Strawberry and Date Jar...............163
Fruity Banana Sea Moss Milk...............158	Vanilla Pumpkin Banana Drink...............163
Mango Banana Sea Moss Drink...............158	

Chapter 13: Sauce and Dressing — 165

Enchilada Sauce...............165	Ginger Onion Sauce...............168
Coconut White Sauce...............165	Easy Spiced Tomato Sauce...............168
Easy Bean Chili...............165	Lime Avocado Dressing...............168
Curried Eggplant Sauce...............166	Sesame Orange Dressing...............168
Vinaigrette Dressing with Variations...............166	Cucumber Dill and Lime Dressing...............170
Easy Homemade Sweet Barbecue Sauce...............166	Garlic Chimichurri Sauce...............170
Lemon Cilantro Salad Dressing...............167	Ginger Tomato Onion Dressing...............170
Cashew Almond Cheese Sauce...............167	Quick Barbecue Sauce...............170
Lime Papaya Seed and Mango Dressing...............167	Italian Infused Grape Seed Oil...............171
Simple Homemade Ketchup...............167	Sweet Whipped Coconut Cream Topping...............171

Garlicky Sun-Dried Tomato Sauce 171	Avocado Onion Sauce 172
Almond Milk Coconut Sauce 171	Nondairy Tzatziki Dill Sauce 172
Easy Spicy Infused Oil 172	Creamy Brazil Nut Sauce 173
Quick Ranch Dressing 172	Vanilla Coconut Whipped Cream 173

Appendix 1: Measurement Conversion Chart   174

Appendix 2: Recipes Index   175

Introduction

Most people nowadays are aware of healthy eating and nutrition balance. People think that a "balanced" diet consists of the food pyramid. However, this is the cause of overweight and all sorts of disease. Have you ever wondered what a "balanced" diet actually is? In order to keep healthy, one should focus more on a diet that regulates the pH level of the body which our alkaline diet does. Balanced pH level for the body promotes tissues and cells to rebuild and will eventually lead to a healthy body.

I wrote this book to share my experience of alkaline diet and healthy menu for your choice. Since alkaline diet is very beneficial and meaningful to one's life, you shouldn't miss it! I listed some foods to eat and some to avoid eating in the book. Foods that most people cling to are always rich in sugar, starch, caffeine, protein, fat and so on, which may lead to their over acidity. And it is the cause of some degenerative disease and autoimmune illnesses. Such problems may only be solved by an alkaline diet. It will help cleanse the body of harmful toxins that people have day to day and get rid of infections or diseases brought about by fungi, bacteria, virus, etc., which like to be in acid-based environment.

After reading this book, I think you will know yourself better and love cooking. With a healthy body and relaxed mind, every day will be beautiful, rich and full!

Chapter 1: Understanding the Alkaline Diet 101

What is the Alkaline Diet?

The alkaline diet promotes balance between acidic and non-acidic foods in the body, creating an ideal pH level for optimal health. The alkaline diet encourages the consumption of foods that are low in acid, on the theory that highly acidic foods throw the body's systems out of balance. There is also evidence that suggests certain cancers thrive in acidic environments, so it stands to reason that if you limit the amount of acidic foods you eat, then you can reduce your risk of getting some cancers. Proponents of the alkaline diet suggest that, if we are constantly consuming lots of highly acidic foods, then our bodies have no energy to do much besides trying to metabolize all that acid. Thus, we tend to put on weight and suffer from chronic health conditions. Finally, there are millions of people who suffer from acid reflux, heartburn, GERD, and other gastrointestinal issues that arise from the consumption of acidic foods. Though the alkaline diet isn't directly intended to target these kinds of issues—it is more concerned with metabolic balance in the body—it can be helpful for people who have them.

The diet encourages practitioners to make smart eating choices in a general sense, and it doesn't necessarily forbid any particular foods. Rather, the alkaline diet emphasizes foods that are low in acidity in order to maintain a balanced metabolism; thus, you will likely be eating a lot of those specific foods while mostly avoiding others. However, you can realign your body's pH balance with an abundance of alkaline-forming foods.

The alkaline diet also suggests that you avoid other substances besides foods that are acidic or can be disruptive to the body's balance, including alcohol and nicotine products, coffee, and soda. Stimulants in general are considered bad for the body's ideal balance. Lastly, the alkaline diet, like many other healthy lifestyles, recommends drinking plenty of water, getting regular exercise, and maintaining other healthy habits.

Understanding PH Balance in the Body

Alkaline is the reverse of acidic, meaning that alkaline substances can neutralize acidic substances. The alkaline diet is all about that balance, promoting a blood pH level of 7 or higher. Higher levels of acidity are reflected in smaller numbers. The pH scale numbers the acidic content of foods and other

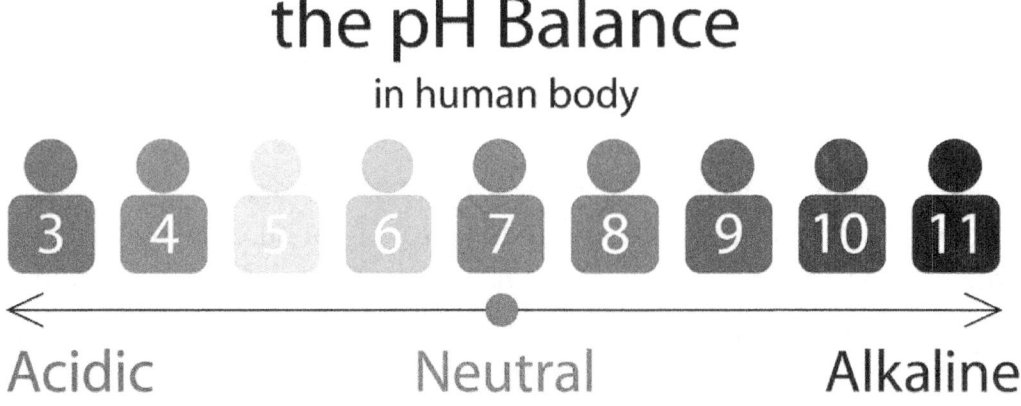

substances rate on a scale from 0-14, with acidic foods rated from 0-6, 6 being the least acidic, and alkaline foods rated 7-14. These alkaline substances are also called "bases," so within the framework of the alkaline diet, there are acidic foods and basic foods. Some of these are listed below for handy reference.

Within the body, your pH levels work to help certain organs and systems function normally. In particular, the lungs and kidneys are primarily responsible for regulating your body's pH balance, as well as being most impacted by a pH imbalance. Normally, functioning blood pH levels hover at around 7.4, but they can vary slightly.

When your body loses its healthy balance between alkaline and acidic compounds, it can have profound repercussions: acidosis describes the condition of having a low pH number (below 7.35), while alkalosis describes the condition of having a high pH number (above 7.45). Oftentimes, these conditions are the result of irregularities with either lung or kidney function; many diabetics must monitor their pH balance because diabetes impacts the kidneys in a variety of ways. Thus, the alkaline diet is one that appeals to many people who suffer from Type 2 diabetes, a chronic and widespread condition in many communities today. Diabetic ketoacidosis (DKA) occurs when the kidneys produce too many ketones and cause dangerous changes to the blood pH levels. With regard to lung function, acidosis can be caused by severe asthma or pneumonia, wherein the body cannot exhale enough carbon dioxide to keep the system in balance.

While this indicates that pH balance is, of course, very important to the normal functioning of the body, most experts agree that what you eat is not likely to be the primary cause of a pH imbalance—usually, it is the result of underlying conditions, such as diabetes or asthma, which more directly impact pH levels. Essentially, what we eat does not specifically impact our blood pH levels, though it can alter the pH levels in urine and saliva, suggesting that an alkaline diet does influence the body's balance in some manner, even if that isn't fully understood at this time. In addition, most experts also agree that the alkaline diet can be very healthy for anyone who follows it, as it largely recommends the consumption of lots of plant-based foods while avoiding red meats high in saturated fats. The alkaline diet might be particularly beneficial for individuals who are suffering from diabetes. For more on what foods to eat (and what foods to avoid) on the alkaline diet, see the sections below.

The Benefits of Alkaline Diet and Alkaline-Forming Foods

While many experts agree, as mentioned above, that what we eat likely doesn't significantly or directly impact our body's blood pH, the alkaline diet is considered to be a healthy and reasonable diet with many potential benefits. In addition, even if the alkaline diet does not directly impact our blood pH levels, some research has clearly shown that low acid foods can have positive results for our general health. Here are some of the benefits of the alkaline diet and alkaline-forming foods:

- An alkaline diet has been linked to **weight loss**. As it tends to be lower in calories with its emphasis on plant-based foods, the alkaline diet is an excellent way to lose weight and maintain a healthy weight over time.

- The most important benefit of the alkaline diet, and one that has been proven through scientific study, is that it can be **beneficial to the kidneys**. These studies suggest that following a diet low in acid can prevent or improve certain kinds of kidney diseases. This is especially relevant to people who are trying to manage Type 2 diabetes.

- Many proponents of the alkaline diet claim that it helps in **preventing certain kinds of cancer**. While there is no specific scientific consensus on this, it is definitely true that many of the foods emphasized by the alkaline diet are considered as cancer-fighting foods that are high in phytochemicals and other nutrients that can prevent some cancers.

- There are similar claims about **cardiovascular health**, and an alkaline diet promotes heart-healthy eating. As the alkaline diet suggests that you avoid foods that are high in fat (like red meat) or high in sodium (like processed foods), the end result is that it can reduce your risk for heart disease and Type 2 diabetes. This is also the result of the alkaline diet's role in helping followers maintain a healthy weight.

- Some preliminary research indicates that the alkaline diet can also **improve growth hormone levels**, which, in turn, can promote better memory and brain health. Most experts agree that a diet rich in plant-based foods is better for the brain. Thus, the alkaline diet can also prove beneficial in potentially warding off neurological conditions.

- Another benefit of the alkaline diet might be that it helps to **prevent osteoporosis**, the weakening of bones as you age. This benefit comes from eating lots of vegetables and lean proteins, so those following a low-protein alkaline diet might not get the same results.

- Finally, there is some evidence to suggest an alkaline diet can improve, or at least maintain, **muscle mass** as we age. Keeping muscle mass becomes important for our general health in many ways: it helps in maintaining a healthy weight since muscles burn more calories than fat; it is instrumental in preventing injuries from falls because of improved balance and strength; and a healthy muscle mass can ward off chronic pain, such as lower back pain.

Following the 80/20 Rule

While the "80/20 Rule" didn't originate with the alkaline diet, it is a concept that makes following the diet fairly straightforward: 80% of the food you eat should be alkaline-forming food, while only 20% of it should be acidic. Measure this by volume, rather than by weight or by caloric counts. This is the most important application of the 80/20 Rule in the alkaline diet, but it has greater implications for healthy decisions and routines overall.

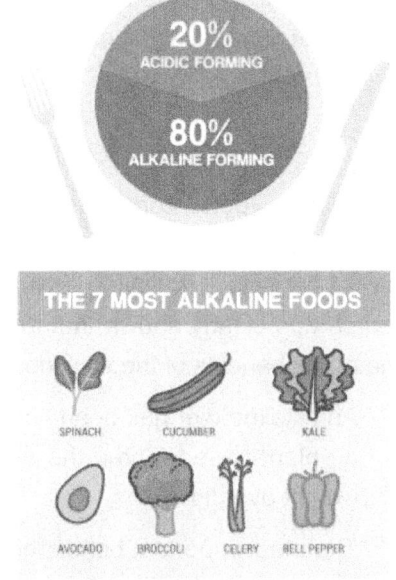

For simplicity, think about how you apply this to each plate of food: fill 80% of your plate with healthy, alkaline-forming food such as vegetables, fruits, whole grains, etc., and only leave 20% of the room for potentially less healthy yet acceptable foods like healthy fats and lean protein. By using this simple strategy, you can make following the alkaline diet easier and more straightforward--no measurements necessary.

Since the alkaline diet itself is literally about creating and maintaining balance—keeping your body's pH balance in harmony—the 80/20 Rule is an easy way to help you balance with a minor amount of indulgence. Using it helps avoid lots of complex rules or calorie counting; you just apply a simple rule and basic common sense to how you maintain your diet. How you implement this into your schedule and eating habits is up to you: you might compose each plate with 80% alkaline and 20% acidic as suggested previously; you could choose to consume only alkaline-forming food throughout the week, saving your acidic splurge for the weekends; or, you could limit acidic foods to one reasonable meal or snack portion each day. As long as you keep track of what kinds of food you are eating, you can successfully follow the alkaline diet in a number of ways. You should also get comfortable with identifying which foods are alkaline forming versus which foods (and other substances) are acidic. The sections below will help you become familiar with what to enjoy and what to avoid, guiding your grocery lists and meal plans.

Alkaline-Forming Foods to Enjoy

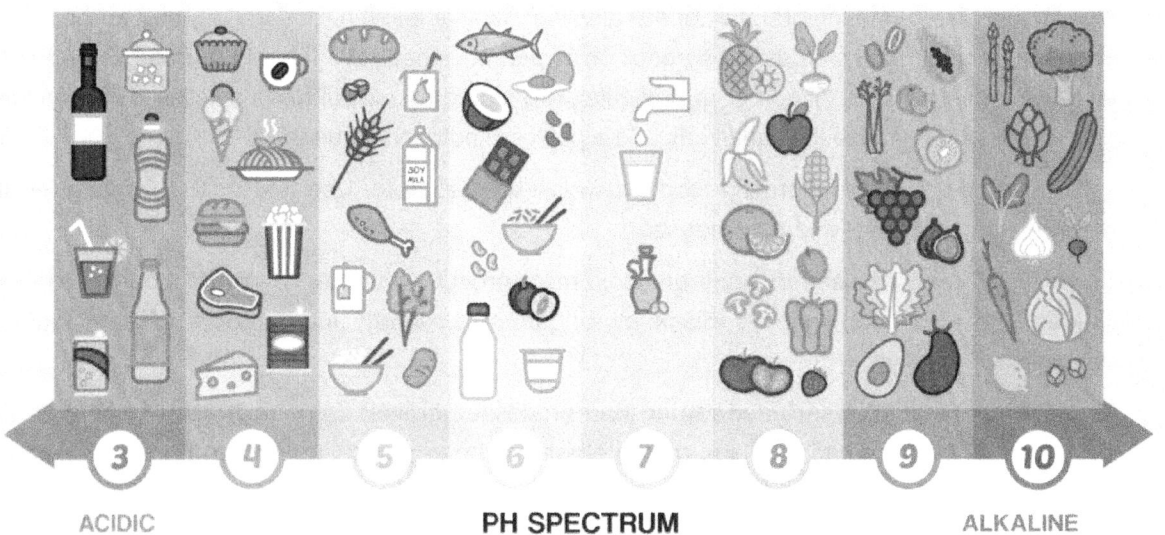

The alkaline diet emphasizes the same kinds of healthy, nutrient-rich, natural (rather than processed) foods that most experts agree are key for good health in general. Thus, it is not terribly different from an overall healthy diet that places an emphasis on plant-based foods for most of what you eat. An alkaline diet consists largely of fresh vegetables and fruits, whole grains, and lean proteins, limiting fatty and sugary foods such as red meat and desserts. But the alkaline diet also emphasizes the alkaline-forming compounds of certain foods; thus, while some fruits are fine (apples and bananas are good), other fruits are excellent (avocados), and some are best avoided in certain instances (like citrus, if you struggle with acid reflux).

The following list highlights some of the best alkaline-forming foods that you will want to incorporate into your diet on a regular basis:

- **Leafy green vegetables** are some of the healthiest foods you can eat, for many reasons: they are rich in phytochemicals and antioxidants. Indeed, leafy greens are considered "superfood" for their health benefits. These include collard greens, kale, spinach, arugula, and other deep green cousins.
- **Cruciferous vegetables**, such as broccoli, cauliflower, and Brussels sprouts, are also considered cancer-fighting superstars and increase your alkaline profile.
- **Various root vegetables** can also help to maintain a healthy balance in the body, but for maximum health benefits. Stick to brightly colored varieties that have a more impressive nutritional profile than typical potatoes: beets, sweet potatoes, carrots are all candidates for best nutritional value. Ginger, though we don't often think of it as a root vegetable, is another important ingredient boasting other

health benefits as well in the alkaline diet.

- **Alliums,** such as onions and garlic, can boost your alkaline balance. Garlic also aids in digestion and is considered an anti-inflammatory.
- **Herbs,** especially parsley and basil, are considered alkalizing foods. In addition, these two widely available herbs are incredibly versatile and can be used in a number of dishes.
- **Fruits** should also be included in the alkaline diet, especially alkaline-friendly fruits such as avocados and pineapples. Tomatoes, though they can be acidic, are not considered an acid-forming food in the body and contain high levels of lycopene, a nutrient thought to ward off cancer. Avoid sweetened fruit juices, though, as their high sugar content undoes any potential health benefits.
- **Nuts** should also be an integral part of the alkaline diet—at least in moderation, due to their high fat content. A handful of nuts a day, as a snack or as part of a meal, are thought to improve heart health along with other benefits. Almonds, in particular, are touted as crucial to an alkaline diet. Don't forget about seeds, either: these little additions add a powerful nutritional punch.
- **Soy products** are alkaline-forming food, as well, especially tofu. Use tofu as a substitute for acidic and unhealthy red meats and rich cheeses.
- **Legumes** can also be used in place of acidic meat products in order to get adequate protein. This includes all of your bean varieties (black, pinto, garbanzo, kidney, and so on), as well as lentils and peanuts.
- **Whole grains** should be included rather than processed grains: think brown rice instead of white; whole grain breads instead of white; and interesting whole grains like quinoa, farro, cracked wheat (bulgur), and the like. Some alkaline diet practitioners warn us against eating grains derived from cereals, while emphasizing grains like quinoa and wild rice.
- **Lean protein** is acceptable in small amounts as well, though red meat (even if lean) is thought to be acid-forming so should be generally avoided. Stick with chicken and seafood for best results, but again, most followers of the alkaline diet keep these to a minimum.

Acid-Forming Foods to Avoid

It is important to make a distinction here between acid-forming foods and foods with an acidic PH. Acid-forming food, like citrus, need not be avoided unless you are struggling with acid reflux or GERD. Citrus can be healthy and instrumental in keeping the body in balance; in fact, many alkaline diets recommend lemon water as a natural hydrating health boost. Indeed, not all foods with an acidic pH actually create a more acidic bodily environment. But, foods that create an acidic environment in the body should be limited, as in the list below:

- **Red meat,** as mentioned above, should be avoided or consumed in very limited quantities. That includes beef, of course, but also most pork, lamb, and goat.
- **Processed foods,** like cured meats (lunch meat, canned meat products), chips and crackers, premade dinners and other highly manipulated food products, should generally be avoided. These kinds of foods are usually high in fat, sodium, and sugar, making them unhealthy for just any diet.
- **Dairy products,** for the most part, should be avoided, especially high fat milk and yogurt, as well as hard cheeses such as parmesan and cheddar.

- Eggs should be eaten in limited quantities, and the yolk itself is considered acid-forming. Thus, you might want to stick with egg-white in only omelets and meals.
- Alcohol, in general, is considered an acid-forming substance and should be mostly avoided. If you do desire a drink now and again, stick with wine rather than hard alcohol or beer.
- Soda is another product to avoid pretty much all together, especially darker sodas with caffeine. Not only are these acidic substances, but they are also loaded with refined sugar or high fructose corn syrup, making them bad for any variety of diet.

Neutral Foods to Limit

It should also be noted that there are some foods that are considered neutral: neither alkaline-forming or acidic. While it is thought that these foods do not contribute to the balance (or imbalance) of the body's metabolic system in general, they should typically be limited so as not to throw off the overall balance in general. Partly, this is due to the fact that these foods are calorically dense and potentially unhealthy in other ways. Here are a few ideas of neutral foods you can include in your diet, but in limited ways:

- Naturally occurring fats, particularly of the unsaturated kind, can be consumed within limits. This includes olive oil and butter, as well as the fats that you get along with other dairy products such as milk and cream.
- Starchy food, in general, is considered neutral, with regard to the alkaline diet. Potatoes, breads, pastas, and rice can be consumed in limited amounts. In general, refined starches (white breads and pastas) are less healthy than whole-grains starches.
- Sugar is the most refined starch or carbohydrate of them all, and we are all aware that consuming large amounts of sugar is detrimental to our overall health. It's pH level, however, is considered neutral within the confines of the alkaline diet, so it can be consumed, just in limited quantities. Again, eating less is a good rule to follow within any healthy diet.

Tips and Techniques for Adhering to the Alkaline Diet

- Structure your meals around vegetables and fruits, rather than meats and starches, as a general guideline. Fill up your plate with vegetables first, limiting the space you have for acidic foods like red meat and sweets.
- Follow the 80/20 Rule, as described above, not just for every meal but also with snacks and beverages. However, don't try for perfection at all times; all diets take time to adjust to.
- Plan meals so that you are always prepared to create healthy, alkaline-forming meals. Cooking at home rather than eating out gives you much more control over your diet, though eating out at restaurants or picking up food becomes easier once you know how to choose foods according to

alkalinity.

- Advanced prep work can also be crucial to sticking with the plan: when you buy vegetables, wash them immediately and store them properly so that they are noticeable when you can be ready to cook.
- Or, wash and prepare salad greens to take salad into almost every meal: this is an excellent way to get enough of one of the best alkaline-forming foods, leafy greens. Using flax oil, another alkaline-forming food, in your vinaigrette, boosts the healthy factor.
- Also be mindful of your snacks by having healthy alkaline-forming options on hand, such as nuts and seeds. Make your own trail mix with a variety of alkaline-friendly nuts, seeds, and dried fruits.
- Hydration is important in any healthy diet, and the alkaline diet is no exception. If you become bored with plain water, try to add some unsweetened flavors to it, or experiment with alkalized waters, which are increasingly available at well-stocked markets.
- Always go for quality when shopping for foods: if you are going to follow a particular diet, then why not get the best possible products for your somewhat limited range of choices? The better the quality, the more satisfied you are with what you are eating.
- In addition, think about what you do eat in terms of pleasure: enjoy everything that you eat, not just the splurge foods. That is, discover how to enjoy the 80% just as much (or more than) the 20%. Finding good recipes will help out with that.
- There are also a variety of other things that you can do to get the most out of following the alkaline diet: first, engaging in regular physical activities is important for overall health in general, so incorporate some exercise routines into your schedule. Also be aware of how you deal with stress, and use mindfulness or meditation practices to keep your mental health strong. Finally, strive to get adequate sleep each night, one of the most important factors in creating good health outcomes.
- Explore the variety of resources available about what and how to eat on an alkaline diet, so you can become very knowledgeable quickly and follow this diet successfully. Knowing the guidelines regarding alkaline versus acidic will help you get started more easily.

Alkaline Diet FAQs

1. Is it actually possible to change the body's pH balance?

While most experts suggest that you cannot change your blood pH level, there is agreement that you can change the pH of your saliva and urine, which suggests that what you eat does affect the body's pH balance. Proponents of the alkaline diet also suggest that following these guidelines helps your body maintain proper pH balance without working so hard to do so. The alkaline diet alleviates the burden your body undertakes to keep it balanced.

2. Why are lemons sometimes recommended, if they're so acidic?

While lemons are an acidic food by nature, they are not an acid-forming food. Once consumed, lemon breaks down into its alkalizing minerals, including potassium and magnesium. This has an alkalizing effect on the body overall.

3. Why are there inconsistencies in the lists of alkaline and acidic foods?

There are various methods by which pH levels are detected in foods and in the body. For example, one method for testing pH levels in food calls for heating it to extremely high temperatures, then measuring the pH left behind in the "ash." Some claim that this method produces inaccurate results, mostly due to the fact that most of the sugar (which can be acidifying) is burned off in the process. Other methods instead test blood pH levels in conjunction with food consumption. The inconsistencies, typically, are minor and shouldn't discourage you from following an alkaline diet after doing some research.

4. Can you determine if a food is alkaline-friendly by its taste?

Not at all: most foods that are acidic don't taste acidic, right? Most foods that are alkaline (also called "basic") aren't bland, either. In addition, remember that acidic-tasting foods, like lemons, may not always be acid-forming foods.

5. How do I get enough protein?

While you want to limit (or entirely avoid) red meats (some proponents say all meats), you can still get enough protein from nuts, legumes, and certain whole grains. Eating non-red meats in moderation should suffice for your protein needs.

6. How do I test my pH levels?

You can buy pH testing strips for either saliva or urine. Follow the instructions on the packaging to test your pH levels. Saliva tests are considered to be more accurate, as urine tests fluctuate more due to how the kidneys function when processing food. A saliva pH of 6.75-7.0 is considered ideal. It's natural for saliva to test a little bit acidic, so your level won't typically measure at the 7.4 base that you can find via a blood test.

7. Do I need dietary supplements if I follow the alkaline diet?

Not necessarily. As long as you follow a balanced diet with plenty of vegetables and enough lean protein, you should be fine. However, there are some supplements that can aid in your quest for pH balance, including pH drops (which can raise the pH of your drinking water), Omega 3 oils, and alkalized salts.

8. Does the alkaline diet impact allergies?

There is some anecdotal evidence to suggest that an alkaline diet protects against many common allergens, including pet dander and various pollen.

9. How does the alkaline diet affect my weight?

Most people who follow the alkaline diet initially lose weight, and if they stick to the diet, they can maintain that lower weight. Some proponents of the alkaline diet claim that problems with weight, whether it be overweight or underweight, are linked to an imbalance in your pH levels. Thus, when you begin an alkaline diet, you can lose fat and gain muscle mass.

10. Can I become too alkaline?

Technically, that is possible, but it is highly unlikely to occur based on the foods that you consume. Indeed, without an underlying disease or chronic health condition, the body regulates your pH levels quite well. By following the alkaline diet, you are merely helping the body to regulate those levels without lots of additional effort.

Chapter 2: Breakfast

Kale Sweet Potato and Onion Breakfast Hash

Prep Time: 10 minutes, Cook Time: 15 minutes, Serves: 1 or 2

INGREDIENTS:

- 1 tsp. avocado oil
- ½ cup chopped kale
- 2 cups peeled and cubed sweet potatoes
- ½ cup diced onion
- ½ tsp. sea salt
- ½ tsp. freshly ground black pepper
- 1 to 2 tsps. sesame seeds or hemp seeds (optional)
- ½ avocado, cubed (optional)

DIRECTIONS:

1. Heat the avocado oil in a large skillet over medium heat. Add the kale, sweet potatoes, onion, salt, and pepper, and sauté for 10 to 15 minutes, or until the sweet potatoes are soft. Turn off the heat.
2. Stir in the sesame seeds and avocado (if using) gently, transfer to 1 large or 2 small plates, and serve.

VARIATIONS TIP:
Transform this dish into a breakfast wrap by adding it to a fresh collard green leaf and wrapping like a burrito.

Nutrition Info per Serving:
Calories: 277; Total Fat: 21.41 g; Carbohydrates: 21.9 g; Protein: 5.4 g; Fiber: 12.3 g

Baked Squash and Apples

Prep Time: 10 minutes, Cook Time: 35 minutes, Serves: 2

INGREDIENTS:

- 1 ½ pounds (680 g) butternut squash, peeled, deseeded, cut into chunks
- 2 tbsps. grapeseed oil
- ½ tsp. sea salt
- 2 apples, cored, cut into ½-inch pieces
- 2 tbsps. agave syrup

DIRECTIONS:

1. Preheat the oven to 375°F (190°C).
2. While the oven preheats, spread the squash pieces on a baking sheet.
3. Add the oil and salt in a small bowl, stir until mixed, and then drizzle over the squash pieces.
4. Use the foil to cover the pan and bake for 20 minutes.
5. While the squash pieces bake, in a medium bowl, add the apple pieces, drizzle with the agave syrup, and then toss until coated.
6. After baking, unwrap the baking sheet, spoon into the bowl containing apple and then stir until mixed.
7. Evenly spread apple-squash mixture on the baking sheet and then continue to bake for 15 minutes.
8. After baking, serve immediately.

Nutrition Info per Serving:
Calories: 126.4; Fats: 4.9 g; Carb: 22.2 g; Protein: 1.1 g; Fiber: 5.1 g

Garlicky Spaghetti Squash Hash Browns

Prep Time: 10 minutes, Cook Time: 10 minutes, Serves: 2

INGREDIENTS:

- 2 cups cooked spaghetti squash
- 1 tsp. garlic powder
- ½ cup finely chopped onion
- ½ tsp. sea salt
- Cooking spray

DIRECTIONS:

1. Squeeze any excess moisture from the spaghetti squash with paper towel. Put the squash in a medium bowl. Add the garlic powder, onion, and salt. Mix to combine.
2. Use cooking spray to grease a medium nonstick skillet, set it over medium heat.
3. Add the squash mixture to the pan. Cook for 5 minutes, untouched. Flip the hash browns with a spatula. It's okay if the mixture falls apart. Cook for about another 5 minutes, or until the desired level of crispness.

VARIATIONS TIP:
Make sure you squeeze as much moisture as you can from the spaghetti squash so it will be crisp.

Nutrition Info per Serving:
Calories: 44; Total Fat: 0.6 g; Carbohydrates: 9.7 g; Protein: 0.9 g; Fiber: 0.6 g

Overnight Mango Banana Oats

Prep Time: 10 minutes, Cook Time: 0, plus overnight chilling, Serves: 1

INGREDIENTS:

½ medium banana, sliced
¼ cup rolled oats
½ cup frozen mango, cut into ½-inch cubes
1 tsp. chia seeds
⅛ tsp. vanilla extract
1 tbsp. unsweetened finely shredded coconut
Pinch sea salt
½ cup unsweetened almond milk

DIRECTIONS:

1. Combine all of the ingredients except the almond milk in a small glass jar with a lid, and gently mix.
2. Pour in the almond milk and seal the jar.
3. Place the jar in the refrigerator to chill overnight. Serve the next morning or store in the refrigerator for up to 4 days.

VARIATIONS TIP:

If you are out of shredded coconut, you can swap in an equal amount of sliced almonds or almond meal.

Nutrition Info per Serving:
Calories: 230; Fat: 14 g; Carbohydrates: 33 g; Protein: 6 g; Fiber: 6 g; Sodium: 185 mg; Iron: 2 mg

Maple Oat Coconut Flax Granola

Prep Time: 15 minutes, Cook Time: 30 to 45 minutes, Serves: 6

INGREDIENTS:

2 tbsps. avocado oil
2 tbsps. unsweetened finely shredded coconut
2 tbsps. almond meal
2 tbsps. flax meal
2 tbsps. maple syrup, or
5 to 6 small dates, pitted
¼ tsp. vanilla extract
2 tbsps. brown rice flour
Pinch sea salt
¾ cup rolled oats

DIRECTIONS:

1. Preheat the oven to 350°F (180°C).
2. Combine the oil, coconut, almond meal, flax meal, and maple syrup in a food processor, process until smooth.
3. Pour the mixture into a bowl and stir in the vanilla, flour, and salt. Stir in the oats.
4. Evenly spread the mixture on a baking sheet and bake for 30 to 45 minutes, turning every 15 minutes, until golden brown. After baking, allow to cool. Store in an airtight container.

VARIATIONS TIP:

For variety, mix in ¼ cup raisins and ¼ cup sliced almonds when the granola is fresh out of the oven.

Nutrition Info per Serving:
Calories: 150; Fat: 9 g; Carbohydrates: 15 g; Protein: 3 g; Fiber: 2 g; Sodium: 28 mg; Iron: 1 mg

Margherita Pizza with Veggies

Prep Time: 25 minutes, Cook Time: 1 hour, Serves: 4

INGREDIENTS:

CRUST:
1 ½ cups of spelt flour
½ tsp. of basil
½ tsp. of pure sea salt
½ tsp. of onion powder
½ tsp. of oregano
1 cup of spring water
CHEESE:
1 tsp. of sea moss gel
1 cup of soaked brazil nuts (overnight or for at least 3 hours)
½ tsp. of oregano
½ tsp. of basil
¼ tsp. of pure sea salt
½ tsp. of onion powder
¼ cup of homemade hemp seed milk
1 tsp. of key lime juice
½ cup of spring water
TOPPINGS:
"garlic" sauce
sliced red onions
sliced plum or cherry tomatoes
chopped fresh basil

DIRECTIONS:

1. Preheat the oven to 350°F (180°C).
2. Add the spelt flour and seasonings in a medium bowl, and mix well. Pour in ½ cup of spring water and mix. Continue to add more water until the dough can be formed into a ball.
3. Spread the flour on your working surface. Use a rolling pin to roll the dough out, adding more flour as necessary to avoid sticking.
4. Spread the dough out on a baking sheet, use the grape seed oil to brush, and use a fork to make holes. Place in the oven and bake 10 to 15 minutes.
5. In a blender, add all of the ingredients for the cheese. Blend well until consistency is smooth.
6. Take the dough out from the oven. Spread with "garlic" sauce and prepared cheese. Place the onions, sliced tomatoes, basil, and more cheese on the top of the pizza.
7. Bake on the bottom rack for 10 to 15 minutes at 425°F (220°C).
8. Serve warm.

Nutrition Info per Serving:
Calories: 463; Fat: 24.25 g; Carbohydrates: 54.31 g; Protein: 15.02 g; Fiber: 9.9 g

Chilled Vanilla Granola Bars

Prep Time: 25 minutes, Cook Time: 0, Serves: 6 bars or 12 squares

INGREDIENTS:

1 tbsp. coconut oil
1 cup quick rolled oats
½ cup almond butter
2 tbsps. brown rice syrup
¼ tsp. ground cinnamon
¼ tsp. vanilla bean powder
¼ tsp. sea salt

DIRECTIONS:

1. Use parchment paper to line a 9-by-5-inch loaf dish.
2. Combine all of the ingredients in a food processor, process them together until well combined.
3. Place the mixture onto the prepared loaf dish, and use your hand and fingertips to press down firmly and evenly.
4. Place in the refrigerator to chill for 15 to 20 minutes, or until the mixture firms up.
5. Cut into 6 bars or 12 squares, and serve. Keep leftovers in the refrigerator; the bars will get soft and lose their shape at room temperature.

VARIATIONS TIP:
You can customize these by adding chopped almonds or pumpkin seeds to the mixture after processing.

Nutrition Info per Serving:
Calories: 218; Total Fat: 14.71 g; Carbohydrates: 18.33 g; Protein: 6.15 g; Fiber: 3.6 g

Chilled Pumpkin Seed-Protein Oats Balls

Prep Time: 25 minutes, Cook Time: 0, Serves: 18 to 20 balls

INGREDIENTS:

3 tbsps. 100% organic pumpkin seed protein powder
½ cup almond butter
1½ cups quick rolled oats
1 tbsp. coconut oil
½ cup raw pumpkin seeds
3 tbsps. brown rice syrup
1 tsp. vanilla bean powder
1 tsp. ground cinnamon
2 to 4 tbsps. coconut milk

DIRECTIONS:

1. Use parchment paper to line a baking sheet.
2. Combine all of the ingredients in a food processor, process them together until well combined, not overprocess.
3. Scoop a tablespoonful and use your hands to roll into a ball. Arrange on the prepared baking sheet, and repeat with the remaining mixture.
4. Place in the refrigerator to chill for 15 to 20 minutes, or until firm, and serve. Remember to store in the refrigerator; the balls will get soft and lose their shape at room temperature.

VARIATIONS TIP:
If you can't find pumpkin seed protein powder, you can omit it.

Nutrition Info per Serving:
Calories: 102; Total Fat: 7.27 g; Carbohydrates: 6.85 g; Protein: 1.8 g; Fiber: 37.4 g

Breakfast Mixed Vegetable Fajitas

Prep Time: 15 minutes, Cook Time: 10 minutes, Serves: 2

INGREDIENTS:

Cooking spray
1 sweet onion, such as Vidalia, chopped
1 bell pepper, any color, cored, seeded, and sliced
½ cup sliced mushrooms
1 cup cooked broccoli florets
½ cup sliced zucchini, or other squash
1 cup cherry tomatoes, halved if large
2 garlic cloves, peeled and chopped
1 jalapeño, chopped (optional)
½ tsp. cumin
1 tsp. sea salt
2 tbsps. fresh cilantro
Juice of ½ lime
salsa fresca, for serving

DIRECTIONS:

1. Use cooking spray to grease a large nonstick skillet and place it over medium heat.
2. Stir in the onion, bell pepper, mushrooms, broccoli, zucchini, tomatoes, garlic, and jalapeño (if using). Cook for about 7 minutes, or until the desired level of tenderness, stirring.
3. Add the cumin, salt, and cilantro. Cook for another 3 minutes, stirring.
4. Turn off the heat and add the lime juice.
5. Evenly divide between two plates and serve with salsa fresca.

VARIATIONS TIP:
There is a source link in the Resources section for coconut-flour tortillas. Wrap one of those around these fajitas for a filling breakfast.

Nutrition Info per Serving:
Calories: 86; Total Fat: 0.07g; Carbohydrates: 17.4 g; Protein: 4.1 g; Fiber: 5.1 g

Sushi Avocado Hand Roll

Prep Time: 10 minutes, Cook Time: 0, Serves: 1

INGREDIENTS:
- 2 nori seaweed squares
- ¼ cup cooked brown rice, divided
- Wasabi, for garnish (optional)
- ½ cucumber, peeled and diced, divided
- ½ avocado, diced, divided
- 1 tsp. sesame oil, divided
- 1 tsp. toasted sesame seeds, divided

DIRECTIONS:
1. Take one nori sheet and put in your hand. Add 2 tablespoons brown rice, wasabi (if using), half of the diced cucumber, and half of the diced avocado.
2. Drizzle over with ½ teaspoon of sesame oil. Sprinkle with ½ teaspoon of the sesame seeds.
3. Wrap the nori around the filling and make it looks like a cone. Then set on a plate.
4. Repeat with the remaining ingredients for another roll.
5. Serve and eat immediately.

VARIATIONS TIP:
You can use quinoa instead of the brown rice for a change of pace.

Nutrition Info per Serving:
Calories: 457; Total Fat: 27.1 g; Carbohydrates: 51.1 g; Protein: 7 g; Fiber: 9.5 g

Banana Alkaline Breakfast Bars

Prep Time: 10 minutes, Cook Time: 10 minutes, Serves: 2

INGREDIENTS:
- 2 baby burro bananas
- 1 tbsp. agave nectar
- ½ cup spelt flour
- 1/16 tsp. sea salt
- 1 cup quinoa flakes
- Extra:
- ¼ cup grapeseed oil
- ½ cup alkaline blackberry jam

DIRECTIONS:
1. Preheat the oven to 350°F(180°C).
2. While the oven preheats, in a medium bowl, add the peeled burro bananas and use a fork to mash them.
3. Add the oil and agave nectar to the bowl, stir until well combined, and then stir in the flour, salt, and quinoa flakes until a sticky dough comes together.
4. Use parchment sheet to line a square dish, spread two-thirds of the prepared dough in its bottom, layer with blackberry jam, and place the remaining dough on the top.
5. Bake for 10 minutes and then allow the dough to cool for 15 minutes.
6. Cut the dough into four bars and serve.

Nutrition Info per Serving:
Calories: 108.6; Fats: 3 g; Carb: 19.4 g; Protein: 1.6 g; Fiber: 1.6 g

Creamy Vegan Mayonnaise Deviled Eggs

Prep Time: 15 minutes, Cook Time: 0, Serves: 4

INGREDIENTS:
FOR THE DEVILED EGGS
- 4 hard-boiled eggs
- ¼ tsp. yellow mustard
- ⅛ tsp. sea salt

FOR THE CREAMY VEGAN MAYONNAISE
- ⅛ tsp. veggie seasoning salt, such as Mrs. Dash or Herbamare
- ¼ cup aquafaba
- 1 cup avocado oil

DIRECTIONS:

TO MAKE THE DEVILED EGGS
1. Peel each hard-boiled egg and slice in half lengthwise. Scoop out the yolks and add the yolks into a small bowl. Set the egg whites aside. Add the mustard and salt to the bowl, then mash the yolks and set aside.

TO PREPARE THE CREAMY VEGAN MAYONNAISE
2. Combine the veggie seasoning salt and aquafaba in a food processor, pulse for 30 seconds, until frothy.
3. Slowly drizzle in the oil while the food processor running on low, and process until the liquid emulsifies into creamy mayonnaise.
4. Add 2 tablespoons of the mayonnaise to the egg yolks and mix well. Place the remaining mayonnaise into a small jar with a tight-fitting lid and keep in the refrigerator for 3 to 4 days. Evenly scoop the egg yolk mixture into the cavity of each egg white with a teaspoon and serve.

VARIATIONS TIP:
If you don't want to use eggs, replace them with ¼ cup cooked shelled edamame and 4 button mushrooms, cleaned and stemmed. Mash the edamame with the sea salt and mustard and mix in the mayo, then scoop the mixture into the mushroom caps.

Nutrition Info per Serving:
Calories: 100; Fat: 8 g; Carbohydrates: 1 g; Protein: 6 g; Fiber: 0 g; Sodium: 149 mg; Iron: 1 mg

Baked Apples with Walnuts

Prep Time: 10 minutes, Cook Time: 55 minutes, Serves: 2

INGREDIENTS:
- 4 apples, large, cored, sliced
- 3 tbsps. agave syrup
- 1 tbsp. chopped walnuts
- ⅛ tsp. ground cloves

DIRECTIONS:
1. Preheat the oven to 350°F(180°C).
2. While the oven preheats, place the apple slices in a large bowl, drizzle with the agave syrup and toss until evenly coated.
3. Place the nuts in a small bowl, add the cloves, and stir until mixed.
4. Sprinkle the nuts mixture over the apple and allow it to rest for 5 minutes or more until the apples start releasing their juices.
5. Arrange apple slices on a medium casserole dish, and bake for 15 minutes.
6. Use the foil to cover the casserole dish and continue to bake for 40 minutes until bubbly.
7. After baking, allow the apples to cool for 10 minutes and serve.

Nutrition Info per Serving:
Calories: 346; Fats 6.4 g; Carb: 78 g; Protein: 1.5 g; Fiber: 6.2 g

Banana Date Muffins

Prep Time: 5 minutes, Cook Time: 15 minutes to 18 minutes, Serves: 12

INGREDIENTS:
- Cooking spray
- 1 cup dates
- 2 ripe bananas
- ½ cup coconut flour
- ¼ cup coconut oil, melted
- ½ cup roasted creamy almond butter
- ½ tsp. sea salt
- 2 tsps. baking soda
- 1 vanilla bean, split lengthwise and seeds scraped out

DIRECTIONS:
1. Preheat the oven to 350°F(180°C).
2. Use paper liners to line a muffin pan and spray the liners with cooking spray.
3. Combine the dates and bananas in a food processor, blend until smooth.
4. Add the remaining ingredients to the processor and pulse until a thick batter forms.
5. Scoop the batter into the lined muffin tins with an ice cream scoop, filling each two-thirds full.
6. Put the muffins in the preheated oven and bake for 15 to 18 minutes, or until a toothpick inserted into a muffin comes out clean.
7. After baking, allow to cool and serve.

VARIATIONS TIP:
When your bananas are starting to get ripe, peel them and freeze them. You can use them in smoothies or banana "ice cream," but you can also use them in this muffin recipe. They get a bit mushy, but since they're blended, it doesn't matter.

Nutrition Info per Serving:
Calories: 181; Total Fat: 10.1 g; Carbohydrates: 21.7 g; Protein: 3.8 g; Fiber: 2.6 g

Carrot Fruit Breakfast Porridge

Prep Time: 10 minutes, Cook Time: 5 minutes, Serves: 2

INGREDIENTS:
- ¼ cup red seedless grapes (approximately 12 grapes)
- ½ ripe medium banana (save the other half for a same-day snack)
- 2 small dates, pitted
- ¼ cup shredded carrots
- ⅛ tsp. vanilla extract
- ⅛ tsp. ground cinnamon
- 2 tbsps. unsweetened shredded coconut
- ½ cup plus 2 tbsps. rolled oats, divided
- ½ cup unsweetened almond milk

DIRECTIONS:
1. Combine the grapes, banana, dates, carrots, vanilla, cinnamon, coconut, and 2 tablespoons of oats in a food processor. Process for 1 to 2 minutes, until well combined.
2. Mix in the remaining ½ cup of oats and pulse a few times to leave a bit of oat texture.
3. Place the mixture into a small saucepan and add the almond milk, stir well. Heat on medium-low heat for about 5 minutes, until warmed.

VARIATIONS TIP:
Make a double batch of the breakfast porridge and use the extra batch to make carrot cake muffins. Mix the porridge with ¼ cup avocado oil and 1 medium egg in a large bowl. Stir in ½ cup flax meal, ½ cup all-purpose flour, and 1 tablespoon baking powder. Bake in a preheated 350°F(180°C) oven for 20 to 25 minutes, until a toothpick inserted into the center of a muffin comes out clean.

Nutrition Info per Serving:
Calories: 208; Fat: 6 g; Carbohydrates: 37 g; Protein: 5 g; Fiber: 6 g; Sodium: 62 mg; Iron: 2 mg

Walnut Kamut Porridge, page 19

Overnight Mango Banana Oats, page 12

Chilled Pumpkin Seed-Protein Oats Balls, page 13

Carrot, Hemp Seed and Oat Muffins, page 17

Chickpea Salad Burritos

Prep Time: 10 minutes, Cook Time: 5 minutes, Serves: 2

INGREDIENTS:
- 2 tbsps. tahini butter, homemade
- 1 tbsp. key lime juice
- ¼ cup cherry tomatoes
- ¾ cup cooked chickpeas
- 2 ounces (57 g) arugula
- 2 Kamut flour tortillas
- ¼ tsp. salt
- ¼ tsp. cayenne pepper

DIRECTIONS:
1. Place the tahini butter in a small bowl, stir in the lime juice until mixed.
2. Place the tomatoes in a medium bowl, add the chickpeas and arugula, drizzle with the dressing, toss until mixed, then cover the bowl and allow it to rest in the refrigerator for 20 minutes.
3. Once ready to eat, warm the tortillas in a skillet, fill them with the chickpeas mixture, sprinkle with salt and cayenne pepper, and then roll to serve.

Nutrition Info per Serving:
Calories: 274; Fats: 9.1 g; Carb: 39 g; Protein: 11.5 g; Fiber: 4.4 g

Carrot, Hemp Seed and Oat Muffins

Prep Time: 15 minutes, Cook Time: 25 minutes, Serves: 12 muffins

INGREDIENTS:
- 1 tbsp. ground flaxseed
- 3 tbsps. water
- 2 cups oat flour
- 1 carrot, shredded
- 1 cup almond milk (boxed)
- ½ cup unrefined whole cane sugar, such as Sucanat
- 2 tbsps. hemp seeds
- 1 tbsp. chopped Lacinato kale
- 6 tbsps. cashew butter
- 1 tbsp. baking powder
- ⅛ tsp. vanilla bean powder
- Pinch sea salt

DIRECTIONS:
1. Preheat the oven to 350°F(180°C).
2. To prepare a flax egg, whisk together the flaxseed and water in a small bowl.
3. Transfer the flax egg to a medium bowl, and add the remaining ingredients, stirring until well combined.
4. Evenly divide the mixture among 12 muffin cups, bake for 20 to 25 minutes, and serve immediately.

VARIATIONS TIP:
Unrefined whole cane sugars, like Sucanat, are much less processed than regular sugar and have a higher molasses content as well. You can find Sucanat and other unrefined whole cane sugars at natural food stores or online.

Nutrition Info per Serving:
Calories: 150; Total Fat: 7.21 g; Carbohydrates: 18.46 g; Protein: 4.2 g; Fiber: 2 g

Blueberry Flax Oats Muffins

Prep Time: 10 minutes, Cook Time: 20 to 25 minutes, Serves: 12

INGREDIENTS:
- ½ cup flax meal
- 12 small dates, pitted
- ½ cup almond meal
- ¼ cup unsweetened shredded coconut
- ½ cup gluten-free rolled oats
- ½ cup gluten-free flour
- 1 tbsp. baking powder
- ¼ tsp. sea salt
- ¼ cup grape seed oil or avocado oil
- 1⅓ cups unsweetened soy milk
- ½ tsp. vanilla extract
- 1 medium egg
- 1 cup fresh blueberries

DIRECTIONS:
1. Preheat the oven to 400°F(205°C). Use paper liners to line a 12-cup muffin tin.
2. Combine the flax meal, dates, almond meal, and coconut in a food processor, process until well combined.
3. Pour the mixture into a medium bowl. Stir in the oats, flour, baking powder, and salt into the mixture.
4. Combine the oil, soy milk, vanilla and egg in a separate bowl, and stir until well blended.
5. Add the wet mixture to the dry mixture and stir until well combined. Allow the mixture to sit for 2 to 3 minutes, until it starts to thicken to a batter consistency.
6. Fold in the blueberries.
7. Evenly scoop the batter into the prepared muffin cups, each using about ½ cup of the batter.
8. Bake until a toothpick inserted into the center of a muffin comes out clean, about 20 to 25 minutes.

VARIATIONS TIP:
Enjoy a freshly baked muffin now, then freeze the rest for later. These are perfect for a grab-and-go breakfast. Simply thaw overnight in the fridge and reheat in the toaster oven or in the microwave for 30 seconds.

Nutrition Info per Serving:
Calories: 172; Fat: 10 g; Carbohydrates: 17 g; Protein: 5 g; Fiber: 4 g; Sodium: 189 mg; Iron: 1 mg

Herbed Breakfast Bean Sausage

Prep Time: 20 minutes, Cook Time: 30 minutes, Serves: 4

INGREDIENTS:

1 small onion, quartered
2 garlic cloves
1 carrot, peeled and cut into large chunks
½ tsp. fennel seeds
Water, as needed
1 (15-ounce, 425 g) can pinto beans, drained
1 tbsp. nutritional yeast
1 tbsp. almond flour or almond meal
½ tsp. dried oregano (1 tsp. fresh)
1 tsp. smoked paprika
½ tsp. dried thyme (1 tsp. fresh)
½ tsp. dried sage (1 tsp. fresh)
½ tsp. dried basil (1 tsp. fresh)
½ tsp. sea salt

DIRECTIONS:

1. Preheat the oven to 400°F(205°C).
2. Use a silicone mat or parchment paper to line a baking sheet.
3. Add the onion, garlic, and carrot in a food processor. Chop until fine, or use hand to chop.
4. Add the onion-carrot mixture, and the fennel seeds into a medium skillet, cook over medium heat for about 4 minutes or until the vegetables are soft, adding water if needed. Remove from the heat and allow to cool.
5. Add the pinto beans to the food processor, pulse until roughly chopped, but not to a paste. Add the onion-carrot mixture to the processor, and process until blended.
6. Pour the contents into a medium bowl. Add the yeast, almond flour, oregano, paprika, thyme, sage, basil, and salt. Mix until combined.
7. Measure ¼ cup of sausage and use your hand to shape into a patty. Then place each patty on the prepared pan carefully. Continue with the remaining sausage.
8. Bake for 25 to 30 minutes, until crispy on the outside but still moist on the inside.
9. After baking, remove from the oven and allow to cool for a few minutes and serve.

VARIATIONS TIP:

You can dry fry these sausage patties by cooking them in a nonstick pan sprayed with cooking spray. Fry for about 5 minutes per side.

Nutrition Info per Serving:
Calories: 69; Total Fat: 1.7 g; Carbohydrates: 10.7 g; Protein: 3.5 g; Fiber: 3 g

Homemade Nutty Amaranth

Prep Time: 10 minutes, Cook Time: 30 minutes, Serves: 2

INGREDIENTS:

1 cup amaranth
2 cups of spring water
¼ tsp. salt
2 tbsps. agave syrup
2 tbsps. chopped walnuts

DIRECTIONS:

1. Place a medium saucepan over medium-high heat, add the amaranth, pour in the water, and bring it to a boil.
2. Reduce the heat to medium, cook for 25 minutes until all the liquid has been absorbed, and then add the salt and stir well.
3. Remove the pan from the heat, allow the amaranth to rest for 10 minutes, and evenly distribute between two bowls and top with the agave syrup and nuts.
4. Serve immediately.

Nutrition Info per Serving:
Calories: 175; Fats: 0 g; Carb: 42 g; Protein: 1.3 g; Fiber: 4 g

Mushroom Pepper Fajitas

Prep Time: 10 minutes, Cook Time: 8 minutes, Serves: 2

INGREDIENTS:

1 tbsp. grapeseed oil
¾ of red bell pepper, sliced
½ of onion, peeled, sliced
2 Portobello mushroom caps, ⅓-inch sliced
⅓ tsp. salt
¼ tsp. cayenne pepper
¼ tsp. onion powder
2 spelt flour tortillas
½ of key lime, juiced

DIRECTIONS:

1. Heat the oil in a medium skillet pan over medium heat, add the red pepper and onion, and cook for 2 minutes until tender-crisp.
2. Add the mushrooms slices, sprinkle with the salt, cayenne pepper and onion powder, stir until mixed, and cook for 5 minutes until the vegetables turn soft.
3. Heat the tortillas until warm, divide the vegetables into their center, drizzle with the lime juice, and then roll tightly.
4. Serve immediately.

Nutrition Info per Serving:
Calories: 337; Fats: 3.7 g; Carb: 73.3 g; Protein: 2.6 g; Fiber: 21.3 g

Spelt Banana Walnut Bread

Prep Time: 10 minutes, Cook Time: 20 minutes, Serves: 2

INGREDIENTS:
1 ⅓ cup of burro banana
¼ cup agave syrup
1 ⅓ tbsps. olive oil
⅔ cup spelt flour
⅓ cup chopped walnuts
⅛ tsp. salt

DIRECTIONS:
1. Preheat the oven to 350°F(180°C).
2. While the oven preheats, in a medium bowl, add the burro banana, use a fork to mash it and stir in the agave syrup and oil until combined.
3. Place the flour in a separate medium bowl, add the nuts and salt, stir until mixed, and then stir in the burro banana mixture until smooth.
4. Pour the batter into a parchment-lined loaf pan and bake for 20 minutes until firm and the top turn golden brown.
5. After baking, allow the bread to cool for 10 minutes, then cut into slices and serve.

Nutrition Info per Serving:
Calories: 186; Fats: 11.3 g; Carb: 22 g; Protein: 1.3 g; Fiber: 2 g

Walnut Kamut Porridge

Prep Time: 5 minutes, Cook Time: 10 minutes, Serves: 2

INGREDIENTS:
½ cup Kamut
¼ tsp. salt
2 cups walnut milk, homemade
½ tbsp. coconut oil
2 tbsps. agave syrup
1/8 cup blueberries or strawberries

DIRECTIONS:
1. Plug in a high-speed food processor or blender, add the Kamut in its jar, and then pulse until cracked.
2. Transfer the Kamut into a medium saucepan, add the salt, pour in the milk and then stir until combined.
3. Bring the Kamut mixture to a boil over high heat, then reduce the heat to medium-low and simmer for 5 to 10 minutes until thickened to your desired level.
4. Remove the pan from the heat, stir the oil and agave syrup into the porridge, evenly divide between two bowls.
5. Garnish the porridge with blueberries and serve.

Nutrition Info per Serving:
Calories: 183; Fats: 2 g; Carb: 30 g; Protein: 10 g; Fiber: 4 g

Nori Avocado Zucchini Burritos

Prep Time: 10 minutes, Cook Time: 0, Serves: 2

INGREDIENTS:
2 nori sheets
1 cucumber, deseeded, cut into round slices
1 avocado, peeled, sliced
1 tbsp. tahini butter
1 zucchini, sliced
2 tsps. sprouted hemp seeds
2 tsps. sesame seeds

DIRECTIONS:
1. Working on one nori sheet at a time, shiny-side-down, place it on a cutting board and arrange half of each cucumber, avocado, tahini butter and zucchini slices on it, leaving 1-inch wide spice to the right.
2. Start folding the sheet over the fillings from the edge that is closest to you, cut into thick slices, and sprinkle with 1 teaspoon of sesame seeds and sprouted hemp seeds.
3. Repeat with the remaining nori sheet, and serve immediately.

Nutrition Info per Serving:
Calories: 90; Fats: 1.5 g; Carb: 12.5 g; Protein: 1.5 g; Fiber: 1 g

Healthy Kamut Porridge with Dates

Prep Time: 5 minutes, Cook Time: 15 minutes, Serves: 2

INGREDIENTS:
1 cup rolled Kamut flakes
2 cups spring water
⅛ tsp. salt
1 cup dates, pitted,
chopped
1 tsp. agave syrup (optional)

DIRECTIONS:
1. In a small saucepan, add the Kamut flakes, pour in the water, and allow to soak for overnight.
2. After soaking, stir in the salt, cook over medium-high heat and bring the mixture to a slow boil.
3. Reduce the heat to medium-low and continue to cook for 10 minutes or more until all the liquid has absorbed.
4. Remove the pan from the heat, add the dates into the porridge and then stir until mixed.
5. Ladle the porridge into two bowls, drizzle with agave syrup if needed, and serve.

Nutrition Info per Serving:
Calories: 132; Fats: 1 g; Carb: 30.2 g; Protein: 0.3 g; Fiber: 2 g

Amaranth Porridge with Walnuts

Prep Time: 5 minutes, Cook Time: 30 minutes, Serves: 2

INGREDIENTS:
1 cup amaranth, soaked
1 cup soft-jelly coconut milk
1 cup spring water
2 tbsps. chopped walnuts
Extra:
2 tbsps. agave syrup
1/16 tsp. salt

DIRECTIONS:
1. Drain the soaked amaranth well, add to a medium pot, pour in the milk and water.
2. Bring the mixture over medium-high heat to a boil, then reduce the heat to medium and cook for 25 minutes or more until amaranth has cooked.
3. Add the agave syrup and salt, stir well and remove the pan from the heat and divide between two bowls.
4. Place the nuts over the amaranth and serve.

Nutrition Info per Serving:
Calories: 373; Fats: 9 g; Carb: 64 g; Protein: 14 g; Fiber: 14 g

Amaranth Walnut Polenta

Prep Time: 5 minutes, Cook Time: 15 minutes, Serves: 2

INGREDIENTS:
1 ½ cups vegetable broth, homemade
¾ cup amaranth
¼ tsp. onion powder
¼ tsp. salt
6 tbsps. walnut milk, homemade
¼ cup cooked chickpeas
Extra:
⅛ tsp. cayenne pepper

DIRECTIONS:
1. Place a medium pot over medium heat, pour in the broth, add the salt and stir well, bring it to a boil.
2. Reduce the heat to medium-low level, add the amaranth and whisk well, cook for 10 to 20 minutes until slightly thick mixture comes together.
3. Stir in all of the remaining ingredients except chickpea, mix well and continue to cook for 5 minutes.
4. Serve the polenta with the chickpeas.

Nutrition Info per Serving:
Calories: 172; Fats: 7.3 g; Carb: 18.5 g; Protein: 4.5 g; Fiber: 1.8 g

Sweet Oatmeal Porridge with Mango-Chia Fruit Jam

Prep Time: 5 minutes, Cook Time: 5 minutes, Serves: 2

INGREDIENTS:
1 cup quick rolled oats
1 (14-ounce, 397 g) can full-fat coconut milk
2 tbsps. unrefined whole cane sugar, such as Sucanat
1 to 2 tbsps. mango chia seed fruit jam

DIRECTIONS:
1. Add the oats, coconut milk and sugar into a small saucepan, cook over medium-low heat for 3 to 5 minutes, or until the oats are soft, stirring occasionally.
2. Place the oatmeal onto 2 serving bowls, place the mango chia Seed fruit jam on the top, and serve.

VARIATIONS TIP:
Canned coconut will give the oatmeal an extra-creamy texture, but substitute with boxed almond or coconut milk, if you like.

Nutrition Info per Serving:
Calories: 211; Total Fat: 3.31 g; Carbohydrates: 39.85 g Protein: 6.32 g; Fiber: 5.7 g

Amaranth and Black Quinoa Porridge

Prep Time: 5 minutes, Cook Time: 15-30 minutes, Serves: 2

INGREDIENTS:
½ cup amaranth, cooked
½ cup black quinoa, cooked
2 cups spring water
2 tbsps. agave syrup
½ cup soft-jelly coconut milk

DIRECTIONS:
1. Place a medium saucepan over medium heat, add the amaranth and cooked quinoa, pour in the water, stir until mixed, and then bring it to a boil.
2. Reduce the heat to low and then simmer for 10 to 25 minutes until the grains have absorbed all the liquid.
3. Add the milk and agave syrup, stir until mixed, and then simmer for an additional 5 minutes until thoroughly cooked and slightly thickened.
4. Serve immediately.

Nutrition Info per Serving:
Calories: 204; Fats: 4 g; Carb: 33 g; Protein: 8 g; Fiber: 3 g

Vegan Baked Portobello with Avocado

Prep Time: 10 minutes, Cook Time: 20 minutes, Serves: 2

INGREDIENTS:

2 tbsps. olive oil
¼ tsp. salt
½ tsp. cayenne pepper
1 tsp. dried oregano
2 tsps. dried basil
2 Portobello mushroom caps
½ of avocado, sliced
1 cup purslane

DIRECTIONS:

1. Preheat the oven to 425°F(220°C).
2. Meanwhile, prepare the marinade, in a small bowl, add the oil, salt, cayenne pepper, oregano, and basil and stir until mixed.
3. Use a foil to line a cookie sheet, brush with oil, arrange with the mushroom caps, evenly pour the marinade over the mushroom caps and allow them to marinate for 10 minutes.
4. Bake the mushroom caps for 20 minutes, flipping halfway, until tender and cooked.
5. After baking, transfer the mushroom caps onto two plates, top with the avocado and purslane evenly and serve.

Nutrition Info per Serving:
Calories: 354; Fats: 32.8 g; Carb: 14.4 g; Protein: 3.7 g; Fiber: 4.4 g

Zucchini Hummus and Lettuce Wrap

Prep Time: 10 minutes, Cook Time: 8 minutes, Serves: 2

INGREDIENTS:

1 tbsp. grapeseed oil
1 zucchini, sliced
¼ tsp. salt
⅛ tsp. cayenne pepper
2 spelt flour tortillas
4 tbsps. homemade hummus
½ cup iceberg lettuce
2 cherry tomatoes, sliced

DIRECTIONS:

1. Use the oil to grease a grill pan, preheat it over medium-high heat.
2. While the pan preheats, in a large bowl, add the zucchini slices, sprinkle with the salt and cayenne pepper, drizzle with the oil and toss until coated.
3. On the grill pan, arrange with the zucchini slices and cook for 2 to 3 minutes per side until developed grill marks.
4. Heat the tortillas on the grill pan until warm and develop grill marks and spread 2 tablespoons of hummus over each tortilla.
5. Divide the grilled zucchini slices over the tortillas, place the lettuce and tomato slices on the top, and wrap tightly.
6. Serve immediately.

Nutrition Info per Serving:
Calories: 264.5; Fats: 5.1 g; Carb: 34.5 g; Protein: 8.5 g; Fiber: 5 g

Chapter 3: Vegetable

Cucumber Asparagus Hummus Sandwiches

Prep Time: 10 minutes, Cook Time: 0, Serves: 2

INGREDIENTS:
½ cup healthy hummus
1 cucumber, peeled and sliced into ¼-inch rounds
4 asparagus spears, trimmed, cooked, cooled, and finely chopped

DIRECTIONS:
1. Top one cucumber round with 1 teaspoon of hummus. Then place ½ teaspoon of the asparagus over the hummus. Place a second cucumber round on top. Place the sandwich on the serving plate carefully.
2. Repeat with the remaining ingredients.

VARIATIONS TIP:
You can quickly cook the asparagus in the microwave and then run it under cold water to cool it.

Nutrition Info per Serving:
Calories: 126; Total Fat: 6.2 g; Carbohydrates: 14.4 g; Protein: 5.9 g; Fiber: 4.5 g

Barbecued Mango Zucchini Stuffed Mushroom Sliders

Prep Time: 15 minutes, Cook Time: 10 minutes, Serves: 2

INGREDIENTS:
4 portobello mushroom caps, gills removed
1 mango, peeled, pitted, and cut into large pieces
¼ cup homemade barbecue sauce
1 zucchini, peeled and julienned

DIRECTIONS:
1. Preheat a grill or a grill pan on the stovetop to medium heat.
2. Place the mango in a food processor, purée it. Add the homemade barbecue sauce. Pour the mixture into a medium bowl. Add the zucchini and stir well to combine.
3. Fill half of the mango-zucchini mixture into 1 mushroom cap. Top with another mushroom cap.
4. Repeat with remaining ingredients for a second slider.
5. Arrange the sliders on the grill and cook for 10 minutes, or until the desired level of tenderness.
6. Serve immediately.

VARIATIONS TIP:
If you don't have zucchini, substitute 1 cup of cooked, shredded spaghetti squash instead.

Nutrition Info per Serving:
Calories: 135; Total Fat: 0.6 g; Carbohydrates: 32.2 g; Protein: 1.7 g; Fiber: 3.1 g

Brussels Sprouts with Ginger Sauce

Prep Time: 15 minutes, Cook Time: 10 minutes, Serves: 2

INGREDIENTS:
FOR THE SAUCE
1 tsp. freshly squeezed lime juice
½ cup light unsweetened coconut milk
½ tsp. chili-garlic sauce
1½ tsps. ground ginger
1 packet stevia

FOR THE BRUSSELS SPROUTS
1 tbsp. coconut oil
¾ pound (341 g) Brussels sprouts, ends removed, trimmed, and halved
½ tsp. sea salt

DIRECTIONS:
TO MAKE THE SAUCE
1. Combine all of the sauce ingredients in a blender, blend them together until smooth.
TO MAKE THE BRUSSELS SPROUTS
2. Preheat the broiler.
3. Add the coconut oil, Brussels sprouts and sea salt in a medium bowl. Toss to combine.
4. Transfer to a ovenproof skillet or medium cast-iron pan. Sauté over medium heat for 5 minutes.
5. Place the skillet under the broiler and broil until the leaves are slightly browned, about 3 minutes.
6. Place the Brussels sprouts into a medium bowl. Pour in the sauce and toss to coat. Serve immediately.

Nutrition Info per Serving:
Calories: 169; Total Fat: 8.7 g; Carbohydrates: 19.4 g; Protein: 7.9 g; Fiber: 6.5 g

Sautéed Eggplant and Spinach with Quinoa

Prep Time: 10 minutes, Cook Time: 25 minutes, Serves: 4

INGREDIENTS:
2 tsps. extra-virgin olive oil
1 medium eggplant, chopped
1 tbsp. taco spice blend
4 cups raw spinach
2 cups cooked quinoa
1 cup mango salsa

DIRECTIONS:
1. Heat the oil and the taco spice blend in a skillet over medium heat. Add the eggplant and cook for about 25 minutes, until thoroughly softened, turning the pieces occasionally.
2. Place the spinach to the pan and cook until the spinach wilts.
3. Evenly divide the cooked quinoa among four bowls and top with the eggplant mixture.
4. Garnish with the salsa and serve.

VARIATIONS TIP:
Mix a pinch of sea salt into the prepared quinoa. It will remove any bitterness and enliven the sweet, nutty flavor of the grain.

Nutrition Info per Serving:
Calories: 240; Fat: 5 g; Carbohydrates: 45 g; Protein: 8 g; Fiber: 11 g; Sodium: 277 mg; Iron: 3 mg

Spicy Eggplant and Bell Pepper Stir-Fry

Prep Time: 10 minutes, Cook Time: 5 minutes, Serves: 2 to 4

INGREDIENTS:
3 tbsps. avocado oil
2 garlic cloves, crushed
2 tbsps. coconut aminos
3 cups cubed eggplant (about three-quarters of an eggplant)
½ tsp. sea salt
½ tsp. freshly ground black pepper
½ yellow bell pepper, diced
½ orange bell pepper, diced
½ red bell pepper, diced
Chopped scallions and/or sesame seeds, for garnish (optional)

DIRECTIONS:
1. Heat the avocado oil in a large skillet over medium-high heat. Add the garlic, coconut aminos, eggplant, salt, and pepper, and sauté for 3 to 5 minutes, or until the eggplant is soft.
2. Reduce the heat to low, add the bell peppers, and toss just long enough to coat everything well.
3. Turn off the heat, transfer to 2 large or 4 small plates, and garnish with scallions and/or sesame seeds (if using) and serve.

VARIATIONS TIP:
Try adding the stir-fry to red lentil penne pasta or even spaghetti squash for variety.

Nutrition Info per Serving:
Calories: 276; Total Fat: 21.74 g; Carbohydrates: 19.54g; Protein: 3.63g; Fiber: 6.7 g

Baked Cheesy Potato and Onion

Prep Time: 10 minutes, Cook Time: 45 minutes, Serves: 4

INGREDIENTS:
1 tbsp. avocado oil
1½ onions, diced small
8 small new potatoes, sliced thin
1 tbsp. chopped fresh tarragon
1 tsp. freshly ground black pepper
1 tsp. sea salt
1 recipe cashew cheese sauce

DIRECTIONS:
1. Preheat the oven to 375°F(180°C).
2. Add the avocado oil, onions and potatoes into a large bowl, mix to coat well. Add the tarragon, pepper and salt, toss again.
3. Layer the potatoes in 3 rows in an 8-by-8-inch baking dish. Overlap and stand them up as necessary to fit in the dish. Sprinkle the diced onions between the potato slices and rows.
4. Bake for about 45 minutes, or until the potatoes are soft.
5. After baking, remove from the oven, and top the potatoes with the cheese sauce. Transfer to 4 plates and enjoy immediately, or place the baking dish back in the oven to warm the sauce for 5 minutes before serving.

VARIATIONS TIP:
Change this recipe up by using sliced sweet potatoes instead! Just bake at 350°F(180°C) for 30 minutes, or until they become soft.

Nutrition Info per Serving:
Calories: 350; Total Fat: 5.02 g; Carbohydrates: 69.85 g; Protein: 8.77 g; Fiber: 8.8 g

Carrot Fennel Slaw with Dijon Vinaigrette

Prep Time: 15 minutes, Cook Time: 0, Serves: 4

INGREDIENTS:
FOR THE SLAW
1 cup shredded carrots
1 cup chopped fennel
3 tbsps. raisins
¼ cup sliced almonds
FOR THE DIJON VINAIGRETTE
1 tbsp. avocado oil
1 tsp. apple cider vinegar
1 tsp. Dijon or yellow mustard
1 tbsp. freshly squeezed lemon juice
1 tsp. finely grated fresh ginger, or 1 cube frozen ginger

DIRECTIONS:
TO MAKE THE SLAW
1. Combine the carrots, fennel, raisins and almonds in a medium bowl, toss well and set aside.

TO MAKE THE DIJON VINAIGRETTE
2. Add all of the vinaigrette ingredients into a small bowl, whisk them together until well combined.
3. Pour over the slaw with the dressing and toss until evenly coated.
4. Serve cold or at room temperature. Place any leftovers in an airtight container and store in the refrigerator for up to 1 week.

Nutrition Info per Serving:
Calories: 167; Fat: 9 g; Carbohydrates: 19 g; Protein: 5 g; Fiber: 6 g; Sodium: 195 mg; Iron: 1 mg

Stuffed Mushroom Mini-Pizzas

Prep Time: 15 minutes, Cook Time: 15 minutes, Serves: 4

INGREDIENTS:
Cooking spray
1 tbsp. garlic powder
1 (6-ounce, 170 g) can organic tomato paste
1 tsp. dried oregano
1 tbsp. onion powder
4 tbsps. sun-dried tomatoes
½ tsp. sea salt, plus a pinch, divided
4 portobello mushroom caps, gills removed
4 slices fresh tomato

DIRECTIONS:
1. Preheat the oven to 350°F(180°C).
2. Use cooking spray to coat a baking pan.
3. Mix together the garlic powder, tomato paste, oregano, onion powder, sun-dried tomatoes, and sea salt in a small bowl.
4. Divide the tomato mixture evenly into the four mushroom caps. Place 1 tomato slice and a pinch of the sea salt on each top.
5. Place the pizzas into the baking pan, and bake for 15 minutes, or until the pizzas are hot and bubbly.

VARIATIONS TIP:
If you don't have tomato paste, you can substitute it for jarred pizza sauce. Just be sure to use a brand with no added oil or sugar.

Nutrition Info per Serving:
Calories: 66; Total Fat: 1.3 g; Carbohydrates: 13.4 g; Protein: 2.9 g; Fiber: 2.8 g

Jalapeño, Cilantro and Lentil "Burgers"

Prep Time: 15 minutes, Cook Time: 30 minutes, Serves: 2

INGREDIENTS:
½ cup dry lentils (equals 1 cup cooked)
½ cup diced onion
½ to 1 jalapeño, diced
½ cup almond flour
½ cup chopped cilantro leaves
2 garlic cloves, crushed
½ tsp. sea salt
½ tsp. freshly ground black pepper
1 tbsp. coconut flour
1 tbsp. avocado oil

DIRECTIONS:
1. According to the package directions to prepare the dry lentils. Set aside to cool.
2. Place the cooled lentils, onion, jalapeño, almond flour, cilantro, garlic, salt and pepper in a medium bowl, stir them together until well combined.
3. Transfer half of the lentil mixture to a food processor, process until it reaches a paste-like consistency.
4. Place the processed lentil mixture back into the bowl with the other half of the mixture, and stir until well combined. The mixture should be very moist, so mix in the coconut flour to help it hold together.
5. Take one-quarter of the mixture, squeeze it together in your hand, and use your palms to flatten it into a small burger. Repeat to make 3 more patties with the remaining lentil mixture.
6. Heat the avocado oil in a large skillet over medium-high heat. Add the burgers; cook for 4 to 6 minutes per side, or until they become golden, flipping them gently; and serve.

Nutrition Info per Serving:
Calories: 169; Total Fat: 10.6 g; Carbohydrates: 14.89 g Protein: 5.13g Fiber: 4.75 g

Almond Spiced Baked Onion Rings

Prep Time: 15 minutes, Cook Time: 10 minutes, Serves: 2

INGREDIENTS:

Cooking spray
1 tsp. garlic powder
⅔ cup almond meal
½ tsp. paprika
1 tsp. onion powder
½ tsp. sea salt
½ cup almond milk
1 large onion, sliced into ¼-inch-thick slices

DIRECTIONS:

1. Preheat the oven to 425°F(220°C).
2. Use cooking spray to grease a baking sheet.
3. Mix together the garlic powder, almond meal, paprika, onion powder and sea salt on a plate.
4. In a medium bowl, add the almond milk.
5. Dip one onion slice first into the milk. Then dredge it in the seasoned almond meal and put it on the baking sheet. Repeat with the remaining onion slices.
6. Put the sheet in the preheated oven and bake for 6 minutes. Turn each slice over and bake for another 4 minutes, or until crispy.
7. After baking, serve warm.

VARIATIONS TIP:

For a sweeter onion ring, choose a sweet onion like Vidalia or Maui.

Nutrition Info per Serving:
Calories: 210; Total Fat: 14.1 g; Carbohydrates: 6.4 g; Protein: 6.3 g; Fiber: 3.2 g

Baby Potato Fries with Mushroom

Prep Time: 10 minutes, Cook Time: 20 minutes, Serves: 2

INGREDIENTS:

4 medium baby white potatoes
½ sweet white onion, chopped
2 ounces (57 g) vegetable broth
1 red bell pepper, seeded and diced
½ cup sliced mushrooms
1 tsp. garlic powder
1 tsp. sea salt

DIRECTIONS:

1. Microwave the potatoes in a medium microwave-safe bowl for 4 minutes, or until soft. Allow to cool.
2. Add the onion, broth, and red bell pepper into a large nonstick skillet, sauté over medium heat for about 5 minutes, or until soft.
3. Meanwhile, cut the potatoes into quarters.
4. Add the mushrooms, potatoes, garlic powder and salt to the skillet. Stir to combine. Cook for about 10 minutes, or until the potatoes are crisp.
5. Serve warm.

VARIATIONS TIP:

You can also use small red potatoes for this recipe. It's best to avoid the brown russet potatoes typically used for baking as they contain a lot of starch.

Nutrition Info per Serving:
Calories: 337; Total Fat: 0.8 g; Carbohydrates: 74.8 g; Protein: 9.3 g; Fiber: 12.4 g

Avocado Toast with Spinach Basil Walnut Pesto

Prep Time: 15 minutes, Cook Time: 0, Serves: 2

INGREDIENTS:

FOR THE AVOCADO TOAST
½ medium avocado, halved
2 slices whole-grain bread, toasted
FOR THE VEGAN SPINACH-BASIL PESTO
3 tbsps. extra-virgin olive oil
4 cups baby spinach
1 cup fresh basil leaves
1 garlic clove, peeled, or 1 tsp. garlic powder
3 tbsps. walnuts
⅛ tsp. sea salt

DIRECTIONS:

TO MAKE THE AVOCADO TOAST
1. Cut slices into the flesh of the avocado and scoop out of the skin. Evenly spread the avocado over each piece of toast. Use plastic wrap to tightly wrap the remaining avocado half (with pit intact) and refrigerate for up to 2 days.

TO MAKE THE VEGAN SPINACH-BASIL PESTO
2. Combine all of the pesto ingredients in a high-speed blender, and blend for 1 to 2 minutes, until it reaches your desired consistency.
3. Place 1 tablespoon of the pesto on the top each avocado-smeared slice of toast and serve. Place the leftover pesto in an airtight container and store in the refrigerator for 4 to 5 days.

VARIATIONS TIP:

Replace the pesto with a crunchy veggie such as sliced radishes or cucumber and top with cilantro.

Nutrition Info per Serving:
Calories: 205; Fat: 13 g; Carbohydrates: 18 g; Protein: 6 g; Fiber: 6 g; Sodium: 97 mg; Iron: 2 mg

Roasted Garlic

Prep Time: 5 minutes, Cook Time: 45 minutes, Serves: 1

INGREDIENTS:
- 1 garlic head
- 1 tsp. avocado oil
- Pinch sea salt

DIRECTIONS:
1. Preheat the oven to 375°F(190°C).
2. Remove the outer papery layer of the garlic head. Cut the top off, and add the entire garlic head into a paper muffin cup in a muffin pan. Drizzle over with the avocado oil, be sure that it's evenly distributed in all the crevices, and sprinkle with the salt.
3. Roast for 45 minutes. Allow to cool until easy to handle.
4. Squeeze or peel each clove out of the paper shell gently. Use in any recipe that calls for roasted garlic.

VARIATIONS TIP:
Save time by roasting several heads of garlic at once and freezing. To freeze, remove the roasted cloves from their skins, spread evenly on a baking pan, and place in the freezer. After they are frozen, transfer to a freezer-safe container.

Nutrition Info per Serving:
Calories: 44; Total Fat: 4.52 g; Carbohydrates: 0.99 g Protein: 0.19 g Fiber: 0.1 g

Garlic Broccoli Bites

Prep Time: 5 minutes, Cook Time: 20 minutes, Serves: 3 cups

INGREDIENTS:
- ½ cup nutritional yeast
- ½ cup almond flour
- ½ tsp. sea salt
- ½ tsp. garlic powder
- ¼ to ½ tsp. ground cayenne pepper (optional)
- 3 cups bite-size broccoli florets
- 2 tbsps. avocado oil

DIRECTIONS:
1. Preheat the oven to 400°F(205°C). Use parchment paper to line a baking sheet.
2. Combine all of the ingredients except the broccoli and avocado oil in a small bowl, stir them together.
3. Add the broccoli and avocado oil into a medium bowl, toss to coat.
4. Sprinkle over the broccoli with half the seasoning mixture, toss gently until all pieces are coated, and bake for 10 minutes.
5. Remove from the oven, and return the broccoli pieces to the medium bowl. Sprinkle with the remaining half of the seasoning mix, and toss to coat.
6. Place back in the oven and bake for another 5 to 10 minutes, and serve.

VARIATIONS TIP:
Add these bite-size pieces of broccoli to a salad as a healthy replacement for croutons.

Nutrition Info per Serving:
Calories: 554; Total Fat: 30.22 g; Carbohydrates: 35.19 g Protein: 38.81 g Fiber: 13 g

Stuffed Sweet Potato with Broccoli-Almond Pesto

Prep Time: 10 minutes, Cook Time: 1 ½ hours, Serves: 2

INGREDIENTS:
- 2 large sweet potatoes
- 2 tbsps. avocado oil
- 2½ cups broccoli
- 2½ cups almonds
- 2 garlic cloves
- ½ cup fresh basil leaves
- ¼ cup onion
- ¼ cup nutritional yeast
- ½ tsp. sea salt

DIRECTIONS:
1. Preheat the oven to 350°F(180°C).
2. Use a fork to pierce the sweet potatoes all over. Add the sweet potatoes onto a baking sheet, and bake for 1 hour and 15 minutes, or until they are soft.
3. While the sweet potatoes bake, prepare the pesto. Combine the remaining ingredients in a food processor, pulse until the broccoli and almonds are ground into tiny pieces. Adjust the seasonings, if needed.
4. When the potatoes are ready, cut them in half lengthwise, and scoop out the insides of the potato gently, not to tear the potato skin; add the baked potato filling to a medium bowl, then add the pesto mixture; stir together gently.
5. Divide the mixture in half, fill each half into the two empty potato skins, and serve.

VARIATIONS TIP:
The pesto is a great alternative for a topping in the pizza recipe here, or as a spread on a wrap or even as a dip for fresh veggies!

Nutrition Info per Serving:
Calories: 765; Total Fat: 31.24 g; Carbohydrates: 97.44 g Protein: 28.94 g Fiber: 20.3 g

Chapter 3: Vegetable

Tomato Zoodles with Avocado Sauce

Prep Time: 10 minutes, Cook Time: 0, Serves: 2

INGREDIENTS:
2 avocados, peeled, pitted
½ cup walnuts
2 cups basil leaves
⅓ tsp. salt
4 tbsps. key lime juice
½ cup spring water
2 zucchinis, spiralized into noodles
24 cherry tomatoes, sliced

DIRECTIONS:
1. Prepare the sauce, in a food processor, add all of the ingredients except for the zucchini noodles and tomatoes, pulse until smooth.
2. Place the zucchini noodles in a large bowl, add the tomato slices, pour in the prepared sauce and toss until coated.
3. Serve immediately.

Nutrition Info per Serving:
Calories: 330; Fats: 20.7 g; Protein: 7.1 g; Carb: 35.3 g; Fiber: 7.8 g;

Sweet Potato "Toast" with Spicy Garlic Avocado Topping

Prep Time: 10 minutes, Cook Time: 10 minutes, Serves: 4

INGREDIENTS:
1 unpeeled sweet potato, cut into 4 (½-inch-thick) lengthwise slices
2 garlic cloves
½ to 1 jalapeño
2 avocados
1 tbsp. chopped onion
1 tbsp. fresh cilantro leaves
¼ to ½ tsp. sea salt
Sliced red onion, sliced radish, or dulse flakes, for topping (optional)

DIRECTIONS:
1. Place a sweet potato slice in each toaster slot, and toast through about 4 cycles, or until cooked through, and can use a fork to pierce. Use tongs to carefully remove, and repeat with the remaining slices.
2. Meanwhile, combine the garlic, jalapeño, avocados, onion, cilantro and salt in a food processor, process them together until creamy and smooth. Adjust the salt level as desired.
3. Spread over the sweet potato "toast" with the avocado topping; place the red onion, radish, or dulse flakes (if using) on the top; and serve.

Nutrition Info per Serving:
Calories: 195; Total Fat: 14.8 g; Carbohydrates: 16.6 g Protein: 2.79 g Fiber: 7.9 g

Red Pepper Tapenade Eggplant Rollups

Prep Time: 15 minutes, Cook Time: 13 minutes, Serves: 6

INGREDIENTS:
FOR THE TAPENADE
1 (12-ounce, 340 g) jar packed-in-water roasted red peppers
¼ onion, chopped
¼ tsp. red pepper flakes
1 tbsp. freshly squeezed lemon juice
3 fresh basil leaves
1 garlic clove
FOR THE EGGPLANT
2 eggplants, tops removed, thinly sliced lengthwise (about 24 slices)
Cooking spray
2 tsps. sea salt

DIRECTIONS:
TO MAKE THE TAPENADE
1. Add of the tapenade ingredients into a food processor. Pulse until blended but still chunky.
TO MAKE THE EGGPLANT
2. Preheat the grill to medium, or preheat the broiler.
3. On a baking sheet, lay the eggplant slices and spray with cooking spray. Sprinkle with salt.
4. Place the eggplant slices onto the grill and grill for 3 minutes, or until grill marks form. If you don't have a grill, place the baking sheet in the broiler and broil instead.
5. Then transfer the eggplant back to the baking sheet (or remove the baking sheet from the oven).
6. If using a grill, preheat the oven to 375°F(190°C).
7. If using a broiler for the eggplant slices, reduce the oven heat to 375°F(190°C).
8. On one end of each eggplant slice, add 1 to 2 tablespoons of tapenade. Roll the slices up and over the filling, finishing seam-side down. Put the sheet back in the oven and bake the rolls for 10 minutes or until heated.
9. After baking, serve the rolls warm.

VARIATIONS TIP:
To make sure you always have roasted red peppers on hand, just pop some in the oven in a baking pan and let them roast as you put away the other groceries. It should take about 15 minutes at 350°F(180°C).

Nutrition Info per Serving:
Calories: 37; Total Fat: 0.3 g; Carbohydrates: 8.7 g; Protein: 1.4 g; Fiber: 3.5 g

Spiced Tomato Okra Curry

Prep Time: 5 minutes, Cook Time: 10 minutes, Serves: 2

INGREDIENTS:
- ½ tbsp. grapeseed oil
- 1 medium onion, peeled, sliced
- 6 tsps. spice mix
- 8 cherry tomatoes, chopped
- ¾ cup vegetable broth, homemade
- ¼ tsp. salt
- ¼ tsp. cayenne pepper
- ¾ cup tomato sauce, alkaline
- 6 tbsps. soft-jelly coconut milk
- 1 ½ cup okra

DIRECTIONS:
1. Heat the oil in a large skillet pan over medium heat, add the onion, and cook for 5 minutes until golden brown.
2. Place the spice mix in the skillet pan, then add all of the remaining ingredients except for the okra, stir until mixed, and bring the mixture to a simmer.
3. Stir in the okra and mix well, reduce the heat to medium-low, cook for 10 to 15 minutes until cooked.
4. Serve immediately.

Nutrition Info per Serving:
Calories: 137; Fats: 8.4 g; Carb: 15 g; Protein: 4 g; Fiber: 5.6 g

Healthy Stir-Fry Mixed Vegetables

Prep Time: 15 minutes, Cook Time: 5 minutes, Serves: 2

INGREDIENTS:
- 2 tbsps. coconut oil
- 1 yellow bell pepper, cored, seeded, and julienned
- 1 red bell pepper, cored, seeded, and julienned
- ½ cup thinly sliced red onion
- 1 cup small broccoli florets
- 1 cup sliced yellow squash
- 1 cup fresh mung bean sprouts
- 2 cups sliced bok choy
- ½ cup snow peas
- ¼ tsp. sea salt
- 1 garlic clove, minced
- 2 tbsps. lime juice
- 2 tbsps. sesame oil

DIRECTIONS:
1. Heat the coconut oil in a wok or large skillet over medium-high heat for 1 to 2 minutes.
2. While stirring constantly, add the yellow bell pepper, red bell pepper, and onion.
3. Add the broccoli, yellow squash, bean sprouts, bok choy, and snow peas. Stir-fry for 2 minutes. Stir in the salt and garlic.
4. Stir in the lime juice and combine well.
5. Remove from the heat and stir in the sesame oil.
6. Serve immediately.

Nutrition Info per Serving:
Calories: 354; Total Fat: 12.8 g; Carbohydrates: 24.1 g; Protein: 8.4 g; Fiber: 8.4 g

Zucchini and Kale Pesto with Spaghetti Squash

Prep Time: 20 minutes, Cook Time: 50 minutes, Serves: 2

INGREDIENTS:
FOR THE SQUASH
- 1 spaghetti squash
- 2 tsps. avocado oil
- Sea salt
- Freshly ground black pepper

FOR THE PESTO
- 2 tbsps. avocado oil
- 2 stalks kale, stemmed
- 1 zucchini peeled
- ¼ cup chopped onion
- ½ cup raw cashews
- 2 garlic cloves
- 1 tbsp. freshly squeezed lemon juice
- 1 tbsp. nutritional yeast
- ½ tsp. sea salt

DIRECTIONS:
1. Preheat the oven to 350°F(180°C). Use parchment paper to line a baking sheet.

TO PREPARE THE SQUASH
2. Cut the spaghetti squash in half lengthwise, scoop out the seeds, rub the avocado oil onto the insides and outer rims of both halves, sprinkle with salt and pepper, and transfer to a baking sheet. Bake for 45 to 50 minutes, or until tender.

TO PREPARE THE PESTO
3. While the squash bakes, add all of the pesto ingredients into a food processor, process until well blended. Adjust seasonings, if needed.

TO ASSEMBLE
4. Scrape out the insides of the squash into long, pasta-like strands with a fork. Transfer to a medium bowl.
5. Add the pesto, and gently toss until well mixed. Transfer to 2 plates or bowls and serve.

VARIATIONS TIP:
The Zucchini and Kale Pesto is so versatile. You can use it as the base sauce for the Veggie Pizza here, toss it with red lentil penne pasta, or use it as a spread in a wrap or even as a dip for fresh veggies.

Nutrition Info per Serving:
Calories: 258; Total Fat: 22.22 g; Carbohydrates: 12.23 g Protein: 5.03 g Fiber: 2.65

Homemade Roated Garlic Cabbage

Prep Time: 5 minutes, Cook Time: 45 minutes, Serves: 4

INGREDIENTS:
1 (2-pound, 907 g) head organic green cabbage, cut into 1-inch-thick slices (about 8 slices)
1½ tbsps. coconut oil
2 to 3 large garlic cloves, smashed
Pinch sea salt

DIRECTIONS:
1. Preheat the oven to 425°F(220°C).
2. In a baking pan, add the cabbage slices and use the coconut oil to brush on both sides.
3. Rub the garlic onto each cabbage slice and sprinkle with salt.
4. Place the pan in the preheated oven and roast for 20 minutes. Flip the cabbage slices over and roast for an additional 20 to 25 minutes, until the edges are brown and crisp.

VARIATIONS TIP:
Try using purple cabbage instead of green; it basically tastes the same but offers a more dramatic presentation.

Nutrition Info per Serving:
Calories: 90; Total Fat: 5.3 g; Carbohydrates: 10.3 g; Protein: 2.3 g; Fiber: 4.5 g

Root Vegetable Chips

Prep Time: 10 minutes, Cook Time: 20 minutes, Serves: 4

INGREDIENTS:
1 large carrot, peeled
1 parsnip, peeled
1 sweet potato, peeled
1 beet, peeled
1 tsp. sea salt
Cooking spray

DIRECTIONS:
1. Preheat the oven to 375°F(190°C).
2. Slice the carrot, parsnip, sweet potato and beet into very thin slices with a food processor attachment, mandoline, or food slicer. Lay the slices flat on a paper towel and sprinkle with the salt. Use a paper towel to cover and allow to sit for 15 minutes.
3. Blot any moisture on the vegetable slices.
4. Use cooking spray to grease a baking sheet.
5. On the baking sheet, place the vegetable slices in a single layer. Spray the vegetables with cooking spray.
6. Put the sheet in the preheated oven and bake until crisp, about 20 minutes.

VARIATIONS TIP:
Toss these chips with garlic powder, chili powder, curry powder, or other alkaline-friendly seasonings to add variety.

Nutrition Info per Serving:
Calories: 69; Total Fat: 0.2 g; Carbohydrates: 16.1 g; Protein: 1.4 g; Fiber: 3.5 g

Garlic Almond Breadsticks

Prep Time: 5 minutes, Cook Time: 20 minutes, Serves: 12 pieces

INGREDIENTS:
FOR THE BREADSTICKS
1 tbsp. ground flaxseed
3 tbsps. water
1 tbsp. avocado oil
2 cups almond flour
1 tbsp. chopped fresh oregano
½ tsp. freshly ground black pepper
½ tsp. sea salt
FOR THE TOPPING
1 tbsp. avocado oil
1 tbsp. chopped fresh oregano
4 garlic cloves, crushed
⅛ tsp. sea salt
⅛ tsp. freshly ground black pepper

DIRECTIONS:
1. Preheat the oven to 350°F(180°C). Use parchment paper to line a baking sheet.

TO PREPARE THE BREADSTICKS
2. To prepare a flax egg, add the flaxseed and water in a small bowl, whisk them together until well blended.
3. Combine the flax egg, avocado oil, almond flour, oregano, pepper and salt in a medium bowl, stir them together until well combined.
4. Place the mixture onto the prepared baking sheet, and form the mixture into a ball. Lay another sheet of parchment paper on top of the ball, and over the paper, roll the dough into a 5-by-8-inch rectangle shape with a rolling pin.

TO PREPARE THE TOPPING
5. Combine all of the topping ingredients in a small bowl, stir them together until well combined. Pour over the dough with the topping mixture, and spread it evenly with the back of a spoon.
6. Bake until the edges are golden brown, about 18 to 20 minutes.
7. After baking, take out from the oven, slice into 12 pieces, and serve.

Nutrition Info per Serving:
Calories: 358; Total Fat: 33.97 g; Carbohydrates: 13.64 g Protein: 4 g; Fiber: 6.9 g

Zucchini Linguine with Avocado Sauce

Prep Time: 10 minutes, Cook Time: 8 minutes, Serves: 2

INGREDIENTS:
- 1 tbsp. grapeseed oil
- ¼ cup chopped cilantro
- ½ cup sliced mushrooms
- ½ cup alkaline avocado sauce
- ⅓ tsp. salt
- ⅛ tsp. cayenne pepper
- ½ tsp. dried thyme
- ½ tsp. dried oregano
- 2 zucchini, spiralized

DIRECTIONS:
1. Heat the oil in a skillet pan over medium heat. When hot, add the cilantro and mushrooms, cook for 3 to 5 minutes until tender.
2. Pour in the avocado sauce, season with the salt, pepper, thyme and oregano, stir until mixed and cook for 1 to 2 minutes until warmed.
3. In a large bowl, add the zucchini noodles, drizzle with some oil, and then toss until well coated.
4. Add the mushroom avocado mixture to the bowl, toss until combined, and serve.

Nutrition Info per Serving:
Calories: 284; Fats: 23.6 g; Carb: 18.8 g; Protein: 5.7 g; Fiber: 9.7 g

Rosemary, Carrot and Sweet Potato Medallions

Prep Time: 10 minutes, Cook Time: 35 to 45 minutes, Serves: 6

INGREDIENTS:
- 4 tsps. avocado oil or extra-virgin olive oil
- 1 cup chopped carrots
- 2 large sweet potatoes, sliced into rounds
- 2 tsps. fresh rosemary
- ¼ tsp. sea salt

DIRECTIONS:
1. Preheat the oven to 400°F(205°C).
2. Combine the oil, carrots, sweet potatoes, rosemary, and salt in a large bowl or resealable plastic bag, mix until the sweet potatoes and carrots are well coated.
3. Transfer the vegetables into a rectangular glass baking dish and arrange them in a single layer to evenly cook.
4. Roast for 35 to 45 minutes, until the thickest sweet potato rounds are soft; use a paring knife insert to check.

VARIATIONS TIP:
Try multicolored carrots (purple, white, and orange) to add color to your dish.

Nutrition Info per Serving:
Calories: 95; Fat: 3 g; Carbohydrates: 16 g; Protein: 1 g; Fiber: 3 g; Sodium: 149 mg; Iron: 1 mg

Potato, Cauliflower and Broccoli Mash

Prep Time: 15 minutes, Cook Time: 7 minutes, Serves: 2

INGREDIENTS:
- 1 sweet potato, peeled and diced
- 2 cups cooked cauliflower florets
- 1 tsp. sea salt, divided
- 1 cup almond milk, room temperature, divided, plus additional as needed
- 2 cups cooked broccoli florets

DIRECTIONS:
1. In a small pan, add the sweet potato, pour in the water. Bring the water to a boil. Cook the sweet potato for 7 minutes, or until it is soft. Drain and set aside.
2. Meanwhile, in a large mixing bowl, add the cauliflower. Add ⅓ teaspoon salt and ⅓ cup almond milk. Mash the cauliflower until smooth, adding additional almond milk if needed. Remove from the mixing bowl and set aside.
3. Add the broccoli, ⅓ teaspoon salt and ⅓ cup almond milk into the same large mixing bowl. Mash the broccoli until smooth. Remove from the mixing bowl and set aside.
4. Add the warm sweet potatoes, the remaining ⅓ teaspoon salt and the remaining ⅓ cup almond milk in the same large mixing bowl. Mash the sweet potato until smooth.
5. In the bottom of each of two medium bowls, add one-half of the mashed sweet potato, top each with one-half of the mashed cauliflower. Layer that with one-half of the mashed broccoli in each bowl. Serve warm.

VARIATIONS TIP:
Add a layer of mashed baby or new potatoes if you wish. If you add these new foods, you'll just need to update the recipe's nutritional information.

Nutrition Info per Serving:
Calories: 158; Total Fat: 0.5 g; Carbohydrates: 27.1 g; Protein: 7.7 g; Fiber: 6.8 g

Easy Baked Sweet Potato and Apple

Prep Time: 5 minutes, Cook Time: 40 minutes, Serves: 1

INGREDIENTS:
1 medium sweet potato
1 medium apple, peeled and diced
Pinch sea salt
½ tsp. cinnamon

DIRECTIONS:
1. Preheat the oven to 350°F(180°C).
2. Cut lengthwise of the sweet potato, about 1 inch deep. Spread the potato open and put it in a baking dish.
3. Inside the sweet potato's opening, add the apple. Sprinkle over with the salt and cinnamon.
4. Use aluminum foil to cover. Put the dish in the preheated oven and bake for 40 minutes, or until the potato is soft.
5. After baking, allow to cool slightly and serve warm.

Nutrition Info per Serving:
Calories: 198; Total Fat: 0.2 g; Carbohydrates: 48.7 g; Protein: 2.3 g; Fiber: 8.2 g

Garlic Mushroom Pâté

Prep Time: 15 minutes, Cook Time: 15 minutes, Serves: 6

INGREDIENTS:
Cooking spray
1 onion, chopped
2 garlic cloves, minced
2 pounds (907 g) fresh mushrooms, any kind, finely chopped
¼ tsp. finely chopped fresh rosemary
1 tbsp. chopped fresh parsley
1 tbsp. freshly squeezed lemon juice
½ tsp. sea salt

DIRECTIONS:
1. Use cooking spray to coat a medium saucepan. Add the onion and cook over medium heat for about 5 minutes, or until translucent.
2. Add the garlic and mushrooms to the pan. Cook for another 10 minutes, until cooked through.
3. Remove from the heat and place the mixture into a food processor. Add the rosemary, parsley, lemon juice and salt. Pulse to a desired consistency.
4. Serve.

VARIATIONS TIP:
For variation, experiment with different kinds of mushrooms. Also, if you're feeling luxurious, drizzle a tiny bit of truffle oil on top before serving.

Nutrition Info per Serving:
Calories: 43; Total Fat: 0.6 g; Carbohydrates: 7.1 g; Protein: 5 g; Fiber: 3.5 g

Garlic Bell Pepper-Stuffed Portobello Mushrooms

Prep Time: 10 minutes, Cook Time: 20 minutes, Serves: 2

INGREDIENTS:
FOR THE MUSHROOMS
2 large portobello mushrooms
Avocado oil, for rubbing
Freshly ground black pepper
Sea salt
FOR THE STUFFING
2 tsps. avocado oil
2 garlic cloves, crushed
½ red bell pepper, diced
½ orange bell pepper, diced
½ yellow bell pepper, diced
¼ cup diced red onion
½ tsp. sea salt
½ tsp. freshly ground black pepper

DIRECTIONS:
1. Preheat the oven to 350°F(180°C). Use parchment paper to line a baking sheet.
TO PREPARE THE MUSHROOMS
2. Quickly rinse and dry the mushrooms. Remove the stems, and scoop out the black gills with the tip of a spoon. Rub the avocado oil all over of the mushrooms, and sprinkle with pepper and salt.
3. Transfer the mushrooms to the prepared baking sheet, and bake for 15 to 20 minutes, or until the mushrooms are as soft as you like.
TO PREPARE THE STUFFING
4. While the mushrooms bake, stir together the avocado oil, garlic, bell peppers, onion, salt, and pepper in a small bowl until well combined.
TO ASSEMBLE
5. After baking, remove the mushrooms from the oven, and discard any accumulated liquid.
6. Evenly divide the stuffing mixture between the 2 mushrooms and serve immediately.

VARIATIONS TIP:
You can turn this dish into a salad by cutting up the mushrooms after baking and tossing them with the veggies and your favorite salad green.

Nutrition Info per Serving:
Calories: 323; Total Fat: 29.47 g; Carbohydrates: 14.99 g Protein: 3.86 g Fiber: 3 g

Cheesy Baked Kale Chips, page 35

Garlic Broccoli Bites, page 27

Tomato Zoodles with Avocado Sauce, page 28

Roasted Garlic, page 27

Chapter 3: Vegetable   33

Cauliflower Popcorn

Prep Time: 10 minutes, Cook Time: 30 minutes, Serves: 4

INGREDIENTS:

3 tbsps. coconut oil
1 cauliflower head, separated into small florets
1 tsp. sea salt

DIRECTIONS:

1. Preheat the oven to 400°F(205°C).
2. Combine the coconut oil, cauliflower, and salt in a large bowl.
3. Place the cauliflower on a baking sheet and evenly spread it into a single layer.
4. Put the sheet in the oven and roast for about 30 minutes, until golden brown and slightly crisp.

VARIATIONS TIP:

Don't use frozen cauliflower for this recipe. It will be too soggy.

Nutrition Info per Serving:
Calories: 107; Total Fat: 10.3 g; Carbohydrates: 3.5 g; Protein: 1.3 g; Fiber: 1.7 g

Garlic Lentil and Sweet Potato Taco Wraps

Prep Time: 10 minutes, Cook Time: 30 minutes, Serves: 2 warps

INGREDIENTS:

FOR THE SWEET POTATO
1 sweet potato, peeled and cut into bite-size cubes
2 tsps. avocado oil
⅛ tsp. ground paprika
1 garlic clove, crushed
⅛ tsp. sea salt
FOR THE LENTILS
¾ cup dry lentils, cooked according to package directions
1 tbsp. avocado oil
2 garlic cloves, crushed
½ to 1 jalapeño
1 cup fresh cilantro leaves
1 tbsp. freshly squeezed lemon juice
1 tsp. sea salt
½ tsp. freshly ground black pepper
FOR ASSEMBLING
2 collard green leaves
Nondairy sour cream, for garnish (optional)

DIRECTIONS:

1. Preheat the oven to 350°F(180°C).
TO PREPARE THE SWEET POTATO
2. Place the sweet potato in a small bowl, toss with the avocado oil to coat. Add the paprika, garlic, and salt, and toss to coat again. Bake for 25 to 30 minutes, or until soft.
TO PREPARE THE LENTILS
3. Add the cooked lentils, avocado oil, garlic, jalapeño, cilantro, lemon juice, salt and pepper into a food processor, pulse until well combined, not overprocess.
TO ASSEMBLE
4. Spread half the lentil mixture onto a collard green leaf, and place half the sweet potatoes on the top, and drizzle with nondairy sour cream (if using). Repeat with the remaining ingredients and enjoy.

VARIATIONS TIP:

Want to save some time? Substitute the baked sweet potato cubes with cubed or sliced avocado.

Nutrition Info per Serving:
Calories: 305; Total Fat: 16.83g; Carbohydrates: 32.32g Protein: 8.85g Fiber: 9.3g

Cauliflower, Almond and Date Porridge

Prep Time: 10 minutes, Cook Time: 7 minutes, Serves: 2

INGREDIENTS:

2 cups chopped cauliflower
¼ cup almond meal
4 dates, pitted
2 tsps. flax meal
½ cup unsweetened almond milk

DIRECTIONS:

1. Set a steamer basket inside a small pot, covered and steam the cauliflower over boiling water for 7 minutes, or until soft.
2. Remove the steamer basket, place the cauliflower into a bowl, and use a fork to mash it or whisk until it reaches the desired consistency. Set aside.
3. Combine the almond meal, dates, and flax meal in a high-speed blender, blend until smooth. Add the mixture to the cauliflower and stir to combine.
4. Evenly divide the porridge between two bowls and stir in ¼ cup of the almond milk. Eat immediately or reheat when ready to serve.

VARIATIONS TIP:

If you have a nut allergy, swap out the almond milk for unsweetened oat milk.

Nutrition Info per Serving:
Calories: 188; Fat: 10 g; Carbohydrates: 22 g; Protein: 8 g; Fiber: 8 g; Sodium: 69 mg; Iron: 2 mg

Cheesy Baked Kale Chips

Prep Time: 5 minutes, Cook Time: 10 minutes, Serves: 1 or 2

INGREDIENTS:

4 or 5 stalks curly kale, stemmed and torn (2 cups, packed)	1 tbsp. avocado oil
	¼ tsp. sea salt
	1 tbsp. nutritional yeast

DIRECTIONS:
1. Preheat the oven to 350°F(180°C). Use parchment paper to line a baking sheet.
2. Place the kale in a medium bowl, toss with the avocado oil to coat.
3. Sprinkle over the kale with the salt and nutritional yeast, and toss to coat again.
4. Place the coated kale onto the prepared baking sheet, and bake for 5 to 6 minutes. Turn them over and bake for another 5 to 6 minutes, or until they are crispy, not to burn them.
5. After baking, allow to cool and serve.

VARIATIONS TIP:
These are also great to crumble over a salad as a topping.

Nutrition Info per Serving:
Calories: 188; Total Fat: 14.76 g; Carbohydrates: 9.28 g Protein: 7.04 g; Fiber: 3.5 g

Roasted Zucchini Lasagna

Prep Time: 10 minutes, Cook Time: 25 minutes, Serves: 2

INGREDIENTS:

4 zucchini, sliced lengthwise into ¼-inch noodles	1 cup sun-dried tomato sauce
	1 cup White sauce

DIRECTIONS:
1. Preheat the oven to 350°F(180°C).
2. On a baking sheet, add the zucchini noodles. Roast for 10 minutes, then remove from the oven.
3. Cover the bottom with one layer of zucchini strips in a small lasagna pan. Pour in ¼ cup sun-dried tomato sauce over. Then add another layer of zucchini strips, placed crosswise from the first layer. Cover with another ¼ cup sun-dried tomato sauce. Lay a third layer of zucchini crosswise from the second layer and another ¼ cup sun-dried tomato sauce. Repeat with the remaining zucchini and ¼ cup sun-dried tomato sauce.
4. Place the White sauce on top of the finished lasagna. Use the aluminum foil to cover, and bake for 15 minutes, or until hot and bubbly.
5. Remove from the oven and allow to cool for 5 minutes before slicing and serving.

Nutrition Info per Serving:
Calories: 184; Total Fat: 3.6 g; Carbohydrates: 16.1 g; Protein: 5.4 g; Fiber: 4.6 g

Nori Vegetable Rolls with Avocado-Jalapeño Spread

Prep Time: 10 minutes, Cook Time: 0, Serves: 2 large rolls

INGREDIENTS:

FOR THE AVOCADO-JALAPEÑO SPREAD	2 collard green leaves
¼ cup fresh cilantro leaves	2 nori sheets
1 avocado, pitted and halved	½ orange bell pepper, sliced
½ to 1 jalapeño	½ red bell pepper, sliced
2 tbsps. freshly squeezed lemon juice	½ yellow bell pepper, sliced
¼ tsp. sea salt	½ cup chopped purple cabbage
FOR THE ROLLS	2 tbsps. chopped fresh cilantro leaves

DIRECTIONS:
TO PREPARE THE AVOCADO-JALAPEÑO SPREAD
1. Combine all of the spread ingredients in a blender, blend them together until smooth.

TO PREPARE THE ROLLS

2. Lay 1 collard green leaf flat, over the top place with 1 nori sheet.
3. Down the center of the nori sheet, spread with half the avocado-jalapeño mixture.
4. Top the avocado-jalapeño spread over the nori sheet, add half of the bell peppers, cabbage, and cilantro. Roll like a burrito. Repeat with the remaining nori, collard green leaf, bell pepper, cabbage, and cilantro.
5. Serve each roll whole or halved.

VARIATIONS TIP:
You can also make a "deconstructed" vegetable roll by turning it into a salad: Just break the nori sheet into small pieces, stem and chop the collard greens, and add both to a salad bowl. Then toss with the veggie filling and use the jalapeño spread as a dressing!

Nutrition Info per Serving:
Calories: 264; Total Fat: 15.89 g; Carbohydrates: 30.14 g; Protein: 6.1 g; Fiber: 9.45 g

Vanilla Spiced Quinoa Pumpkin Casserole

Prep Time: 15 minutes, Cook Time: 15 minutes, Serves: 6

INGREDIENTS:

Cooking spray
3 cups cooked quinoa
1 vanilla bean, split lengthwise and seeds scraped out
1 (15-ounce, 425 g) can pumpkin purée
½ cup water
½ tsp. nutmeg
½ tsp. ground ginger
1 tsp. cinnamon
¼ tsp. grated fresh ginger
¼ tsp. sea salt

DIRECTIONS:
1. Preheat the oven to 350°F(180°C).
2. Spray a 4-cup casserole dish and set aside.
3. Add the quinoa and the remaining ingredients in a medium bowl, stir them together.
4. Place the mixture onto the prepared casserole dish. Bake for 15 minutes, or until golden and bubbly.

VARIATIONS TIP:
You can actually microwave this dish to make it even faster. Simply pop the mixture into the microwave for 7 minutes on high, or until the pumpkin is set.

Nutrition Info per Serving:
Calories: 26; Total Fat: 5 g; Carbohydrates: 57.1 g; Protein: 12 g; Fiber: 7.7 g

Nutty Spinach, Artichoke and Tomato Dip

Prep Time: 10 minutes, Cook Time: 20 minutes, Serves: 6

INGREDIENTS:

Cooking spray
¾ cup unsweetened almond milk
1 garlic clove
¾ cup raw cashews
2 tbsps. freshly squeezed lemon juice
¾ tsp. sea salt
1 tbsp. nutritional yeast
2 cups baby spinach leaves
1 cup baby tomatoes
2 cups artichoke hearts, frozen or canned in water, not oil

DIRECTIONS:
1. Preheat the oven to 425°F(220°C).
2. Use cooking spray to coat a medium baking dish.
3. Add the almond milk, garlic, cashews, lemon juice, salt and yeast into a blender. Blend until very smooth.
4. Add the spinach, tomatoes and artichoke hearts to the blender. Pulse to combine, but still leaving chunks of vegetables.
5. Place the dip into the prepared baking dish. Place the dish in the preheated oven and bake for 20 minutes.
6. After baking, remove from the oven, allow to cool for 5 minutes, and serve warm.

VARIATIONS TIP:
You can use frozen spinach in this recipe if you prefer. Just be sure to squeeze out all of the water.

Nutrition Info per Serving:
Calories: 178; Total Fat: 15.3 g; Carbohydrates: 10.3 g; Protein: 4.4 g; Fiber: 2.3 g

Tomato Mushroom Stuffed Eggplant

Prep Time: 10 minutes, Cook Time: 30 minutes, Serves: 4

INGREDIENTS:

1 large eggplant, cut in half lengthwise
3 tbsps. extra-virgin olive oil or avocado oil, divided
⅛ tsp. sea salt
1 tsp. taco spice blend
2 garlic cloves, crushed, or 2 frozen garlic cubes
1 cup canned low-sodium diced tomatoes
2 cups sliced mushrooms
1 cup canned low-sodium chickpeas, drained and rinsed

DIRECTIONS:
1. Preheat the oven to 425°F(220°C). Use aluminum foil to line a baking sheet.
2. Put the eggplant on the baking sheet and use 1½ teaspoons of oil to brush each side. Sprinkle both sides with salt.
3. Place the eggplant halves on the baking sheet, cut-side down, bake for 30 to 40 minutes, until the flesh softens and the outer skin puckers.
4. While the eggplant is baking, heat the remaining 1 tablespoon of oil in a skillet on medium heat. Add the taco spice blend and garlic, cook for 2 minutes.
5. Stir the tomatoes and mushrooms into the skillet and cook for an additional 10 minutes, or until the mushrooms are soft.
6. Add the chickpeas and cook for 3 minutes more, or until warmed through. Turn off the heat and cover.
7. Evenly divide the mushroom mixture between the eggplant halves and cut each in half to make four servings.

Nutrition Info per Serving:
Calories: 183; Fat: 8 g; Carbohydrates: 23 g; Protein: 6 g; Fiber: 9 g; Sodium: 365 mg; Iron: 2 mg

Quinoa Vegetable Stuffed Peppers

Prep Time: 5 minutes, Cook Time: 20 minutes, Serves: 2

INGREDIENTS:

Cooking spray
1 tsp. coconut oil
½ cup chopped vegetables, zucchini, carrots, or broccoli
1 cup cooked quinoa
1 tsp. onion powder
1 tsp. garlic powder
1 tsp. sea salt
2 bell peppers, any color, cored and seeded; tops removed and reserved

DIRECTIONS:
1. Preheat the oven to 350°F(180°C).
2. Use cooking spray to coat a baking pan.
3. Add the coconut oil and chopped vegetables in a medium saucepan, sauté over medium heat for 5 minutes, or until softened.
4. Stir in the quinoa, onion powder, garlic powder, and salt. Combine well.
5. Place each bell pepper upright in the prepared pan. Stuff each pepper with one-half of the quinoa-vegetable mix. Use its reserved top to cover each pepper.
6. Use aluminum foil to cover, and bake for 15 minutes, or until the peppers are soft.

Nutrition Info per Serving:
Calories: 213; Total Fat: 5.1 g; Carbohydrates: 34.8 g; Protein: 7.2 g; Fiber: 5.5 g

Baked Buffalo Cauliflowers

Prep Time: 10 minutes, Cook Time: 25 minutes, Serves: 4

INGREDIENTS:

1 tsp. onion powder
1 tsp. garlic powder
1 tsp. sea salt
1 cauliflower head, broken into florets
½ tsp. cayenne pepper
2 tbsps. coconut oil, melted

DIRECTIONS:
1. Preheat the oven to 450°F(235°C).
2. Mix together the onion powder, garlic powder and salt in a small bowl.
3. Use the spice mix to season the cauliflower. Put the seasoned cauliflower in a baking pan and place in the preheated oven. Bake for 10 minutes, turn the cauliflower over, and bake for another 10 minutes.
4. Meanwhile, combine the cayenne pepper and coconut oil in a large bowl.
5. After baking, transfer the hot cauliflower to the large bowl with the coconut oil. Toss to coat thoroughly and place the cauliflower back in the baking pan.
6. Bake for another 5 minutes, until the sauce is absorbed.
7. Remove from the oven and allow to sit for 10 minutes and serve.

VARIATIONS TIP:
Instead of the cayenne pepper, try your favorite brand of hot sauce. Just be sure to avoid traditional hot wing sauce as it's usually loaded with sugar and oil.

Nutrition Info per Serving:
Calories: 82; Total Fat: 6.9 g; Carbohydrates: 4.6 g; Protein: 1.5 g; Fiber: 1.8 g

Lettuce, Zucchini and Hummus Wrap

Prep Time: 15 minutes, Cook Time: 15 minutes, Serves: 2

INGREDIENTS:

1 tbsp. of grape seed oil
1 sliced zucchini
Pure sea salt, to taste
Cayenne, to taste
2 tortillas
4 tbsps. of homemade hummus
1 cup of romaine lettuce
1 sliced plum tomato
¼ sliced red onion

DIRECTIONS:
1. In a grill pan, add the grape seed oil and warm on medium heat.
2. Add the sliced zucchini to the pan and season with the pure sea salt and cayenne.
3. Cook on medium heat for about 3 minutes then flip and cook for another 2 minutes. Remove it from the heat.
4. Place each of the tortillas on the grill and cook for 1 minute until warm. Remove from the grill.
5. Place 2 tablespoons of homemade hummus, lettuce, onion, tomato, zucchini slices in the center of each tortilla.
6. Wrap it tightly and serve.

VARIATIONS TIP:
If you don't want to use romaine lettuce, add wild arugula instead.
If you don't have plum tomatoes, you can add 6 cherry tomatoes instead.
If you don't have a grill, cook in a skillet pan.

Nutrition Info per Serving:
Calories: 221.5; Total Fat: 5.55 g; Carbohydrates: 37.62 g; Protein: 5.82 g; Fiber: 3.35 g

Grilled Vegetable Stuffed Mushrooms

Prep Time: 10 minutes, Cook Time: 20 minutes, Serves: 2

INGREDIENTS:

½ eggplant, sliced into ¼-inch-thick slices
2 portobello mushrooms, stemmed and gills removed
1 red bell pepper, seeded and sliced lengthwise
1 yellow bell pepper, seeded and sliced lengthwise
1 red onion, peeled and sliced
½ cup healthy hummus, divided
1 tsp. sea salt, divided

DIRECTIONS:
1. Preheat the grill or a broiler.
2. Grill the eggplant, mushroom caps, red bell peppers, yellow bell peppers, and onion over medium coals or a gas flame (or under a broiler, if using), grill for 20 minutes, turning occasionally.
3. Fill ¼ cup of hummus into one mushroom cap. Top with half of the eggplant, half of the red peppers, half of the yellow peppers, and half of the onion slices. Sprinkle over with ½ teaspoon of salt. Set aside.
4. Repeat with the second mushroom cap and remaining ingredients. Serve warm.

Nutrition Info per Serving:
Calories: 179; Total Fat: 3.1 g; Carbohydrates: 15.7 g; Protein: 3.9 g; Fiber: 3.6 g

Mixed Vegetable Pancakes

Prep Time: 5 minutes, Cook Time: 5 minutes, Serves: 2

INGREDIENTS:

1 carrot, peeled and roughly chopped
1 yellow squash, roughly chopped
1 medium zucchini, roughly chopped
½ small onion, grated
4 scallions
½ tsp. garlic powder
¼ cup almond flour
1 tsp. sea salt
¼ cup filtered water, as needed
Cooking spray for greasing the pan

DIRECTIONS:
1. In a food processor, add all of the ingredients except the water and cooking spray. Pulse until blended.
2. Add just enough water to make the mixture moist, not runny. The batter will be fairly thick.
3. Use cooking spray to coat a large nonstick skillet or griddle. Place the skillet over medium-high heat.
4. Once the oil is hot, drop the batter into the skillet with an ice cream scoop or ¼-cup measure. Using a fork to spread the batter evenly, pressing down on the pancakes. Cook until nicely browned on both sides, about 5 minutes total, turning once.
5. Serve hot or at room temperature.

VARIATIONS TIP:
You can make your own almond flour by grinding raw almonds in a food processor.

Nutrition Info per Serving:
Calories: 254; Total Fat: 12.1 g; Carbohydrates: 33.4 g; Protein: 6.3 g; Fiber: 7.2 g

Garlic Cashew Cream–Stuffed Mushrooms

Prep Time: 15 minutes, Cook Time: 5 minutes, Serves: 12 mushrooms

INGREDIENTS:

FOR THE MUSHROOMS
12 cremini mushrooms, stemmed
1½ tsps. avocado oil
Pinch freshly ground black pepper
Pinch sea salt

FOR THE STUFFING
2 garlic cloves
1 cup raw cashews
1 tsp. apple cider vinegar
¼ cup freshly squeezed lemon juice
¼ tsp. sea salt

DIRECTIONS:
TO PREPARE THE MUSHROOMS
1. Rinse the mushroom caps and dry them.
2. Heat the avocado oil in a medium skillet over medium heat. Add the mushroom caps, sprinkle with pepper and salt, sauté for 2 to 4 minutes, or until they soften. Discard any liquid that may accumulate.

TO PREPARE THE STUFFING
3. Combine all of the stuffing ingredients in a high-speed blender, blend them together until a thick paste forms.
4. Evenly spoon the stuffing mixture among the 12 mushroom caps and serve.

VARIATIONS TIP:
The stuffing here has all the hallmarks of a delicious pasta sauce. Add a bit of water while the blender is still going to create a luscious pasta sauce, and top with a dash fresh of lemon zest.

Nutrition Info per Serving:
Calories: 176; Total Fat: 15.07 g; Carbohydrates: 9.71 g Protein: 3.69 g Fiber: 2.5 g

Baked Sweet Potato Fries

Prep Time: 10 minutes, Cook Time: 30 minutes, Serves: 2

INGREDIENTS:

2 sweet potatoes, peeled and cut into fries
Cooking spray
1 tsp. sea salt

DIRECTIONS:

1. Preheat the oven to 425°F(220°C).
2. Use cooking spray to grease a baking sheet.
3. On the sheet, place the fries in a single layer. Coat the fries with cooking spray and sprinkle with the salt.
4. Place the sheet in the preheated oven and bake for 15 minutes. Turn the fries over and bake for another 15 minutes, or until crisp.
5. After baking, serve warm.

VARIATIONS TIP:

There is a difference between sweet potatoes and yams. Sweet potatoes have an orange flesh and yams have a white flesh. Both are delicious when made into fries.

Nutrition Info per Serving:
Calories: 71; Total Fat: 0.02 g; Carbohydrates: 5.8 g; Protein: 2.1 g; Fiber: 0.3 g

Mixed Vegetable Potpie

Prep Time: 15 minutes, Cook Time: 25 minutes, Serves: 4

INGREDIENTS:

Cooking spray
1 large carrot, peeled and finely chopped
1 large sweet potato, peeled and chopped into ½-inch pieces
1 medium onion, finely chopped
1 celery stalk, finely chopped
¾ cup chopped broccoli florets (optional)
1 large shiitake mushroom, or 4 to 5 white mushrooms, chopped
⅓ cup frozen peas
4 to 6 garlic cloves, finely chopped
2 cups vegetable broth
1 tsp. dried oregano
1 to 2 tsps. sea salt
1 bay leaf
Pinch red pepper flakes
1 all-purpose pie crust

DIRECTIONS:

1. Preheat the oven to 350°F(180°C).
2. Use cooking spray to spray a medium skillet. Add the carrot, sweet potato, onion, celery, broccoli, mushrooms, peas, and garlic. Sauté over medium heat for 5 minutes, or until slightly softened.
3. Stir in the broth, oregano, salt, bay leaf, and red pepper flakes. Simmer the mixture for about 5 minutes, or until thickened and bubbly. Remove from the heat and allow to cool slightly.
4. Evenly divide the vegetable mixture among four individual ramekins.
5. Roll the pie dough to a ¼-inch thickness. Cut the dough into circles larger than the ramekins slightly.
6. Top one dough disc of each ramekin. Press the edges down to seal. Cut an opening in the top with a sharp knife to let steam escape while cooking.
7. Arrange the filled ramekins on a baking sheet. Bake for 15 minutes. Remove from the oven and let cool slightly.
8. Serve warm.

Nutrition Info per Serving:
Calories: 195; Total Fat: 4.1 g; Carbohydrates: 247.1 g; Protein: 7.1 g; Fiber: 4.5 g

Lentil Tacos with Onions and Bell Peppers

Prep Time: 15 minutes, Cook Time: 20 minutes, Serves: 4

INGREDIENTS:

1 tsp. taco spice blend
2 cups cooked lentils
2 tsps. extra-virgin olive oil
2 cups sliced bell peppers (frozen is fine)
1 medium onion, sliced
8 (6-inch) corn tortillas
2 tbsps. chopped fresh cilantro

DIRECTIONS:

1. Add the taco spice blend and lentils into a small bowl, mix them together.
2. Heat the oil in a skillet on low. Add the bell peppers and onion, and cook for about 15 minutes, until the onion is translucent and the bell peppers are soft.
3. Add the seasoned lentils and cook for 3 minutes more, until warmed through.
4. Divide the lentil-vegetable mixture among the tortillas evenly. Garnish with the cilantro and serve.

VARIATIONS TIP:

To keep it on the mild side, replace the taco spice blend with nutmeg to taste and swap out the onion for chopped fresh basil.

Nutrition Info per Serving:
Calories: 267; Fat: 4 g; Carbohydrates: 48 g; Protein: 13 g; Fiber: 10 g; Sodium: 174 mg; Iron: 5 mg

Squash "Noodles" with Tomato Spaghetti Sauce

Prep Time: 15 minutes, Cook Time: 15 minutes, Serves: 2

INGREDIENTS:

1 tsp. coconut oil
¼ onion, chopped
1 tsp. minced garlic
1 tsp. sea salt
½ tsp. red pepper flakes
1 (6-ounce, 170 g) can tomato paste
½ cup water
1 (16-ounce, 454 g) jar spaghetti sauce
2 cups cooked spaghetti squash, shredded into noodles

DIRECTIONS:

1. Add the coconut oil and onion into a medium pot, sauté over medium heat for about 5 minutes, or until tender.
2. Stir in the garlic, salt, red pepper flakes, and tomato paste. Combine well.
3. Add the water and spaghetti sauce. Simmer for 10 minutes.
4. Stir in the spaghetti squash and mix well.
5. Serve immediately.

Nutrition Info per Serving:
Calories: 284; Total Fat: 3.8 g; Carbohydrates: 36.8 g; Protein: 8.6 g; Fiber: 7.7 g

Onion Sautéed Kale

Prep Time: 15 minutes, Cook Time: 10 minutes, Serves: 4

INGREDIENTS:

1 bunch of kale
¼ cup of minced onions
¼ cup of minced red pepper
2 tbsps. of "garlic" infused oil
¼ tsp. of pure sea salt
1 tsp. of crushed red pepper flakes

DIRECTIONS:

1. Rinse the kale leaves and then fold in half and cut off the stems.
2. Dice the kale into small pieces. Spin in a salad spinner until dry.
3. Warm the oil in a wok on high heat.
4. Add minced onions and peppers to the wok and sauté on medium heat for 2 to 3 minutes.
5. Add the kale leaves and pure sea salt to the pan and use a lid to cover. Reduce the heat to low and cook for about 5 minutes.
6. Spread in the crushed red pepper flakes and mix thoroughly. Cover and continue to cook for 3 minutes.
7. Serve warm.

VARIATIONS TIP:
If you don't have "garlic" infused oil prepared, substitute grape seed oil instead.
If you don't have a salad spinner, wait until the kale is dry to continue.

Nutrition Info per Serving:
Calories: 71; Total Fat: 13.77 g; Carbohydrates: 4.93 g; Protein: 1.75 g; Fiber: 1.1 g

Sweet Potato Slices with Garlic Artichoke Spread

Prep Time: 5 minutes, Cook Time: 45 minutes, Serves: 8

INGREDIENTS:

1 red bell pepper, quartered
2 unpeeled sweet potatoes, cut into 4 (¼-inch-thick) lengthwise slices
6 tsps. avocado oil, divided
¼ tsp. freshly ground black pepper, plus 1 pinch
½ tsp. salt, plus 1 pinch
2 garlic cloves
1 (14-ounce, 397 g) can artichoke hearts

DIRECTIONS:

1. Preheat the oven to 350°F(180°C). Use parchment paper to line a baking sheet.
2. Place the bell pepper and sweet potato on the prepared baking sheet, and drizzle with 2 teaspoons of avocado oil, the pinch pepper, and the pinch salt.
3. Bake for 30 minutes. Flip them over and bake for another 15 minutes.
4. Combine the roasted red bell pepper, the remaining ½ teaspoon of salt, the remaining ¼ teaspoon of black pepper, the remaining 4 teaspoons of avocado oil, the garlic and the artichoke hearts in a food processor, pulse until well combined but still chunky. Adjust seasonings, if needed.
5. Top the sweet potato slices with the spread and serve.

VARIATIONS TIP:
This recipe would be great to add to a salad or even use as a dip for fresh veggies.

Nutrition Info per Serving:
Calories: 71; Total Fat: 13.76g; Carbohydrates: 37.98g; Protein: 5.36g Fiber: 8.75 g

Jamaican Jerk Vegetable Patties

Prep Time: 20 minutes, Cook Time: 1 hour, Serves: 3-4

INGREDIENTS:

FILLING:
- ½ cup of diced green pepper
- 1 cup of cooked garbanzo beans
- 1 cup of chopped butternut squash
- ½ cup of diced onions
- 2 cups of chopped mushrooms
- 1 tbsp. of onion powder
- 1 tsp. of ginger
- 2 tsps. of thyme
- 1 tbsp. of agave syrup
- ½ tsp. of cayenne powder
- 1 tsp. of allspice
- ¼ tsp. of cloves
- 1 tsp. of pure sea salt
- 1 chopped plum tomato

CRUST:
- 1 tbsp. of grape seed oil
- 1 ½ cups of spelt flour
- 1 tsp. of pure sea salt
- ⅛ tsp. of ginger powder
- 1 tsp. of onion powder
- 1 cup of spring water
- ¼ cup of aquafaba

DIRECTIONS:
1. Preheat the oven to 350°F(180°C).
2. In a food processor, add all of the vegetables, except the plum tomatoes. Pulse a few times to chop them into large pieces.
3. In a large bowl, combine the blended vegetables with seasonings and tomatoes. This constitutes the filling for the patties.
4. Add the grape seed oil, spelt flour, pure sea salt, ginger powder and onion powder in a separate large bowl, mix well.
5. Pour in ½ cup of spring water and knead the dough into a ball, adding more water or flour as needed.
6. Allow the dough to rest for 5 to 10 minutes. Knead again for a few minutes, then equally divide it into 8 parts.
7. Make each part into a ball and roll each ball out into a 6 to 7-inch circle.
8. Take a dough circle and place ½ cup of the filling in the center. Use the aquafaba to brush all edges of the dough, fold it over in half and use a fork to seal the edges together.
9. Repeat step 8 until all the dough circles are filled.
10. Use a little grape seed oil to lightly coat a baking sheet.
11. Bake filled patties for about 25 to 30 minutes until golden brown.
12. Serve warm.

Nutrition Info per Serving:
Calories: 476; Total Fat: 4 g; Carbohydrates: 97.63 g; Protein: 20.96 g; Fiber: 16.53 g

Fresh Vegetable Pizza with Garlic Tahini-Beet Spread

Prep Time: 10 minutes, Cook Time: 15 minutes, Serves: 4

INGREDIENTS:

FOR THE CRUST
- 3 tbsps. coconut oil
- 1¼ cup almond flour
- ½ tsp. garlic powder
- ½ tsp. sea salt

FOR THE TAHINI-BEET SPREAD
- 1 tbsp. avocado oil
- 2 beets, peeled and cubed
- 1 tbsp. tahini
- 2 garlic cloves
- 1 tbsp. freshly squeezed lemon juice
- ⅛ tsp. sea salt
- Pinch freshly ground black pepper

FOR ASSEMBLING
Mushrooms, red onions, dandelion greens, asparagus, jalapeños, artichokes, arugula, broccoli, basil, dulse flakes (optional toppings)

DIRECTIONS:
1. Preheat the oven to 375°F(190°C). Use parchment paper to line a baking sheet.

TO PREPARE THE CRUST
2. Combine the coconut oil, almond flour, garlic powder and salt in a small bowl, stir them together until well combined.
3. Place onto the prepared baking pan, and squeeze the mixture together until it forms a ball shape. On top of the ball, lay another sheet of parchment paper, and roll the dough out over the parchment paper into a 7-by-7-inch square with a rolling pin.
4. Bake for about 14 minutes, until the edges turn golden brown.

TO PREPARE THE TAHINI-BEET SPREAD
5. At the same time, add all of the tahini-beet spread ingredients into a food processor, process them together until thick and creamy. Adjust the seasonings, if needed.

TO ASSEMBLE
6. When the crust is ready, evenly spread over with the tahini-beet spread, top the pizza with your favorite alkaline veggies, cut into 4 slices, and serve.

VARIATIONS TIP:
The Tahini-Beet Spread would also work great as a salad dressing—just add 1 to 2 tablespoons of water to thin it out.

Nutrition Info per Serving:
Calories: 115; Total Fat: 6.19 g; Carbohydrates: 13.56 g Protein: 2.88 g; Fiber: 3.7 g

Homemade Easy Roasted Vegetables

Prep Time: 15 minutes, Cook Time: 1 hour, Serves: 4

INGREDIENTS:
- 1 baking pumpkin, peeled and cubed
- 2 large carrots, peeled and cubed
- 1 butternut squash, peeled and cubed
- 3 fresh sage leaves, finely chopped
- 2 green apples, peeled, cored, and sliced
- 1 tsp. sea salt
- 2 tsps. coconut oil

DIRECTIONS:
1. Preheat the oven to 350°F(180°C).
2. Combine all of the ingredients in a large bowl. Toss to coat evenly in the oil and seasonings. Transfer the vegetables to a roasting pan, in a single layer.
3. Roast for 60 minutes, stirring occasionally. Then serve warm.

Nutrition Info per Serving:
Calories: 176; Total Fat: 12.4 g; Carbohydrates: 44.3 g; Protein: 4.1 g; Fiber: 6.3 g

Garlic Broccoli Carrot Bake

Prep Time: 10 minutes, Cook Time: 30 minutes, Serves: 2

INGREDIENTS:
- 2 tbsps. coconut oil
- 4 carrots, peeled and sliced
- 1 pound (454 g) broccoli, cut into bite-size pieces
- 3 garlic heads, cloves peeled and chopped, or 3 tbsps. minced
- 2 tsps. lemon zest
- ¼ tsp. mustard powder
- 1 cup vegetable broth
- 1 tsp. sea salt

DIRECTIONS:
1. Preheat the oven to 400°F(205°C).
2. Add all of the ingredients into a medium bowl, stir them together.
3. Spread the mixture evenly into a baking pan. Use aluminum foil to cover and bake for 30 minutes, stirring once.
4. After baking, serve immediately.

Nutrition Info per Serving:
Calories: 270; Total Fat: 15.2 g; Carbohydrates: 28.1 g; Protein: 11.6 g; Fiber: 5.1 g

Avocado Tomato Guacamole

Prep Time: 15 minutes, Cook Time: 0, Serves: 2

INGREDIENTS:
- 2 avocados
- ½ cup of minced red onion
- ½ tsp. of cayenne powder
- ½ cup of chopped cilantro
- ½ tsp. of onion powder
- ½ tsp. of pure sea salt
- Juice from a half of lime
- 1 minced roma tomato

DIRECTIONS:
1. Cut the avocados in half, peel them, and remove the seeds.
2. Chop into small pieces and add to a medium bowl.
3. Add all of the remaining ingredients except the roma tomato to the bowl.
4. Mash them together with a masher until smooth.
5. Add the minced roma tomato to the mixture and combine well.
6. Serve.

Nutrition Info per Serving:
Calories: 350; Total Fat: 29.72 g; Carbohydrates: 23.49 g; Protein: 5.25 g; Fiber: 14.85 g

Hummus, Carrots and Pesto Lettuce Wraps

Prep Time: 10 minutes, Cook Time: 0, Serves: 1

INGREDIENTS:
- 2 crisp romaine lettuce leaves
- 2 tbsps. vegan spinach-basil pesto
- 2 tbsps. simple hummus
- 4 tbsps. shredded carrots or thinly sliced radishes

DIRECTIONS:
1. On a cutting board, place the lettuce leaves.
2. Spread 1 tablespoon of the pesto and 1 tablespoon of the hummus onto each lettuce leaf.
3. Place 2 tablespoons of the carrots on each top.
4. Roll up and serve immediately!

VARIATIONS TIP:
Got one dip and not the other? Simply use one-quarter of a ripe avocado in its place.

Nutrition Info per Serving:
Calories: 198; Fat: 12 g; Carbohydrates: 20 g; Protein: 7 g; Fiber: 6g; Sodium: 168 mg; Iron: 2 mg

Spiced Zucchini Dish

Prep Time: 10 minutes, Cook Time: 20 minutes, Serves: 2

INGREDIENTS:
1 tbsp. onion powder
2 tbsps. agave syrup
1 tsp. liquid smoke
1 tbsp. of sea salt
½ tsp. cayenne powder
¼ cup date sugar
¼ cup spring water
2 zucchini, cut into strips
1 tbsp. grapeseed oil

DIRECTIONS:
1. Place a medium saucepan over medium heat, add all of the ingredients except for the zucchini and oil, cook until the sugar has dissolved.
2. In a large bowl, add the zucchini strips, pour in the mixture from the saucepan, toss until coated, and allow it to marinate for at least 1 hour.
3. When ready to cook, switch on the oven, preheat the oven to 400°F(205°C).
4. Use the parchment paper to line a baking sheet, grease with the oil, arrange the marinated zucchini strips on it, and bake for 10 minutes.
5. Then flip the zucchini, continue to cook for 4 minutes and then allow to cool completely.
6. Serve immediately.

Nutrition Info per Serving:
Calories: 184; Fats: 2 g; Carb: 26 g; Protein: 12 g; Fiber: 2 g

Morning Mixed Vegetables

Prep Time: 10 minutes, Cook Time: 10 minutes, Serves: 2

INGREDIENTS:
1 tbsp. coconut oil
1 medium sweet onion, chopped
1 red bell pepper, cored, seeded, and chopped
2 medium sweet potatoes, peeled and cubed
2 garlic cloves, chopped
4 cups spinach
¼ cup sliced mushrooms, any type
1 tsp. garlic powder
1 tsp. onion powder
½ tsp. bouquet garni herb blend, or other dried herbs such as rosemary or sage
½ tsp. sea salt

DIRECTIONS:
1. Combine all of the ingredients in a medium bowl, toss until the oil and seasonings are distributed evenly on the vegetables.
2. Heat a nonstick frying pan over medium heat, place the combined ingredients in the pan and cook for 10 minutes, or until tender, stirring.
3. Divide into two portions and serve.

VARIATIONS TIP:
Keep a bag of chopped onions in your freezer so you can just measure out what you need. You don't even need to defrost them; just add them to the pan frozen.

Nutrition Info per Serving:
Calories: 181; Total Fat: 1.5 g; Carbohydrates: 37.8 g; Protein: 5.6 g; Fiber: 8.1 g

Pasta with Alkaline Sauce and Veggies

Prep Time: 5 minutes, Cook Time: 0, Serves: 2

INGREDIENTS:
½ cup sliced zucchini
½ cup diced green bell peppers
¼ cup diced onions
¼ cup cherry tomatoes, cut in half
2 cups cooked spelt pasta
Extra:
2 tbsps. olives
½ cup alkaline sauce, homemade

DIRECTIONS:
1. Combine all of the ingredients except the pasta in a large bowl, stir well.
2. Add the pasta into the bowl, and toss until well coated.
3. Serve immediately.

Nutrition Info per Serving:
Calories: 143.7; Fats: 1.8 g; Carb: 29.1 g; Protein: 4.5 g; Fiber: 4.8 g

Chapter 4: Grains and Rice

Alkaline Veggies Fried Rice

Prep Time: 5 minutes, Cook Time: 15 minutes, Serves: 2

INGREDIENTS:
- 1 tbsp. grapeseed oil
- ¼ of a medium onion, peeled, cubed
- ½ cup sliced red bell pepper
- ½ cup sliced mushrooms
- ½ cup sliced zucchini
- 1 cup cooked wild rice
- ½ tsp. salt
- ¼ tsp. cayenne pepper

DIRECTIONS:
1. Heat the oil in a medium skillet pan over medium heat. When hot, add the onion and cook for 5 minutes until browned.
2. Stir in the pepper, mushrooms and zucchini, and cook for 5 minutes until almost soft.
3. Add the rice, stir until combined and cook for 3 minutes until golden brown, season with the salt and cayenne pepper.
4. Serve immediately.

Nutrition Info per Serving:
Calories: 140; Fats: 7 g; Carb: 15 g; Protein: 4 g; Fiber: 1.1 g

Avocado Tomato and Basil Pasta

Prep Time: 15 minutes, Cook Time: 0, Serves: 4

INGREDIENTS:
- 4 cups of cooked spelt pasta
- 1 medium diced avocado
- 2 cups of halved cherry tomatoes
- ¼ cup of olive oil
- 1 tsp. of agave syrup
- 1 minced fresh basil
- ¼ tsp. pure sea salt
- 1 tbsp. key lime juice

DIRECTIONS:
1. In a large bowl, add the cooked pasta.
2. Add the minced basil, diced avocado and halved cherry tomatoes into the bowl. Stir them together until well combined.
3. In another bowl, add the olive oil, agave syrup, basil, pure sea salt and key lime juice, whisk well.
4. Pour the mixture over the pasta and stir until well combined.

5. Enjoy!

Nutrition Info per Serving:
Calories: 797; Fats: 20.12 g; Carb: 129 g; Protein: 26.42 g; Fiber: 22.1 g

Baked Nutty Macaroni

Prep Time: 30 minutes, Cook Time: 50 minutes + 8-12 hours for soaking, Serves: 8-10

INGREDIENTS:
- 1 cup of raw brazil nuts
- 1 cup of spring water + extra for soaking
- 12 ounces (340 g) of any alkaline pasta
- 2 tsps. of grape seed oil
- ¼ cup of chickpea flour
- 2 tsps. of onion powder
- ½ tsp. of ground achiote
- 1 tsp. of pure sea salt
- 1 cup of homemade hempseed milk
- juice from ½ key lime

DIRECTIONS:
1. In a medium bowl, add the brazil nuts and pour in the spring water to cover. Allow them to soak overnight.
2. Cook your favorite alkaline pasta.
3. Preheat the oven to 350°F(180°C).
4. In a baking dish, add the cooked pasta and drizzle the extra grape seed oil to prevent it sticking to the bottom.
5. In a blender, add the soaked brazil nuts and the remaining ingredients and blend for 2 to 4 minutes until smooth.
6. Pour the brazil nut sauce over the pasta and mix well.
7. Bake for about 30 minutes.
8. After baking, serve and enjoy!

VARIATIONS TIP:
If you don't have prepared homemade hempseed milk, add coconut milk instead.
If you want to make the top crispy, broil the pasta for about 5 minutes.

Nutrition Info per Serving:
Calories: 198; Fats: 12.29 g; Carb: 19.1 g; Protein: 5.42g; Fiber: 3.94 g

Vanilla Rice Treats

Prep Time: 5 minutes, Cook Time: 1 minute, Chilling time: 45 minutes, Serves: 12

INGREDIENTS:

Cooking spray
¼ cup coconut oil
⅔ cup brown rice syrup
¼ tsp. sea salt
1 vanilla bean, split lengthwise and seeds scraped out
4 cups brown rice crisp cereal

DIRECTIONS:

1. Use cooking spray to coat a 9-inch baking pan.
2. Add the coconut oil and brown rice syrup into a medium saucepan, bring to a boil over medium heat, and boil for 1 minute. Stir in the salt and vanilla bean seeds.
3. Add the rice cereal in a large bowl. Top with the syrup mixture. Use a wooden spoon to combine thoroughly.
4. Place the rice mixture in the prepared pan. Spray the cooking spray onto your hands and press gently on the rice mixture to distribute it evenly in the pan.
5. Place in the refrigerator to chill for 45 minutes.
6. Once ready to eat, bring to room temperature, cut into 12 bars, and serve.

VARIATIONS TIP:

These treats don't contain marshmallows because marshmallows contain gelatin, an animal by-product. You can find brown rice syrup in your local health food store.

Nutrition Info per Serving:

Calories: 104; Total Fat: 4.6 g; Carbohydrates: 15.8 g; Protein: 0.3 g; Fiber: 4.6 g

Easy Spelt Pasta

Prep Time: 10 minutes, Cook Time: 50 minutes, Serves: 4

INGREDIENTS:

¾ cup of warm spring water
½ tsp. of pure sea salt
2 cups of spelt flour

DIRECTIONS:

1. Add ¾ cup of warm spring water, the pure sea salt and 1 cup of spelt flour in a large bowl, mix together until it can be shaped into a ball.
2. Spread the flour on your work space.
3. Knead the dough for 5 to 8 minutes.
4. Form into a ball and first use the flour and then plastic wrap to cover. Set aside for 15-20 minutes.
5. Unwrap the dough and equally divide into 4 portions.
6. Take 1 portion you are going to work with and re-wrap the others.
7. Use a rolling pin to roll the dough out in one direction a couple of times, then flip it and repeat the rolling process. Remember to add more flour when flipping.
8. Use a pastry cutter to cut the dough into individual pieces of pasta.
9. Repeat steps 6, 7, and 8 with the remaining dough.
10. In a large pot, fill in the spring water and add the pure sea salt, bring to a boil.
11. Cook the pasta in the boiling water for 1 to 2 minutes then strain.
12. Serve immediately!

Nutrition Info per Serving:

Calories: 294; Fat: 2.12 g; Carbohydrates: 61.12 g; Protein: 12.69 g; Fiber:9.3 g

Date Cashew Oat Bites with Raisins

Prep Time: 10 minutes, Cook Time: 10 minutes, Serves: 20 bites

INGREDIENTS:

Nonstick cooking spray
8 small dates, pitted
¾ cup rolled oats
¼ cup cashew butter
¼ cup unsweetened coconut flakes (optional)
½ tsp. vanilla extract
1 tsp. ground cinnamon
3 to 4 tbsps. water
½ cup raisins

DIRECTIONS:

1. Preheat the oven to 350°F(180°C). Use cooking spray to lightly grease a baking sheet.
2. Combine the remaining ingredients except the water and raisins in a food processor. Process until the mixture resembles coarse crumbs.
3. Add the water, 1 tablespoon at a time, until a dough forms and holds together well. Pour the mixture into a bowl and add the raisins, mix until evenly distributed throughout the dough.
4. Scoop small balls of the mixture onto the prepared baking sheet with a mini scoop or rounded teaspoon, evenly spacing them.
5. Bake for 10 minutes, or until just browned. Without overcooking.

VARIATIONS TIP:

Use chocolate chips instead of raisins.

Nutrition Info per Serving:

Calories: 113; Fat: 5 g; Carbohydrates: 17 g; Protein: 2 g; Fiber: 2 g; Sodium: 4 mg; Iron: 1 mg

Walnut, Spinach and Basil Pesto with Pasta

Prep Time: 10 minutes, Cook Time: 10 minutes, Serves: 4

INGREDIENTS:
2 cups dried gluten-free pasta
3 tbsps. avocado oil
3 cups packed baby spinach
½ cup packed fresh basil
1 to 2 garlic cloves, peeled
3 tbsps. walnut pieces
⅛ tsp. sea salt

DIRECTIONS:
1. Pour the water into a pot, and bring to a boil and cook the pasta according to the package instructions. Drain, place into a large bowl, and set aside.
2. Combine the remaining ingredients in a food processor, pulse for 20 to 30 seconds, until it reaches the desired consistency. Toss the pesto with the cooked pasta and serve.

VARIATIONS TIP:
If you are seeking something tangier (and don't suffer from GERD), you can add 1 tablespoon freshly squeezed Meyer lemon juice. You can also replace the walnuts with ¼ cup sliced almonds.

Nutrition Info per Serving:
Calories: 320; Fat: 15 g; Carbohydrates: 43 g; Protein: 6 g; Fiber: 7 g; Sodium: 24 mg; Iron: 2 mg

Baked Vanilla Bean and Cinnamon Granola

Prep Time: 5 minutes, Cook Time: 30 minutes, Serves: 3

INGREDIENTS:
6 tbsps. coconut oil
3 cups quick rolled oats
½ cup brown rice syrup
2 tsps. vanilla bean powder
2 tsps. ground cinnamon
1/8 cup unrefined whole cane sugar, such as Sucanat
¼ tsp. sea salt

DIRECTIONS:
1. Preheat the oven to 250°F(120°C). Use parchment paper to line a baking pan.
2. Add all of the ingredients into a large bowl, mix together until well combined with your hands.
3. Form the mixture together into a ball, and place onto the prepared baking pan.
4. Evenly press the mixture on the baking pan, not to break it up into small pieces. This will allow it to bake in large cluster pieces that you can break apart after baking, if you prefer.
5. Bake until crispy, about 30 minutes, not to overbake.
6. After baking, allow to cool completely and serve. As the granola cools, it will harden and get even crispier. Keep in an airtight container.

VARIATIONS TIP:
Customize your granola by adding some sliced almonds, pumpkin seeds, or unsweetened shredded coconut flakes!

Nutrition Info per Serving:
Calories: 556; Fats: 6.17 g; Carb: 116.39 g; Protein: 13.82 g; Fiber: 13.83 g

Wild Rice, Mushroom Leek and Miso Soup

Prep Time: 10 minutes, Cook Time: 55 minutes, Serves: 1 or 2

INGREDIENTS:
⅓ cup wild rice
½ cup sliced leeks, white part only
1 cup sliced cremini mushrooms
3 cups water
2 tbsps. organic white miso
¼ to ½ tsp. freshly ground black pepper
Sliced scallions, for garnish

DIRECTIONS:
1. According to the package directions to prepare the wild rice.
2. Add the leeks, sliced mushrooms and water into a medium soup pot, and bring to a boil over high heat. Boil for 8 to 10 minutes, or until the mushrooms are soft.
3. Add the miso, cooked wild rice, and black pepper. Mash the miso on the side of the pot to break it down with the back side of a spoon, and then stir it in.
4. Turn off the heat. Ladle into 1 large or 2 small bowls, garnish with the chopped scallions, and serve warm.

VARIATIONS TIP:
Since miso is a high-sodium food, this soup doesn't have added sea salt, but if you prefer, adjust the seasonings to your preference.

Nutrition Info per Serving:
Calories: 146; Fats: 1.42 g; Carb: 28.35 g; Protein: 6.5 g; Fiber: 3.3 g

Stir Fried Kale Mushroom Wild Rice, page 49

Cinnamon Mango Quinoa Porridge, page 49

Vanilla Rice Treats, page 46

Quinoa and Wild Rice with Cherries, page 50

Chapter 4: Grains and Rice

Cinnamon Mango Quinoa Porridge

Prep Time: 10 minutes, Cook Time: 25 to 30 minutes, Serves: 4

INGREDIENTS:

1 cup frozen mango chunks, cut into ½-inch cubes
3 cups cooked quinoa, cooled
¼ tsp. ground cinnamon
¾ cup unsweetened almond milk, plus more for serving
⅛ tsp. sea salt

DIRECTIONS:

1. Combine all of the ingredients in an airtight container, and refrigerate for a couple of hours or up to overnight.
2. Reheat and serve. Add some almond milk for the desired consistency.

Nutrition Info per Serving:
Calories: 217; Fat: 4 g; Carbohydrates: 39 g; Protein: 7 g; Fiber: 5 g; Sodium: 88 mg; Iron: 2 mg

Mixed Vegetable Fried Rice

Prep Time: 15 minutes, Cook Time: 20 minutes + 30 minutes (for boiling), Serves: 2

INGREDIENTS:

½ tbsp. of grape seed oil
¼ diced onion
½ cup of cubed zucchini
½ cup of sliced mushrooms
½ cup of cubed bell peppers
1 cup of cooked wild rice
Pure sea salt, to taste
Cayenne powder, to taste

DIRECTIONS:

1. In a medium pan, add the grape seed oil and heat it over medium heat.
2. Add the diced onion and sauté until golden brown.
3. Stir in the zucchini, mushrooms, and bell peppers and cook for another 5 minutes, until the vegetables become a little softer.
4. Add the boiled wild rice to the pan and continue to sauté until lightly browned, season with the salt and cayenne powder is using.
5. Serve immediately.

VARIATIONS TIP:
If you want, you can use cooked Quinoa instead.

Nutrition Info per Serving:
Calories: 103; Fat: 0.35 g; Carbohydrates: 22.25 g; Protein: 3.97 g; Fiber: 2.1 g

Stir Fried Kale Mushroom Wild Rice

Prep Time: 5 minutes, Cook Time: 15 minutes, Serves: 2

INGREDIENTS:

1 tbsp. grapeseed oil
½ of medium white onion, peeled, diced
10 button mushrooms, sliced
1 cup kale leaves
2 cups cooked wild rice
¼ tsp. cayenne pepper
⅔ tsp. salt

DIRECTIONS:

1. Heat the oil in a large skillet pan over medium heat. When hot, add the onion, and then cook for 4 minutes until tender.
2. Stir in the mushrooms, and cook for 4 minutes until mushrooms are almost tender.
3. Add the kale and wild rice into the pan, season with the cayenne pepper and salt, stir well and cook for 5 minutes until leaves wilts.
4. Serve immediately.

Nutrition Info per Serving:
Calories: 234; Fats: 13 g; Carb: 22 g; Protein: 6 g; Fiber: 6 g

Stir Fried Mushroom Wild Rice

Prep Time: 5 minutes, Cook Time: 1 hour and 25 minutes, Serves: 2

INGREDIENTS:

1 tbsp. grapeseed oil
4 ounces (113 g) sliced mushrooms
¼ of an onion, chopped
1 cup wild rice
⅓ tsp. salt
¼ tsp. cayenne pepper
2 cups vegetable broth, homemade

DIRECTIONS:

1. Heat the oil in a medium pot over medium heat. When hot, add the mushrooms and onion, cook for 4 to 5 minutes until the mushrooms have turned golden brown and the liquid in the pan has evaporated.
2. Stir in the rice, mix well and cook for 1 minute, then stir in salt and cayenne pepper.
3. Pour in the broth, reduce the heat to low and cook for 1 hour and 20 minutes until the rice is tender.
4. Serve immediately.

Nutrition Info per Serving:
Calories: 133; Fats: 1.3 g; Carb: 25.2 g; Protein: 4.5 g; Fiber: 2.4 g

Brown Rice Stevia Porridge

Prep Time: 5 minutes, Cook Time: 5 minutes, Serves: 6

INGREDIENTS:
1 cup almond milk
3 cups cooked brown rice
1 packet stevia

DIRECTIONS:
1. Add the almond milk and brown rice into a medium saucepan. Simmer over medium heat for 5 minutes until the mixture is thick and creamy, stirring constantly.
2. Turn off the heat. Stir in the stevia.
3. Evenly divide among 6 bowls and serve.

VARIATIONS TIP:
You can buy brown rice cereal in the market. Use it instead of regular brown rice in this recipe to make this alkaline-friendly dish even quicker and easier.

Nutrition Info per Serving:
Calories: 236; Total Fat: 1.8 g; Carbohydrates: 48.3 g; Protein: 7 g; Fiber: 3.6 g

Quinoa and Wild Rice with Cherries

Prep Time: 10 minutes, Cook Time: 18 minutes, Serves: 2

INGREDIENTS:
½ tbsp. olive oil
½ cup tricolor quinoa, uncooked
½ cup spring water
½ key lime, zested
½ tsp. salt, divided
⅛ tsp. cayenne pepper
⅛ tsp. ground cardamom
½ cup wild rice, boiled
¼ cup cherry tomato dressing, homemade
2 tbsps. dried cherries

DIRECTIONS:
1. Heat the oil in a medium saucepan over medium heat. When hot, add the quinoa and cook for 3 minutes until softened.
2. Pour in the water, add the lime zest, salt, cayenne pepper and cardamom, stir until mixed, and bring the mixture to a boil.
3. Reduce the heat to medium-low and simmer the quinoa for 10 to 12 minutes until tender.
4. Remove from the heat and allow the quinoa to cool for 10 minutes, use a fork to fluff it and transfer into a medium bowl.
5. Stir in the rice and tomato dressing, add the cherries and toss until mixed.
6. Serve immediately.

Nutrition Info per Serving:
Calories: 132; Fats: 3.5 g; Carb: 22 g; Protein: 4.5 g; Fiber: 2 g

Chapter 5: Bean and Legume

Chapter 5: Bean and Legume

Ginger Green Beans Almondine

Prep Time: 5 minutes, Cook Time: 5 minutes, Serves: 4

INGREDIENTS:
- 2 tsps. avocado oil
- 2 tsps. grated fresh ginger, or 2 cubes frozen ginger
- ¼ cup sliced almonds
- 1 pound (454 g) steamed green beans, chopped

DIRECTIONS:
1. Heat the oil in a skillet on medium heat. Stir in the ginger and cook for 2 to 3 minutes, until fragrant, stirring.
2. Stir in the almonds and toast in the pan until just starting to turn golden, about a couple of minutes.
3. Remove from the heat and add the green beans, mix well.
4. Serve warm or at room temperature.

VARIATIONS TIP:
Swap out the ginger for garlic (if you don't suffer from GERD) for a different take on the dish.

Nutrition Info per Serving:
Calories: 108; Fat: 6 g; Carbohydrates: 10 g; Protein: 5 g; Fiber: 4 g; Sodium: 7 mg; Iron: 2 mg

Chickpea Falafel

Prep Time: 10 minutes, Cook Time: 10 minutes, Serves: 2

INGREDIENTS:
- 2 cups cooked chickpeas
- ½ cup chopped white onion
- ¼ cup green onions, chopped
- ½ cup chickpea flour
- 1 tsp. chopped oregano
- 1 tsp. chopped basil
- 1 tsp. onion powder
- ½ tsp. of sea salt
- ½ tsp. cayenne pepper
- ⅓ cup water from cooked chickpeas
- 1 tbsp. tahini
- 1 tbsp. lime juice
- 1 tbsp. grapeseed oil

DIRECTIONS:
1. In a food processor, add all of the ingredients except for the oil, and pulse until well blended.
2. Tip the mixture into a bowl and form into even sized patties.
3. Heat the oil in a large skillet pan over medium heat. When hot, add the prepared falafel patties and cook for 4 to 5 minutes per side until golden brown and cooked.
4. Serve immediately.

Nutrition Info per Serving:
Calories: 182; Fats: 10 g; Carb: 18 g; Protein: 6 g; Fiber: 4 g

Black Bean Pumpkin Chili

Prep Time: 10 minutes, Cook Time: 20 minutes, Serves: 4

INGREDIENTS:
- 1 tbsp. avocado oil
- 1 cup diced celery
- ⅛ tsp. sea salt
- 1 cup canned pumpkin puree
- 1 cup yellow corn kernels
- 1 (15-ounce, 425 g) can low-sodium black beans, drained and rinsed
- 2 tsps. grated fresh ginger, or 2 cubes frozen ginger
- ¼ tsp. ground cinnamon
- ½ cup low-sodium vegetable broth
- ½ cup water
- ½ tsp. ground cumin
- ¼ tsp. dried thyme
- Juice of ½ lemon

DIRECTIONS:
1. Heat the oil in a pan over medium heat for 1 minute. Add the celery and salt and cook for 5 minutes, or until the celery is soft.
2. Add the remaining ingredients except the lemon juice, heat until thoroughly warmed.
3. Squeeze over with the lemon juice and serve.

VARIATIONS TIP:
Frozen cubes of crushed ginger are available in certain supermarkets and online, and make a convenient way to add fresh ginger without the hassle of peeling and grating it. Each cube is approximately 1 teaspoon for ease of measurement. Dorot Gardens is one brand of these easy-to-use cubes.

Nutrition Info per Serving:
Calories: 202; Fat: 4 g; Carbohydrates: 35 g; Protein: 8 g; Fiber: 12 g; Sodium: 393 mg; Iron: 3 mg

Homemade Easy Chickpea Quinoa Burgers

Prep Time: 10 minutes, Cook Time: 20 minutes, Serves: 2

INGREDIENTS:

¾ cup chickpeas
2 tbsps. chopped onion
¼ cup cooked quinoa
1 tbsp. grapeseed oil
1 tbsp. spring water
⅓ tsp. salt
¼ tsp. cayenne pepper
4 spelt flour burgers
2 tsps. tahini butter

DIRECTIONS:

1. Preheat the oven to 375°F(190°C).
2. While the oven preheats, in a food processor, add the chickpeas, onion and quinoa, and pulse until little chunky mixture comes together.
3. Add the oil, water, salt, and cayenne pepper to the processor, pulse until the dough comes together.
4. Tip the mixture into a medium bowl, use its lid to cover and allow it to rest in the refrigerator for 15 minutes.
5. Form the mixture into two patties, place them on a baking sheet lined with parchment paper, then bake for 20 minutes, turning halfway.
6. Switch on the broiler and continue to cook for 2 minutes per side until golden brown.
7. Serve the patties with spelt flour burgers and tahini butter.

Nutrition Info per Serving:
Calories: 315.4; Fats: 9.4 g; Carb: 47.7 g; Protein: 10.1 g; Fiber: 5.8 g

Alkaline Chickpeas Hot Dogs

Prep Time: 5 minutes, Cook Time: 45 minutes, Serves: 2

INGREDIENTS:

1 cup cooked chickpeas
⅓ cup diced green bell pepper
⅓ cup diced white onion
1 tsp. coriander
Extra:
1 tbsp. grapeseed oil
½ cup liquid from chickpeas
¼ cup diced shallots
1 tbsp. onion powder
½ tsp. dill
2 tsps. sea salt

DIRECTIONS:

1. Heat the oil in a pan over medium heat until hot, add the chickpeas, bell pepper, onion, coriander and shallots, and then cook for 5 minutes.
2. Place the chickpeas and vegetables in a food processor, add all of the remaining ingredients to the processor and pulse until well combined.
3. Form the mixture into hot dog shape rolls, and then use a parchment paper to wrap each hot dog.
4. Pour some water in a pot and bring to a boil, place a steamer on it and arrange the wrapped hot dogs on the steamer and then steam for 30 minutes.
5. After finished, remove the parchment paper and then fry for 10 minutes over medium heat until browned on all sides.
6. Serve the hot dogs.

Nutrition Info per Serving:
Calories: 120; Fats: 2 g; Carb: 8 g; Protein: 16 g; Fiber: 2 g

Broiled Chinese-Style Green Beans

Prep Time: 15 minutes, Cook Time: 15 minutes, Serves: 4

INGREDIENTS:

1 pound (454 g) green beans, ends trimmed
1 tsp. sesame oil
1 tsp. coconut oil
2 garlic cloves, finely chopped
1 tsp. chopped fresh ginger
½ tsp. red pepper flakes
½ tsp. sea salt

DIRECTIONS:

1. Adjust the oven racks to make the top rack is closest to the broiler.
2. Preheat the broiler.
3. In a baking pan, place the green beans in a single layer. Broil the beans for about 10 minutes, or until they start to show black flecks. Take the beans away from the broiler and place them into a large bowl. Set aside.
4. Combine the remaining ingredients in a small saucepan, warm the mixture over medium heat until it begins to shimmer and turn red. Turn off the heat.
5. Pour over the green beans with the warm sauce, toss well to combine.
6. Place the beans back in the baking pan and put under the broiler for 5 minutes.
7. After cooking, remove from the oven, transfer the green beans onto a serving platter, and serve warm.

VARIATIONS TIP:
Try Chinese green beans for a change. They are found in the produce section of some markets.

Nutrition Info per Serving:
Calories: 60; Total Fat: 2.5 g; Carbohydrates: 9 g; Protein: 2.2 g; Fiber: 4 g

Quinoa Vegetable Casserole

Prep Time: 15 minutes, Cook Time: 0, Serves: 6

INGREDIENTS:
2 cups cooked quinoa
¼ cup sprouted black beans
¼ cup chopped fresh cilantro
½ red onion, chopped
½ teaspoon ground cumin
1 avocado, mashed
½ teaspoon sea salt
Juice of 1 lime
1 cup salsa fresca
Assorted raw vegetables, for serving

DIRECTIONS:
1. Combine the beans, quinoa, red onion, cilantro and cumin in a medium bowl.
2. Add the lime juice, avocado and salt in a small bowl, mix well.
3. Spread into the bottom of a serving dish with the quinoa mixture. Place the avocado and salsa on the top.
4. Serve with the raw vegetables.

VARIATIONS TIP:
If you didn't sprout your beans, don't worry. You can use regular, canned black beans. Just consider this recipe part of your 20 percent if you use canned beans.

Nutrition Info per Serving:
Calories: 309; Total Fat: 10.8 g; Carbohydrates: 45.8 g; Protein: 10.7 g; Fiber: 8.1 g

Black Bean Vegetable Tostada with Avocado

Prep Time: 5 minutes, Cook Time: 20 minutes, Serves: 4

INGREDIENTS:
1½ tbsps. avocado oil or extra-virgin olive oil
¼ tsp. dried thyme
½ large onion, sliced
¼ tsp. dried oregano
1 cup sliced mushrooms
1 large zucchini, sliced
¼ cup canned low-sodium diced tomatoes
1 (15-ounce, 425 g) can low-sodium black beans, drained (liquid reserved) and rinsed
1 tbsp. taco spice blend
4 (6-inch) corn tortillas
1 avocado, sliced

DIRECTIONS:
1. Heat the oil in a skillet over medium for 1 minute. Add the thyme, onion, and oregano and cook for 5 to 7 minutes, until softened.
2. Stir in the mushrooms, zucchini, and tomatoes and cook for another 5 to 7 minutes, until softened.
3. Add the beans, ¼ cup of the reserved liquid from the can, and the taco spice blend, heat until warmed.
4. Warm the corn tortillas in a toaster oven or on the stove until lightly browned.
5. Scoop the black beans into the heated tortillas with a slotted spoon, evenly dividing them.
6. Garnish with the avocado slices and serve.

VARIATIONS TIP:
You can swap out the black beans for cooked lentils if you prefer a legume.

Nutrition Info per Serving:
Calories: 322; Fat: 12 g; Carbohydrates: 43 g; Protein: 14 g; Fiber: 12 g; Sodium: 294 mg; Iron: 5 mg

Vegetable and Garbanzo Bean Burger

Prep Time: 20 minutes, Cook Time: 40 minutes, Serves: 3-4

INGREDIENTS:
CUTLET:
1 diced plum tomato
½ cup of diced kale
½ cup of diced green peppers
½ cup of minced onions
2 tsps. of onion powder
2 tsps. of oregano
2 tsps. of basil
1 tsp. of dill
½ tsp. of cayenne
2 tsps. of pure sea salt
½ tsp. of cayenne powder
1 cup of garbanzo bean flour
¼ to ½ cup of spring water
2 tbsps. of grape seed oil
BURGER:
8 flatbreads
1 sliced red onion
2 sliced plum tomatoes
1 cup of sauce

DIRECTIONS:
1. In a large bowl, add all of the vegetables and seasonings, mix well.
2. Add the garbanzo bean flour to it and mix well.
3. Slowly pour in the spring water and mix thoroughly until it can be easily shaped into cutlets. Add more flour if it is too loose.
4. In a skillet, warm the grape seed oil over high heat.
5. Reduce the heat to medium. Add the formed cutlets to the pan and cook for about 2 to 3 minutes on all sides until golden brown.
6. Place the cooked burger cutlet on one flatbread. add the greens, onion, sliced tomatoes, and the sauce.
7. Serve and enjoy!

Nutrition Info per Serving:
Calories: 544; Fats: 12.42 g; Carb: 89.53 g; Protein: 22.12 g; Fiber: 10.9 g

Garlicky Parsley and Tahini Hummus

Prep Time: 10 minutes, Cook Time: 0, Serves: 1 cup

INGREDIENTS:

2 tbsps. avocado oil
¼ cup water
3 tbsps. tahini
1 cup cooked chickpeas
2 tbsps. chopped fresh parsley sprigs, plus more
(optional) for garnish
2 tsps. freshly squeezed lemon juice
½ zucchini, peeled
3 garlic cloves, crushed
½ tsp. sea salt

DIRECTIONS:
1. Add all of the ingredients into a high-speed blender, blend them together until creamy.
2. Garnish with the extra parsley (if using), and serve immediately.

VARIATIONS TIP:
Tahini is ground-up sesame seeds, and you can either purchase it or make your own, which is really easy. Add 1 cup sesame seeds to a food processor, process until they become creamy, and store in an airtight glass jar in the refrigerator. Yields ½ cup tahini.

Nutrition Info per Serving:
Calories: 550; Total Fat: 52.16 g; Carbohydrates: 19.51 g Protein: 8.92 g Fiber: 2.7 g

Tahini Fennel-Seasoned Falafel with Hummus Dressing

Prep Time: 10 minutes, Cook Time: 20 minutes, Serves: 4

INGREDIENTS:

1 cup canned low-sodium chickpeas, drained (liquid reserved) and rinsed
1½ cups arugula
¼ cup chopped fennel
¾ cup almond meal
2 tbsps. tahini
Juice of 1 lemon, divided
1 tsp. low-sodium soy sauce or bragg liquid aminos
½ cup simple hummus or store-bought hummus

DIRECTIONS:
1. Preheat the oven to 350°F(180°C). Use parchment paper or aluminum foil to line a baking sheet, or grease it with oil.
2. Combine the chickpeas, arugula, fennel, almond meal, tahini, half the lemon juice, and the soy sauce in a food processor.
3. Roll the mixture into 1½-inch balls and place them on the prepared baking sheet, 2 inches apart. Bake for 20 minutes, or until golden.
4. Mix the remaining lemon juice and hummus in a small bowl. Add the water, 1 tablespoon at a time, until it reaches the desired consistency.
5. Drizzle over the falafel with 1 to 2 teaspoons of the hummus mixture and serve.

VARIATIONS TIP:
Use nonstick cooking spray to lightly coat the falafel balls before baking to increase their golden crispness.

Nutrition Info per Serving:
Calories: 307; Fat: 19 g; Carbohydrates: 27 g; Protein: 13 g; Fiber: 9 g; Sodium: 362 mg; Iron: 3 mg

Chickpea Mushroom Loaf

Prep Time: 10 minutes, Cook Time: 45 minutes, Serves: 2

INGREDIENTS:

1 tbsp. grapeseed oil
1 red bell pepper, cored, diced
1 tbsp. and ¼ tsp. granulated onion, homemade
½ cup sliced white mushrooms
¼ cup minced basil
½ tsp. sea salt and more
as needed
¼ tsp. cayenne pepper and more as needed
1 ½ cups chickpeas, cooked
¼ cup spelt flour
¾ cup diced onions
⅛ tsp. dried thyme
⅓ tsp. dried sage
¼ tsp. dried oregano

DIRECTIONS:
1. Preheat the oven to 350°F(180°C).
2. While the oven preheats, heat the oil in a large skillet pan over medium-high heat. When hot, add the pepper, onion, and mushroom and cook for 3 minutes or until begin to tender.
3. Stir the minced basil into the pan, and remove the pan from heat, add the salt and cayenne pepper, then stir until mixed.
4. In a food processor, add the chickpeas and pulse until coarsely chopped, then transfer into a medium bowl.
5. Stir the cooked vegetable mixture along with the remaining ingredients into the bowl, mix well and then spoon into a greased loaf pan.
6. Bake the loaf for 30 to 40 minutes until firm and cooked. After baking, allow it to cool slightly, cut into slices and serve.

Nutrition Info per Serving:
Calories: 268.7; Fats: 6.2 g; Carb: 46 g; Protein: 10.3 g; Fiber: 9.4 g

Chickpea Falafel, page 52

Delicious Onion Chickpea Nuggets, page 59

Easy Healthy Hummus, page 58

Roasted Chickpea and Kale, page 57

Easy Homemade PB Frosting

Prep Time: 5 minutes, Cook Time: 0, Serves: ¾ cup

INGREDIENTS:

¾ cup canned low-sodium chickpeas, drained (liquid reserved) and rinsed
2 tbsps. maple syrup, or 8 small dates, pitted
2 tbsps. peanut butter or all-natural nut butter of your choice
⅛ tsp. vanilla extract
⅛ tsp. ground cinnamon
⅛ tsp. sea salt

DIRECTIONS:
1. Combine all of the ingredients in a high-speed blender.
2. Blend until smooth and creamy.

VARIATIONS TIP:

If you replace the chickpeas with black beans and add 1 to 2 tablespoons unsweetened carob powder or cocoa powder, you'll have a delicious chocolate frosting.

Nutrition Info per Serving:
Calories: 76; Fat: 3 g; Carbohydrates: 10 g; Protein: 2 g; Fiber: 2 g; Sodium: 90 mg; Iron: 0 mg

Roasted Chickpea and Kale

Prep Time: 5 minutes, Cook Time: 10 minutes, Serves: 2

INGREDIENTS:

2 cups cooked chickpeas
2 tbsps. grapeseed oil
⅔ tsp. salt
⅓ tsp. cayenne pepper
1 cup kale leaves
⅓ cup soft-jelly coconut cream

DIRECTIONS:
1. Preheat the oven to 425°F(220°C).
2. Spread the chickpeas on a medium baking sheet, drizzle with 1 tablespoon oil, sprinkle with the salt and cayenne pepper, bake for 15 minutes until roasted.
3. Heat the remaining oil in a frying pan over medium heat. When hot, add the kale and cook for 5 minutes.
4. Place the roasted chickpeas in the pan, pour in the cream, stir until mixed and then simmer for 4 minutes, squashing the chickpeas slightly.
5. Serve immediately.

Nutrition Info per Serving:
Calories: 522; Fats: 38 g; Carb: 26 g; Protein: 15 g; Fiber 8 g

Healthy Eggplant Hummus

Prep Time: 15 minutes, Cook Time: 0, Serves: 4

INGREDIENTS:

1 tbsp. sesame oil
1 cup eggplant, roasted and peeled
1 cup chickpeas, canned or cooked
1 garlic clove
1 tsp. sea salt
1 tbsp. freshly squeezed lemon juice
Water, for thinning

DIRECTIONS:
1. Combine all of the ingredients except the water in a food processor.
2. Blend until creamy and smooth. Add water, if needed, to create a creamy consistency.

VARIATIONS TIP:

If you're on the Thyroid-Support Plan, omit the eggplant and substitute an extra cup of chickpeas instead.

Nutrition Info per Serving:
Calories: 219; Total Fat: 6.5 g; Carbohydrates: 31.9 g; Protein: 9.9 g; Fiber: 9.5 g

Tahini Hummus with Crudités

Prep Time: 10 minutes, Cook Time: 0, Serves: 1

INGREDIENTS:

1 (15-ounce, 425 g) can low-sodium chickpeas, drained and rinsed
1 garlic clove, peeled
3 tbsps. tahini
⅛ tsp. sea salt
¼ cup freshly squeezed lemon juice
½ cup raw veggie slices or sticks

DIRECTIONS:
1. Combine all of the ingredients except the raw veggie slices in a high-speed blender, blend until creamy.
2. Serve 2 tablespoons of the hummus with the veggies.
3. Place the remaining hummus in an airtight container and store in the refrigerator for up to 1 week.

VARIATIONS TIP:

Use the remaining hummus as a dressing. Simply add the juice of 1 lime or lemon to ¼ cup of the hummus and mix in about 2 tablespoons warm water until thinned and well blended.

Nutrition Info per Serving:
Calories: 152; Fat: 5 g; Carbohydrates: 24 g; Protein: 6 g; Fiber: 7 g; Sodium: 204 mg; Iron: 1 mg

Chapter 5: Bean and Legume

Whipped Aquafaba Cream

Prep Time: 10 minutes, Cook Time: 0, Serves: 1

INGREDIENTS:
- 1 cup of aquafaba
- ¼ cup of agave syrup

DIRECTIONS:
1. In a bowl, add the agave syrup and aquafaba.
2. Use a stand mixer to mix at high speed around 5 minutes or use a hand mixer to mix for 10 to 15 minutes.
3. Serve and enjoy!

VARIATIONS TIP:
Store in the refrigerator if you don't use it immediately. Whipped Cream will turn back to Aquafaba consistency eventually, just whip it again until thick.

Nutrition Info per Serving:
Calories: 286; Fats: 0.25 g; Carb: 46.8 g; Protein: 24.05 g; Fiber: 0.1 g

Easy Healthy Hummus

Prep Time: 10 minutes, Cook Time: 0, Serves: 1-2

INGREDIENTS:
- 2 tbsps. of olive oil
- 1 cup of cooked garbanzo beans
- ⅓ cup of raw sesame "tahini" butter
- ½ tsp. of onion powder
- pure sea salt, to taste
- 2 tbsps. key lime juice

DIRECTIONS:
1. Add all of the ingredients into a food processor.
2. Blend them thoroughly until it reaches a creamy consistency.
3. Serve and enjoy!

VARIATIONS TIP:
If you don't have a food processor, you can blend with a high-powered blender.

Nutrition Info per Serving:
Calories: 481; Fats: 35.01 g; Carb: 34.29 g; Protein: 13.63 g; Fiber: 9.8 g

Teff Chickpea Sausage

Prep Time: 10 minutes, Cook Time: 6 minutes, Serves: 2

INGREDIENTS:
- 1 tbsp. grapeseed oil
- 2 tbsps. diced red bell pepper
- 2 tbsps. diced onions
- ¼ cup chickpea flour
- ¾ cup cooked teff grain
- 1 tsp. basil

Extra:
- ½ tsp. of sea salt
- ¼ tsp. crushed red pepper
- 1 tsp. oregano

DIRECTIONS:
1. Heat the oil in a medium skillet pan over medium-high heat. When hot, add the peppers and onion, and cook for 2 to 3 minutes until tender.
2. Add the chickpea flour and stir well, transfer the mixture into a medium bowl, then add all of the remaining ingredients to the bowl, stir until well combined, and then form the mixture into evenly sized patties.
3. Heat the skillet pan over medium heat. When hot, add the patties and cook for 3 minutes per side until crisp and cooked.
4. Serve immediately.

Nutrition Info per Serving:
Calories: 88.3; Fats: 2.3 g; Carb: 12.7 g; Protein: 4.6 g; Fiber: 1.6 g

Chickpea Sloppy Joe

Prep Time: 5 minutes, Cook Time: 12 minutes, Serves: 2

INGREDIENTS:
- 1 cup cooked Kamut
- ½ cup cooked chickpeas
- ½ tbsp. grapeseed oil
- ¼ cup chopped green bell pepper
- ¼ cup chopped white onion
- ½ tsp. of sea salt
- ⅛ tsp. cayenne powder
- ¾ cup barbecue sauce, alkaline
- ½ tsp. onion powder

DIRECTIONS:
1. In a food processor, add the Kamut and chickpeas, and pulse until combined.
2. Heat the oil in a large skillet pan over medium-high heat, when hot, add the pepper and onion, stir in the salt and cayenne powder, and cook for 5 minutes until tender.
3. Add the blended chickpea mixture, sauce and onion powder to the skillet, stir until mixed, and then simmer it for 5 minutes.
4. Serve immediately.

Nutrition Info per Serving:
Calories: 166.5; Fats: 2.5 g; Carb: 32.5 g; Protein: 7 g; Fiber 6 g

Mashed Chickpeas

Prep Time: 5 minutes, Cook Time: 10 minutes, Serves: 2

INGREDIENTS:

2 cups cooked chickpeas
1 cup walnut milk, homemade
¼ cup diced green onion
2 tsps. onion powder
2 tsps. sea salt

DIRECTIONS:
1. In a food processor, add the chickpeas, pour in the milk, and pulse for 1 to 2 minutes until blended.
2. Tip the chickpea mixture into a medium saucepan, cook over medium heat, add the green onions and then stir until mixed.
3. Cook the chickpeas until cooked, about 25 to 30 minutes, stirring constantly, season with onion powder and sea salt, and serve.

Nutrition Info per Serving:
Calories: 52; Fats: 2.6 g; Carbohydrates: 6 g; Protein 1.4 g; Fiber 1.2 g

Revitalizing Onion and Chickpea Dish

Prep Time: 10 minutes, Cook Time: 0 (chill 30 mins), Serves: 2

INGREDIENTS:

2 cups cooked chickpeas
¼ cup diced red onion
2 tsps. onion powder
⅛ cup diced green bell pepper
¼ tsp. of sea salt
Extra:
¼ tsp. salt
1 tsp. dill
½ nori sheet, cut into small pieces
⅛ tsp. cayenne pepper
⅔ cup alkaline hemp seed mayo

DIRECTIONS:
1. Place the chickpeas in a large bowl, and use a fork to mash them.
2. Add all of the remaining ingredients to the bowl, stir until well mixed, then place the salad in the refrigerator to chill for at least 30 minutes.
3. After chilling, serve straight away.

Nutrition Info per Serving:
Calories: 259; Fats: 13.7 g; Carb: 27.7 g; Protein: 6.1 g; Fiber: 5.2 g

Delicious Onion Chickpea Nuggets

Prep Time: 10 minutes, Cook Time: 30 minutes, Serves: 2

INGREDIENTS:

2 cups cooked chickpeas
1 tsp. onion powder
½ tsp. salt
⅓ cup and 1 tbsp. bread crumbs

DIRECTIONS:
1. Preheat the oven to 350°F(180°C).
2. While the oven preheats, in a food processor, add the chickpeas and then pulse until crumbled.
3. Tip the chickpeas in a bowl, add the onion powder and salt except for ⅓ cup of breadcrumbs and then stir until a chunky mixture comes together.
4. Form the mixture into evenly sized balls, then form each ball into a nugget, arrange on a baking sheet greased with oil and bake for 15 minutes per side until golden brown.
5. Serve immediately.

Nutrition Info per Serving:
Calories: 291.6; Fats: 3.9 g; Carb: 26.8 g; Protein: 19.9 g; Fiber: 3.4 g

Chapter 5: Bean and Legume

Chapter 6: Salads

Fresh Salsa Fresca

Prep Time: 20 minutes, Cook Time: 0, Serves: 6

INGREDIENTS:
½ sweet onion (Maui or Vidalia), diced
4 fully ripened tomatoes, diced
¼ cup chopped fresh cilantro
¼ cup apple cider vinegar
1 tbsp. toasted cumin seeds
½ tsp. sea salt

DIRECTIONS:
1. Combine all of the ingredients in a large airtight container.
2. Cover and chill in the refrigerator for 15 minutes so the flavors blend, and serve.

VARIATIONS TIP:
Play with spices by adding a seeded, chopped jalapeño or chipotle pepper. Just remember to wear gloves so you don't accidentally get spices in your nose or eyes.

Nutrition Info per Serving:
Calories: 25; Total Fat: 0.4 g; Carbohydrates: 4.6 g; Protein: 1.5 g; Fiber: 1.2 g

Apple Grape Dates Waldorf Salad

Prep Time: 15 minutes, Cook Time: 0, Serves: 6

INGREDIENTS:
5 tbsps. creamy vegan mayonnaise
1 tbsp. freshly squeezed lemon juice
1 cup halved seedless grapes
2 apples, cored and chopped
2 small dates, pitted and finely chopped, or 1 tbsp. raisins
1 cup sliced celery
½ cup hulled pumpkin seeds
3 cups chopped romaine lettuce

DIRECTIONS:
1. Combine the mayonnaise and lemon juice in a medium bowl.
2. Add the remaining ingredients except the lettuce, toss to coat well.
3. On each serving plate, place ½ cup of the lettuce, then evenly divide the fruit mixture among them, and serve.

VARIATIONS TIP:
Swap out the pumpkin seeds for an equal amount of chopped walnuts. These nuts offer heart-healthy omega-3s in addition to vitamin E, vitamin B6, and phosphorus.

Nutrition Info per Serving:
Calories: 199; Fat: 14 g; Carbohydrates: 18 g; Protein: 4 g; Fiber: 3 g; Sodium: 31 mg; Iron: 1 mg

Curried Almond and Raisin Tofu Salad with Greens

Prep Time: 10 minutes, Cook Time: 3 minutes, Serves: 6

INGREDIENTS:
4 tbsps. chopped fresh basil, divided
2 tbsps. sliced almonds, divided
8 ounces (227 g) firm tofu, diced
½ cup shredded carrots
2 tbsps. creamy vegan mayonnaise
2 tsps. curry powder or garam masala
2 tbsps. raisins
½ tsp. ground turmeric
⅛ tsp. sea salt
8 ounces (227 g) salad greens, for serving

DIRECTIONS:
1. Add 3 tablespoons of basil, 1 tablespoon of almonds and the remaining ingredients except the salad greens into a medium bowl, toss them together to combine.
2. Transfer the mixture into a nonstick pan, heat over low heat for 3 minutes or cover the bowl and microwave for 30 seconds.
3. Garnish with the remaining 1 tablespoon each of basil and almonds, and serve warm or at room temperature over a bed of greens.

VARIATIONS TIP:
You can swap out the tofu for 8 ounces (227 g) chopped cooked skinless chicken breast.

Nutrition Info per Serving:
Calories: 144; Fat: 12 g; Carbohydrates: 6 g; Protein: 5 g; Fiber: 2 g; Sodium: 130 mg; Iron: 1 mg

Lime Summer Fruit Salad

Prep Time: 10 minutes, Cook Time: 0, Serves: 4

INGREDIENTS:
- ¼ cup peeled and diced apple
- ¼ cup bite-size watermelon pieces
- ¼ cup grapes
- ¼ cup bite-size cantaloupe pieces
- ¼ cup bite-size honeydew melon pieces
- ¼ cup orange slices
- ¼ cup peeled and diced peaches
- ¼ cup strawberries
- 2 tbsps. freshly squeezed lemon juice
- 2 tbsps. chopped fresh mint

DIRECTIONS:
1. Add all of the ingredients except the mint and lemon juice into a medium bowl, combine well.
2. Mix in the lemon juice and mint. Toss to combine. Cover and refrigerate overnight.
3. Evenly spoon into four bowls, and serve chilled.

VARIATIONS TIP:
If you don't have time to make this the night before, you can make it and serve it right away. It's delicious either way.

Nutrition Info per Serving:
Calories: 32; Total Fat: 0.02 g; Carbohydrates: 7.8 g; Protein: 0.6 g; Fiber: 0.09 g

Garlicky Green Olive Pasta Salad

Prep Time: 10 minutes, Cook Time: 0, Serves: 1 or 2

INGREDIENTS:
FOR THE DRESSING
- 1 cup coconut milk (boxed)
- ½ cup raw cashews
- 2 garlic cloves
- 1 tbsp. apple cider vinegar
- ⅛ tsp. dried dill
- ½ to ¾ tsp. sea salt

FOR ASSEMBLING
- 2 cups cooked lentil pasta
- 2 tbsps. chopped scallions
- 2 tbsps. sliced green olives

DIRECTIONS:
TO PREPARE THE DRESSING
1. Combine all of the dressing ingredients in a blender, blend them until well combined. Adjust the salt, if needed.

TO ASSEMBLE
2. In a medium bowl, add the cooked pasta, the dressing, scallions and green olives, toss until well combined. Transfer the salad into 1 large plates or 2 small plates and serve.

VARIATIONS TIP:
This pasta salad can be enjoyed as a warm or cold salad.

Nutrition Info per Serving:
Calories: 618; Total Fat: 9.19 g; Carbohydrates: 99.22 g; Protein: 41.08 g; Fiber: 35.6 g

Date and Watermelon Tofu "Feta" Salad

Prep Time: 15 minutes, Cook Time: 0, Serves: 4

INGREDIENTS:
FOR THE VEGAN TOFU "FETA"
- 2 tbsps. avocado oil
- 2 tbsps. freshly squeezed lemon juice
- ½ tsp. dried thyme
- 1 tsp. dried oregano
- ¼ tsp. garlic powder
- ¼ tsp. sea salt
- 8 ounces (227 g) firm tofu, cubed

FOR THE SALAD
- 8 dates, pitted
- ¼ cup balsamic vinegar
- 4 cups crisp leafy greens
- 1 cup cubed watermelon
- ¼ cup chopped fresh basil

DIRECTIONS:
TO MAKE THE VEGAN TOFU "FETA"
1. Combine the oil, lemon juice, thyme, oregano, garlic powder, and salt in a small bowl. Add the tofu and allow it to soak up the flavors while you make the salad.

TO MAKE THE SALAD
2. Add the dates and vinegar into a high-speed blender, blend until smooth.
3. Place 1 cup of the leafy greens into each of four salad bowls. Then add ¼ cup of the watermelon to each.
4. Top each bowl with 2 tablespoons of the vegan feta with a slotted spoon. Keep the remaining vegan feta in an airtight container in the refrigerator for up to 5 days.
5. Evenly garnish with the basil. Drizzle over each salad with a tablespoon of the balsamic mixture and serve.

VARIATIONS TIP:
For a simpler option, you can swap out the Vegan Tofu "Feta" for an equal amount of cubed or crumbled tofu.

Nutrition Info per Serving:
Calories: 147; Fat: 5 g; Carbohydrates: 21 g; Protein: 6 g; Fiber: 3 g; Sodium: 156 mg; Iron: 7 mg

Hawaiian Fruit Veggie Salsa

Prep Time: 20 minutes, Cook Time: 0, Serves: 6

INGREDIENTS:
4 fully ripened tomatoes, diced
½ cup diced fresh mango
½ cup diced pineapple
½ sweet onion (Maui or Vidalia), diced
½ tsp. sea salt
¼ cup apple cider vinegar

DIRECTIONS:
1. Combine all of the ingredients in a large airtight container, mix them together.
2. Cover the container and place in the refrigerator to chill for 15 minutes so the flavors blend before serving.

VARIATIONS TIP:
You can use canned, fresh, or frozen pineapple in this recipe. If all you have on hand is frozen pineapple, just be sure to thaw it before using it.

Nutrition Info per Serving:
Calories: 48; Total Fat: 0.2 g; Carbohydrates: 5.3 g; Protein: 0.9 g; Fiber: 1.4 g

Chickpea Rainbow Salad with Mango-Lemon Salsa

Prep Time: 15 minutes, Cook Time: 0, Serves: 4

INGREDIENTS:
FOR THE MANGO-LEMON SALSA
1 cup chopped fennel
2 cups chopped mango
¼ cup fresh chopped basil
⅓ cup chopped scallions
3 tbsps. freshly squeezed lemon juice
¼ tsp. sea salt

FOR THE RAINBOW SALAD
½ cup chopped bell pepper
1 (15-ounce, 425 g) can low-sodium chickpeas, drained (liquid reserved) and rinsed
1 tsp. chopped fresh cilantro, for garnish

DIRECTIONS:
TO MAKE THE MANGO-LEMON SALSA
1. Combine all of the mango-lemon salsa ingredients in a medium bowl, and toss well. For best results, cover and refrigerate for several hours or up to overnight to let the flavors meld.
TO MAKE THE RAINBOW SALAD
2. Combine the bell pepper, chickpeas, and ¼ cup of the salsa in a large bowl. Place the remaining salsa in an airtight container and store in the refrigerator for 5 to 7 days.
3. Garnish with the cilantro and serve.

VARIATIONS TIP:
Save the liquid from the canned chickpeas (known as aquafaba) in an airtight container in the refrigerator for up to 2 days.

Nutrition Info per Serving:
Calories: 126; Fat: 2 g; Carbohydrates: 24 g; Protein: 6g; Fiber: 6 g; Sodium: 366 mg; Iron: 1 mg

Chopped Veggie Salad with Garlic-Avocado Dressing

Prep Time: 10 minutes, Cook Time: 0, Serves: 2

INGREDIENTS:
FOR THE DRESSING
1 tsp. avocado oil
2 garlic cloves
1 avocado, roughly chopped
1 cup fresh cilantro
½ to 1 jalapeño
1 tbsp. freshly squeezed lime juice
2 tbsps. water
½ tsp. sea salt

FOR THE VEGGIES
¼ cup red onion
1 medium carrot
½ orange bell pepper
½ to 1 jalapeño
½ cup broccoli florets

FOR ASSEMBLING
2 to 4 cups mixed salad greens

DIRECTIONS:
TO PREPARE THE DRESSING
1. Add all of the dressing ingredients into a blender, blend them together until creamy and smooth. Adjust the seasonings if needed.
TO PREPARE THE VEGGIES
2. Add the onion, carrot, bell pepper, jalapeño and broccoli into a food processor, process them together until they are chopped into tiny pieces, not to overprocess.
TO ASSEMBLE
3. Combine the salad greens and veggies in a medium bowl, toss them together. Transfer to 2 plates, drizzle with the dressing, and serve.

VARIATIONS TIP:
Add extra nutrients by sprinkling some dulse flakes over the top.

Nutrition Info per Serving:
Calories: 232; Fat: 17.38 g; Carbohydrates: 20.01g; Protein: 4.68 g; Fiber: 10 g

Peach Basil Salad with Sweet Orange Dressing

Prep Time: 10 minutes, Cook Time: 0, Serves: 1

INGREDIENTS:

FOR THE DRESSING
- 1 tbsp. lime juice (fresh squeezed)
- 2 tbsps. orange juice (fresh squeezed)
- 1 pinch sea salt
- 1 tbsp. brown rice syrup

FOR ASSEMBLING
- 2–4 cups chopped romaine leaves
- 1 cup cubed peaches
- 8 large basil leaves, cut into long, thin strips

DIRECTIONS:

TO PREPARE THE DRESSING
1. Combine all of the dressing ingredients in a small bowl, whisk them together until well combined. Adjust seasonings if needed.

TO ASSEMBLE
2. Add the chopped romaine leaves in a serving dish, sprinkle over the top with the peaches, and drizzle with the dressing. Transfer to 1 large or 2 small plates, garnish each with some of the basil, and serve.

VARIATIONS TIP:

Add some texture and crunch to your salad by sprinkling slivered almonds on top!

Nutrition Info per Serving:
Calories: 298; Total Fat: 0.92 g; Carbohydrates: 37.8 g; Protein: 5.53 g; Fiber: 75.12 g

Tofu Salad

Prep Time: 15 minutes, Cook Time: 0, Serves: 4

INGREDIENTS:
- 8 ounces (227 g) extra-firm tofu
- ¼ tsp. yellow mustard
- ½ cup finely chopped celery
- ¼ tsp. sea salt
- ¼ tsp. ground turmeric
- 2 tbsps. creamy vegan mayonnaise
- ¼ cup finely chopped fresh basil
- 4 slices gluten-free bread, for serving (optional)
- 8 ounces (227 g) leafy greens, for serving (optional)

DIRECTIONS:
1. Mash the tofu with a fork in a medium bowl, so it resembles chopped hard-boiled egg.
2. Add the mustard, celery, salt and turmeric, mix well.
3. Stir in the mayonnaise until well combined. Fold in the basil. Place on top of a slice of gluten-free bread or over a base of leafy greens and serve with a bowl of soup.
4. Place the leftovers in an airtight container and keep in the refrigerator for 3 to 4 days.

VARIATIONS TIP:

Want to use eggs instead? You can replace the tofu with 4 hard-boiled eggs, mashed.

Nutrition Info per Serving:
Calories: 115; Fat: 9 g; Carbohydrates: 1 g; Protein: 8 g; Fiber: 0 g; Sodium: 175 mg; Iron: 2 mg

Peach Cilantro Salsa Salad with Sweet Lemon Tahini Dressing

Prep Time: 10 minutes, Cook Time: 0, Serves: 1 or 2

INGREDIENTS:

FOR THE DRESSING
- 3 to 4 tbsps. brown rice syrup
- 4 tbsps. tahini
- 1 tsp. freshly squeezed lemon juice
- ¼ cup water
- Pinch sea salt

FOR THE SALSA
- ¼ cup diced red bell pepper
- 1 tbsp. chopped fresh cilantro
- 1 peach, pitted and cubed
- ½ jalapeño, diced
- 1 tbsp. diced red onion

FOR ASSEMBLING
- 2 to 3 cups mixed salad greens

DIRECTIONS:

TO PREPARE THE DRESSING
1. Add the brown rice syrup, tahini, lemon juice, water and salt into a small bowl, whisk them together until well combined. Adjust the seasonings, if needed.

TO PREPARE THE SALSA
2. Combine all of the salsa ingredients in another small bowl, toss them together.

TO ASSEMBLE THE SALAD
3. On 1 large or 2 small plates, add the mixed salad greens. Place the salsa on the top, drizzle with the dressing, and serve.

VARIATIONS TIP:

You can also enjoy the peach salsa as a regular salsa.

Nutrition Info per Serving:
Calories: 117; Total Fat: 0.86 g; Carbohydrates: 27.21 g; Protein: 4.97 g; Fiber: 6.5 g

Avocado and Orange Salad

Prep Time: 5 minutes, Cook Time: 0, Serves: 2

INGREDIENTS:
- ½ cup cilantro
- ¼ tsp. salt
- 2 tbsps. lime juice
- 2 tbsps. orange juice
- ¼ cup olive oil
- 1 orange, peeled, sliced
- 4 cups greens
- ½ of avocado, peeled, pitted, diced
- 2 tbsps. slivered red onion

DIRECTIONS:
1. In a food processor, add the cilantro and salt, pour in the lime juice, orange juice, and oil, pulse until blended.
2. Tip the dressing into a mason jar, add the remaining ingredients, toss until coated, and transfer to a salad bowl, or serve in the jar.

Nutrition Info per Serving:
Calories: 228; Fats: 18.9 g; Carb: 14.7 g; Protein: 3.3 g; Fiber: 7 g

Pineapple Cabbage Salad with Garlic-Lime Vinaigrette

Prep Time: 10 minutes, Cook Time: 0, Serves: 1 or 2

INGREDIENTS:
FOR THE LIME VINAIGRETTE
- ¼ cup avocado oil
- 2 garlic cloves
- 2 tbsps. freshly squeezed lime juice
- ¼ cup water
- ½ cup chopped scallions
- ½ cup chopped fresh cilantro
- ½ tsp. sea salt

FOR ASSEMBLING
- 2 to 3 cups mixed salad greens
- 1 cup chopped purple cabbage
- ½ cup cubed pineapple
- Dulse flakes, for garnish (optional)

DIRECTIONS:
TO PREPARE THE VINAIGRETTE
1. Add all of the lime vinaigrette ingredients into a blender, blend them together until well combined. Adjust the seasonings, if needed.

TO ASSEMBLE THE SALAD
2. On 1 large or 2 small plates, add the mixed salad greens. Place the purple cabbage, pineapple, and dulse flakes (if using) on the top; drizzle with the dressing; and serve.

VARIATIONS TIP:
If you don't have fresh pineapple, canned pineapple will work, too. Just make sure it doesn't have any added sugar.

Nutrition Info per Serving:
Calories: 326; Total Fat: 27.615 g; Carbohydrates: 21.5 g; Protein: 2.65 g; Fiber: 3.55 g

Lemon and Red Lentil Pasta Salad with Sautéed Vegetables

Prep Time: 15 minutes, Cook Time: 15 minutes, Serves: 2 to 4

INGREDIENTS:
FOR THE PASTA AND DRESSING
- 2 cups red lentil pasta
- 1 tbsp. freshly squeezed lemon juice
- ¼ cup avocado oil
- 2 tbsps. apple cider vinegar
- 2 pinches sea salt
- 1 tsp. dried oregano
- 2 pinches freshly ground black pepper

FOR THE VEGGIES
- 1 tbsp. avocado oil
- 2 garlic cloves, crushed
- 6 asparagus stalks, diced
- ⅓ cup diced red onion
- 1 cup diced orange bell pepper
- ½ summer squash, sliced
- ½ zucchini, sliced

DIRECTIONS:
TO PREPARE THE PASTA AND DRESSING
1. According to package directions to cook the pasta.
2. Meanwhile, add the lemon juice, avocado oil, vinegar, salt, oregano and pepper into a small bowl, whisk them together until well combined. Adjust the seasonings, if needed.

TO PREPARE THE VEGGIES
3. Heat the avocado oil in a skillet over medium-high heat. Add the garlic, asparagus, onion, bell pepper, squash and zucchini, and sauté for 2 to 3 minutes, or just until soft.

TO ASSEMBLE
4. Combine the cooked pasta, veggies and dressing in a large bowl, toss together until well combined. Transfer to 2 large or 4 small plates and serve.

VARIATIONS TIP:
If you can't find red lentil pasta, this would also be good to enjoy with just the sautéed veggies and dressing by itself, over a bed of mixed salad greens or spaghetti squash pasta.

Nutrition Info per Serving:
Calories: 521; Total Fat: 18.3 g; Carbohydrates: 68.15 g; Protein: 25.13 g; Fiber: 11.7 g

Mixed Melon Salad

Prep Time: 15 minutes, Cook Time: 0, Serves: 4

INGREDIENTS:
1 cup bite-size cantaloupe pieces
½ lengthwise-cut watermelon, flesh scooped into balls, shell reserved
1 cup bite-size honeydew melon pieces

DIRECTIONS:
1. Combine the cantaloupe, watermelon balls and honeydew in a large bowl.
2. Transfer the fruit to the watermelon shell and serve.

VARIATIONS TIP:
Summertime is a great time to experiment with different fruits. Have fun and add some exotic melons to this dish.

Nutrition Info per Serving:
Calories: 31; Total Fat: 0.2 g; Carbohydrates: 7.4 g; Protein: 0.8 g; Fiber: 0.7 g

Vegetable and Blueberry Salad with Roasted Garlic and Miso Dressing

Prep Time: 10 minutes, Cook Time: 0, Serves: 1

INGREDIENTS:
FOR THE DRESSING
1 head roasted garlic
2 tbsps. organic white miso
½ cup avocado oil
2 tbsps. freshly squeezed lime juice
¼ cup water
1 tsp. ground black pepper
FOR THE SALAD
2 cups mixed salad greens
¼ cup finely sliced fennel
½ cup blueberries
1 to 2 tsps. chia seeds, for garnish
1 tbsp. fresh mint leaves

DIRECTIONS:
TO PREPARE THE DRESSING
1. Combine 8 of the roasted garlic cloves, miso, avocado oil, lime juice, water and pepper in a blender, blend them together until well combined and smooth. Adjust seasonings to your preference.
TO PREPARE THE SALAD
2. In your serving bowl, add the mixed salad greens, then place the fennel, blueberries, chia seeds and mint on the top.
3. Drizzle over with the salad dressing, or pour it into the salad and toss it in so the entire salad is covered with the dressing.
4. Garnish with chia seeds and serve.

VARIATIONS TIP:
Try it as a pasta sauce over red lentil pasta, a dip for veggies, drizzled over a baked sweet potato, or in a wrap.

Nutrition Info per Serving:
Calories: 1144; Total Fat: 111.77 g; Carbohydrates: 37.55 g; Protein: 7.95 g; Fiber: 7.6 g

Warm Garlic Asparagus Salad with Lemon-Cashew Dressing

Prep Time: 10 minutes, Cook Time: 5 minutes, Serves: 1 or 2

INGREDIENTS:
FOR THE SALAD
1 tsp. avocado oil
3 garlic cloves, crushed
½ cup diced onion
24 asparagus stalks, diced
½ tsp. sea salt
¼ tsp. freshly ground black pepper
FOR THE DRESSING
2 tbsps. freshly squeezed lemon juice
½ cup raw cashews
½ cup water
⅛ tsp. freshly ground black pepper
¼ tsp. sea salt
FOR ASSEMBLING
½ cup raw cashews
½ cup water
2 tbsps. freshly squeezed lemon juice
¼ tsp. sea salt
⅛ tsp. freshly ground black pepper
FOR ASSEMBLING
2 cups mixed salad greens

DIRECTIONS:
TO PREPARE THE ASPARAGUS MIXTURE
1. Heat the avocado oil in a large skillet over medium heat. Add the garlic, onion, asparagus, salt, and pepper, and sauté for 5 to 7 minutes, or until the onion is soft.
TO PREPARE THE DRESSING
2. Add half the asparagus mixture and all of the dressing ingredients into a high-speed blender, blend them together until creamy and smooth.
TO ASSEMBLE THE SALAD
3. On 1 large or 2 small plates, add the mixed salad greens. Place the remaining asparagus mixture on the top, drizzle with the dressing, and serve.

VARIATIONS TIP:
Give your salad a nutritional boost by garnishing with hemp seeds or sesame seeds.

Nutrition Info per Serving:
Calories: 356; Total Fat: 18.18 g; Carbohydrates: 45.84 g; Protein: 15.22 g; Fiber: 11.3 g

Avocado, Cucumber and Quinoa Salad

Prep Time: 10 minutes, Cook Time: 0, Serves: 2

INGREDIENTS:
1 avocado, cut into cubes
1 cup cherry tomatoes, halved
1 cup cooked quinoa, cooled
1 cup cucumber, peeled and diced
¼ cup chopped cilantro
1 tbsp. onion powder
1 tbsp. garlic powder
1 tsp. sea salt
1 tbsp. freshly squeezed lemon juice

DIRECTIONS:
1. Combine all of the ingredients in a large bowl, stir them together.
2. Place in the refrigerator to chill for 15 minutes to allow the flavors to blend.
3. Serve immediately, or store in the refrigerator for 2 to 3 days.

VARIATIONS TIP:
To make this a dish for a holiday party, use red quinoa. The red and green colors will be festive complements to any seasonal buffet.

Nutrition Info per Serving:
Calories: 433; Total Fat: 14.8 g; Carbohydrates: 63.6 g; Protein: 13.7 g; Fiber: 9.9 g

Strawberry Spinach Salad with Mustard Dressing

Prep Time: 15 minutes, Cook Time: 0, Serves: 4

INGREDIENTS:
FOR THE TURMERIC DIJON VINAIGRETTE
3 tbsps. avocado oil
1 tsp. Dijon or yellow mustard
Juice of 1 small lemon
⅛ tsp. sea salt
¼ tsp. ground turmeric
1 tsp. maple syrup (optional)
FOR THE SALAD
¼ cup sliced almonds
4 cups baby spinach
1 cup halved strawberries

DIRECTIONS:
TO MAKE THE TURMERIC DIJON VINAIGRETTE
1. Add all of the vinaigrette ingredients except the maple syrup into a small bowl, whisk them together until well combined. Add the maple syrup (if using) and combine well.
TO MAKE THE SALAD
2. Toss the almonds, baby spinach and strawberries in a large bowl.
3. Drizzle over the salad with the dressing and gently toss to combine. Serve immediately.
4. If you are planning to serve later, refrigerate the undressed salad and the dressing in separate airtight containers and add the dressing to the salad when ready to serve.

Nutrition Info per Serving:
Calories: 160; Fat: 14 g; Carbohydrates: 6 g; Protein: 3 g; Fiber: 3 g; Sodium: 30 mg; Iron: 2 mg

Warm Garlic Sweet Potato Salad with Spicy Cashew Cilantro Dressing

Prep Time: 10 minutes, Cook Time: 25 minutes, Serves: 1 or 2

INGREDIENTS:
FOR THE SWEET POTATOES
2 tbsps. avocado oil
3 medium sweet potatoes, peeled and cubed
1 tsp. ground paprika
2 garlic cloves, crushed
½ tsp. sea salt
FOR THE JALAPEÑO-CILANTRO DRESSING
1 cup raw cashews
½ to 1 jalapeño
1 cup water
¼ cup fresh cilantro leaves
2 tbsps. freshly squeezed lime juice
½ tsp. sea salt
FOR ASSEMBLING
2 cups mixed salad greens

DIRECTIONS:
1. Preheat the oven to 350°F(180°C). Use parchment paper to line a baking sheet.
TO PREPARE THE SWEET POTATOES
2. Combine the avocado oil, potatoes, paprika, garlic and salt in a medium bowl, toss them together.
3. Evenly spread the sweet potato cubes on the prepared baking pan, and bake for 25 minutes, or until soft.
TO PREPARE THE JALAPEÑO-CILANTRO DRESSING
4. While the sweet potatoes bake, add the cashews, jalapeño, water, cilantro, lime juice and salt into a high-speed blender, blend them together until smooth.
TO ASSEMBLE
5. On 1 large or 2 small plates, add the mixed salad greens. Place the warm sweet potatoes on the top, drizzle with the dressing, and enjoy.

Nutrition Info per Serving:
Calories: 408; Total Fat: 20.91 g; Carbohydrates: 52.65 g; Protein: 7.33 g; Fiber: 8.1 g

Garlicky Orange Broccoli Salad

Prep Time: 10 minutes, Cook Time: 0, Serves: 4

INGREDIENTS:

2 seedless oranges, peeled and separated
4 cups cooked broccoli florets, cooled
2 tbsps. sesame oil
⅓ cup freshly squeezed orange juice
½ tsp. sea salt
2 garlic cloves, minced
¼ tsp. red pepper flakes

DIRECTIONS:

1. Combine the orange sections and broccoli in a large bowl.
2. Add the sesame oil, orange juice, salt, garlic and red pepper flakes in a blender. Blend until smooth.
3. Pour the dressing in the bowl over the broccoli salad. Place in the refrigerator to chill for 1 hour to blend the flavors.
4. Serve cold.

VARIATIONS TIP:
Stir-fry this salad and eat it warm for a hearty meal.

Nutrition Info per Serving:
Calories: 103; Total Fat: 7.2 g; Carbohydrates: 13.7 g; Protein: 2.8 g; Fiber: 3.5 g

Asian-Style Vegetable Salad

Prep Time: 15 minutes, Cook Time: 0, Serves: 1

INGREDIENTS:

1 cup shredded red cabbage
1 cup shredded green cabbage
1 cup chopped carrots
¼ cup water chestnuts
3 tbsps. chopped scallions
1 tbsp. cashew butter
1 tbsp. dark sesame oil
½ tsp. ginger powder
¼ tsp. red pepper flakes, or additional as needed
Hot water, as needed
2 tsps. toasted sesame seeds

DIRECTIONS:

1. Layer the red and green cabbage in a medium bowl, then layer the carrots, water chestnuts, and scallions.
2. Combine the cashew butter, sesame oil, ginger powder, red pepper flakes in a blender. Blend until the ingredients emulsify. If the dressing is too thick, add hot water by the teaspoon.
3. Pour over the vegetables with the dressing, add sesame seeds, and serve.

VARIATIONS TIP:
Cashew butter is usually located near the peanut butter in grocery stores. If you can't find cashew butter, you can use almond butter; just make sure it doesn't have added sugar.

Nutrition Info per Serving:
Calories: 317; Total Fat: 24.7 g; Carbohydrates: 20.8 g; Protein: 7.2 g; Fiber: 6.6 g

Garlic Mushroom and Lentil Salad with Lime Tahini Dressing

Prep Time: 15 minutes, Cook Time: 25 minutes, Serves: 1 or 2

INGREDIENTS:

FOR THE MUSHROOM-LENTIL MIXTURE
1 tbsp. avocado oil
1 garlic clove, crushed
⅓ cup dry lentils
1 tbsp. chopped shallot
6 cremini mushrooms, sliced
Pinch sea salt
Pinch freshly ground black pepper

FOR THE DRESSING
1 tsp. avocado oil
1 tbsp. freshly squeezed lime juice
2 tbsps. tahini
3 tbsps. water
Pinch salt
Pinch freshly ground black pepper

FOR ASSEMBLING
2 to 4 cups mixed salad greens

DIRECTIONS:

TO PREPARE THE MUSHROOM-LENTIL MIXTURE
1. According to package directions to prepare the lentils.
2. Heat the avocado oil in a large skillet over medium-high heat. Add the garlic, cooked lentils (you'll need 1 cup), shallot, mushrooms, salt, and pepper, and sauté for 2 to 4 minutes, or until the mushrooms are soft.

TO PREPARE THE DRESSING
3. Add the avocado oil, lime juice, tahini, water, salt, and pepper in a small bowl, whisk them together until well combined.

TO ASSEMBLE
4. On 1 large or 2 small plates, add the mixed salad greens. Place the mushroom-lentil mixture on the top, drizzle with the dressing, and serve.

VARIATIONS TIP:
Save time by making a double batch of lentils so you can use them for more than one recipe!

Nutrition Info per Serving:
Calories: 552; Total Fat: 39.58 g; Carbohydrates: 43.52 g; Protein: 14.98 g; Fiber: 13.2 g

Russian Style Beet Salad

Prep Time: 15 minutes, Cook Time: 0, Serves: 2

INGREDIENTS:
- 1 golden beet, peeled and shredded
- 1 red beet, peeled and shredded
- 2 tbsps. hazelnuts
- 2 carrots, peeled and shredded
- 2 tbsps. golden raisins
- ½ tsp. sea salt

DIRECTIONS:
1. Add the golden beet, red beet, hazelnuts, carrots, golden raisins, and salt in a medium bowl, stir them together.
2. Place in the refrigerator to chill for 15 minutes to blend the flavors. Serve cold.

Nutrition Info per Serving:
Calories: 101; Total Fat: 0.3 g; Carbohydrates: 25.3 g; Protein: 1.9 g; Fiber: 3.2 g

Roasted Vegetable Salad

Prep Time: 10 minutes, Cook Time: 15 minutes, Serves: 2

INGREDIENTS:
- 1 pint cherry tomatoes
- ½ bunch asparagus, trimmed
- 1 carrot, peeled and cut into bite-size pieces
- ½ cup mushrooms, halved
- 1 red or yellow bell pepper, seeded and cut into bite-size pieces
- 1 tbsp. coconut oil
- 1 tsp. sea salt
- 1 tbsp. garlic powder

DIRECTIONS:
1. Preheat the oven to 425°F(220°C).
2. Combine the tomatoes, asparagus, carrot, mushrooms, and bell pepper in a bowl. Add the coconut oil, salt and garlic powder. Toss to evenly coat the vegetables.
3. Place the vegetables into a baking pan, place in the preheated oven, and roast for 15 minutes, or until the vegetables are tender.
4. After roasting, place the vegetables into a large bowl. Refrigerate, if desired.
5. Evenly divide the vegetables into two bowls and serve warm or cold.

VARIATIONS TIP:
This is another one of those dishes that's great to have on hand. You can use these roasted vegetables for smoothies, soups, wraps, or stir-fries.

Nutrition Info per Serving:
Calories: 132; Total Fat: 7.3 g; Carbohydrates: 15.4 g; Protein: 2.9 g; Fiber: 4.2 g

Roasted Artichoke Salad with Sesame Seed Dressing

Prep Time: 5 minutes, Cook Time: 30 minutes, Serves: 1 or 2

INGREDIENTS:
FOR THE ARTICHOKES
- 1 (14-ounce, 397 g) can artichoke hearts, drained
- 1 tbsp. avocado oil
- ⅛ tsp. garlic powder
- ⅛ tsp. freshly ground black pepper
- ⅛ tsp. sea salt
- ⅛ tsp. ground paprika

FOR THE DRESSING
- 1 tbsp. sesame seeds
- 2 tbsps. avocado oil
- 1 tbsp. brown rice syrup
- 2 tbsps. apple cider vinegar
- 1 shallot, diced
- ⅛ tsp. sea salt
- ⅛ tsp. freshly ground black pepper

FOR ASSEMBLING
- 2 to 4 cups mixed salad greens

DIRECTIONS:
1. Preheat the oven to 425°F(220°C). Use parchment paper to line a baking sheet.

TO PREPARE THE ARTICHOKES
2. Cut the artichoke tips off, and then cut each heart in half. Rub all over the artichoke pieces with the avocado oil.
3. Mix together the garlic powder, pepper, salt, and paprika in a small bowl. Transfer the artichokes onto the prepared baking sheet, and sprinkle over with the seasoning, tossing to coat.
4. Roast the artichoke pieces for 30 minutes, tossing halfway through.

TO PREPARE THE DRESSING
5. Meanwhile, combine all of the dressing ingredients in a small bowl, whisk them together until well blended. Adjust the seasonings, if needed.

TO ASSEMBLE
6. Place the roasted artichokes in a large bowl, toss with the mixed salad greens and drizzle with the dressing. Transfer to 1 large or 2 small plates and serve.

VARIATIONS TIP:
The roasted artichokes are great to enjoy by themselves as a snack.

Nutrition Info per Serving:
Calories: 296; Total Fat: 23.87 g; Carbohydrates: 20.93 g; Protein: 3.63 g; Fiber: 7.1 g

Zucchini, Radish and Spring Greens Salad

Prep Time: 5 minutes, Cook Time: 0, Serves: 4

INGREDIENTS:
- ½ cup sliced zucchini
- ½ cup sliced radishes
- 4 cups loosely packed spring greens
- ¼ cup turmeric dijon vinaigrette

DIRECTIONS:
1. Add the zucchini, radishes and greens into a large bowl, toss them together well.
2. Drizzle over with the vinaigrette and toss to coat.

VARIATIONS TIP:
If you are eating for one, add approximately 2 teaspoons dressing per 1 cup prepared salad. Refrigerate the remaining salad and dressing separately in sealed containers.

Nutrition Info per Serving:
Calories: 108; Fat: 10 g; Carbohydrates: 4.3 g; Protein: 2 g; Fiber: 2 g; Sodium: 146 mg; Iron: 2 mg

Amaranth Bowl with Butternut Squash and Collard Greens

Prep Time: 5 minutes, Cook Time: 10 minutes, Serves: 2

INGREDIENTS:
- 10 ounces (283 g) cooked butter squash chunks
- 1 tsp. garam masala
- 8 ounces (227 g) collard greens
- 1 apple, peeled, cored, sliced
- 1 ½ cup cooked amaranth
- Extra:
- ½ tsp. salt
- ¼ tsp. cayenne pepper
- 1 tsp. and 1 tbsp. grapeseed oil

DIRECTIONS:
1. Heat 1 teaspoon oil in a pan over medium heat, when hot, add the squash pieces, sprinkle with ¼ teaspoon salt and garam masala, stir until combined and then cook for 5 minutes until hot.
2. Place the squash mixture into a bowl, add the remaining oil into the skillet, and heat over medium heat, when hot, add the collard green, season with the remaining salt and cayenne pepper, and then cook for 5 minutes until hot.
3. Divide the cooked amaranth between two bowls, top with the collards, squash mixture and apple sliced, and then serve.

Nutrition Info per Serving:
Calories: 325; Fats: 12 g; Carb: 50 g; Protein: 9.2 g; Fiber: 8.1 g

Roasted Carrot and Onion Salad with Cashew-Miso Dressing

Prep Time: 15 minutes, Cook Time: 30 minutes, Serves: 1 or 2

INGREDIENTS:
FOR THE ROASTED VEGETABLES
- ½ cup thinly sliced red onion
- 2 carrots, sliced
- 1 tsp. avocado oil
- Pinch freshly ground black pepper
- Pinch sea salt
- Pinch garlic powder

FOR THE DRESSING
- 2 tsps. organic white miso
- 2 tbsps. cashew butter
- 3 tbsps. water
- Pinch freshly ground black pepper

FOR ASSEMBLING
- 2 to 4 cups arugula

DIRECTIONS:
1. Preheat the oven to 425°F(220°C). Use parchment paper to line a baking pan.

TO PREPARE THE VEGGIES

2. Add the onion and carrots into a medium bowl, toss them in the avocado oil to coat. Season with pepper, salt, and garlic powder.
3. Place the vegetables onto the prepared baking pan, and roast until the carrots and onion are soft, about 25 to 30 minutes.

TO PREPARE THE DRESSING

4. While the vegetables are roasting, add the miso, cashew butter, water and pepper into a small bowl, whisk them together until well combined. Miso is a high-sodium food so the dressing shouldn't need any sea salt, but taste it and add salt, if needed.

TO ASSEMBLE

5. On 1 large or 2 small plates, add the arugula. Place the roasted vegetables on the top, drizzle with the dressing, and serve.

VARIATIONS TIP:
If you can't find organic white miso, you can omit it and add sea salt; the dressing will still work well with this salad.

Nutrition Info per Serving:
Calories: 331; Total Fat: 22.64 g; Carbohydrates: 29.28 g; Protein: 8.01 g; Fiber: 4.5 g

Chapter 6: Salads

Mixed Melon Salad, page 66

Hawaiian Fruit Veggie Salsa, page 63

Curried Almond and Raisin Tofu Salad with Greens, page 61

Zucchini, Radish and Spring Greens Salad, page 70

Chapter 6: Salads   71

Baby Tomato and Kale Salad

Prep Time: 10 minutes, Cook Time: 0, Serves: 2

INGREDIENTS:
2 cups organic baby tomatoes
1 bunch kale, stemmed, leaves washed and chopped
2 tbsps. ranch dressing

DIRECTIONS:
1. Add the tomatoes, kale leaves and ranch dressing in a large bowl, toss them together until the dressing thoroughly coats the leaves.
2. Equally, divide onto two serving plates and enjoy immediately.

VARIATIONS TIP:
Be sure to wash the kale thoroughly. Like most leafy greens, it can have sand in it. Nothing ruins a great salad faster than biting down on gritty sand.

Nutrition Info per Serving:
Calories: 58; Total Fat: 6.9 g; Carbohydrates: 1.6 g; Protein: 1.1 g; Fiber: 6.8 g

Roasted Broccoli Salad with Spicy Cashew Dressing

Prep Time: 15 minutes, Cook Time: 20 minutes, Serves: 1 or 2

INGREDIENTS:
FOR THE BROCCOLI
2 cups bite-size broccoli florets
1 tsp. avocado oil
Pinch freshly ground black pepper
Pinch sea salt
Pinch garlic powder
FOR THE DRESSING
¼ tsp. avocado oil
¼ cup cashew butter
1 tbsp. coconut aminos
1 tbsp. apple cider vinegar
1 tbsp. brown rice syrup
1 tbsp. red pepper flakes
2 to 3 tbsps. water
FOR ASSEMBLING
2 to 4 cups mixed salad greens
3 tbsps. chopped scallions
¼ cup raw cashews
2 tsps. sesame seeds

DIRECTIONS:
1. Preheat the oven to 400°F(205°C). Use parchment paper to line a baking sheet.
TO PREPARE THE BROCCOLI
2. Add the broccoli into a small bowl, toss with the avocado oil to coat. Season with the pepper, salt, and garlic powder.
3. Place the broccoli onto the prepared baking sheet, and roast until the broccoli is soft, about 15 to 20 minutes.
TO PREPARE THE DRESSING
4. While the broccoli is roasting, combine all of the dressing ingredients in a small bowl, whisk them together until well combined.
TO ASSEMBLE
5. On 1 large or 2 small plates, add the mixed greens, and place the roasted broccoli, scallions and cashews on the top. Drizzle with the dressing, garnish with the sesame seeds, and serve.

VARIATIONS TIP:
Coconut aminos is a healthy replacement for soy sauce. It doesn't contain soy, has 73 percent less sodium, and contains 17 naturally occurring amino acids. Use it in any recipe that calls for soy sauce.

Nutrition Info per Serving:
Calories: 359; Total Fat: 26.68 g; Carbohydrates: 27.69 g; Protein: 9.08 g; Fiber: 5 g

Lime Dandelion and Strawberry Salad

Prep Time: 10 minutes, Cook Time: 7 minutes, Serves: 2

INGREDIENTS:
1 tbsp. grapeseed oil
½ of onion, peeled, sliced
¼ tsp. salt
5 strawberries, sliced
2 cups dandelion greens, rinsed
1 tbsp. key lime juice

DIRECTIONS:
1. Heat the oil in a medium skillet pan over medium heat, and let it heat until warm.
2. Stir in the onion, season with ⅛ teaspoon salt, mix well and cook for 3 to 5 minutes until tender and golden brown.
3. While the onion cooks, place the slices of strawberries in a small bowl, drizzle with ½ tablespoon lime juice and then toss until coated.
4. When the onions have turned golden brown, add the remaining lime juice, stir until mixed, and cook for 1 minute.
5. Remove the pan from the heat, transfer the onions into a large salad bowl, add the dandelion greens and strawberries along with their juices and sprinkle with the remaining salt. Toss until mixed and serve.

Nutrition Info per Serving:
Calories: 204; Fats: 16.1 g; Carb: 10.6 g; Protein: 7 g; Fiber: 2.8 g

Warm Spinach Mushroom Salad

Prep Time: 10 minutes, Cook Time: 5 minutes, Serves: 2

INGREDIENTS:
½ cup chopped, toasted almonds
1 (6-ounce, 170 g) package baby spinach leaves
1 tbsp. sesame oil
1 cup chopped shiitake mushrooms
1 tsp. sea salt
1 tbsp. apple cider vinegar
Water, as needed

DIRECTIONS:
1. Combine the almonds and spinach in a large bowl.
2. Add the sesame oil, mushrooms, salt and cider vinegar into a small saucepan, cook over low heat for about 5 minutes, or until the mushrooms soften, adding water if needed.
3. Drizzle over the almond and spinach with the mushroom dressing. Toss well to coat the spinach leaves.
4. Serve immediately.

VARIATIONS TIP:
Sprinkle some nutritional yeast on the salad to enhance the warm flavor and give yourself a boost of B vitamins.

Nutrition Info per Serving:
Calories: 271; Total Fat: 19.4 g; Carbohydrates: 20.3 g; Protein: 10.2 g; Fiber: 7.6 g

Sautéed Onion and Strawberry Dandelion Salad

Prep Time: 15 minutes, Cook Time: 10 minutes, Serves: 2

INGREDIENTS:
2 tbsps. of grape seed oil
pure sea salt, to taste
1 sliced red onion
2 tbsps. key lime juice
10 sliced strawberries
4 cups of dandelion greens
1 tbsp. of sesame seeds

DIRECTIONS:
1. Warm the grape seed oil in a non-stick frying pan over medium heat.
2. Sprinkle the Pure Sea Salt on the Red Onions and place the slices in the warm pan.
3. Sauté until the Onions are slightly golden and soft. Stir often.
4. Add the 1 teaspoon of Key Lime Juice to the pan and continue to cook for 1 to 2 minutes.
5. Mix 1 teaspoon of Key Lime Juice and the sliced Strawberries in a salad bowl.
6. Wash the Dandelion Greens, tear them into medium pieces, and add to the salad bowl.
7. Transfer the cooked Onions with their Juice into the salad bowl.
8. Sprinkle over with the Sesame Seeds and Pure Sea Salt.
9. Enjoy!

Nutrition Info per Serving:
Calories: 111; Total Fat: 3.45g; Carbohydrates: 20.26 g; Protein: 4.47 g; Fiber: 5.8 g

Fresh Herb Potato Salad with Lime Garlic Dressing

Prep Time: 10 minutes, Cook Time: 20 minutes, Serves: 1 or 2

INGREDIENTS:
2 cups peeled and diced small white potatoes
FOR THE DRESSING
¼ cup avocado oil
¼ cup fresh parsley
¼ cup chopped scallions
1 celery stalk
2 tsps. apple cider vinegar
2 garlic cloves
1 tbsp. freshly squeezed lime juice
½ to ¾ tsp. sea salt
FOR ASSEMBLING
2 tbsps. chopped scallions
1 radish, sliced
2 tbsps. diced red onion

DIRECTIONS:
TO PREPARE THE POTATOES
1. Place the potatoes in a medium saucepan, pour in the water to cover about 2 inches over the top. Boil for 18 to 20 minutes, or until the potatoes are soft.
2. Drain and transfer to a medium bowl.
TO PREPARE THE DRESSING
3. While the potatoes are cooking, combine all of the dressing ingredients in a blender, blend them together until well combined. Adjust the seasonings, if needed.
TO ASSEMBLE
4. Pour over the potatoes with the dressing, and stir gently until the dressing is evenly distributed, not to mash the potatoes too much.
5. Gently stir in the scallions, radish, and red onion; place into 1 large or 2 small plates; and serve.

VARIATIONS TIP:
You can enjoy this potato salad warm or cold.

Nutrition Info per Serving:
Calories: 440; Fat: 27.83 g; Carbohydrates: 45.73 g; Protein: 5.76 g; Fiber: 9.4 g

Over-Night Marinated Beans Carrot Salad

Prep Time: 15 minutes, Cook Time: 0, Serves: 4

INGREDIENTS:
- 1 (16-ounce, 454 g) can kidney beans
- 1 (14.5-ounce, 411 g) can whole green beans, drained
- 1 cup button mushrooms
- 1 (14.5-ounce, 411 g) can carrots (or 2 cups steamed fresh carrots)
- 1 (4-ounce, 113 g) jar pimiento peppers, drained
- ¼ cup coconut oil
- 1 cup water
- 2 tbsps. dried oregano
- ¼ cup apple cider vinegar
- 1 tbsp. onion powder
- 1 tbsp. garlic powder
- 1 tsp. sea salt

DIRECTIONS:
1. Combine the kidney beans, green beans, mushrooms, carrots and pimientos in a medium bowl.
2. Add the coconut oil, water, oregano, cider vinegar, onion powder, garlic powder, and salt in a blender. Blend to emulsify the ingredients.
3. Pour the dressing over the vegetables in the bowl. Toss to combine. Cover and chill overnight.

VARIATIONS TIP:
To lower the acidity of this dish even more (so you can eat it more often), sprout your beans and use them in place of the canned kidney beans. Just sprout 2 cups of dried beans and enjoy this meal as often as you like!

Nutrition Info per Serving:
Calories: 198; Total Fat: 9.7 g; Carbohydrates: 11.1 g; Protein: 2.5 g; Fiber: 3.5 g

Broccoli, Asparagus and Quinoa Salad

Prep Time: 15 minutes, Cook Time: 0 (chill 15 mins), Serves: 4

INGREDIENTS:
- 1 cup trimmed and cooked asparagus spears, roughly chopped
- 1 cup cooked broccoli florets, roughly chopped
- 2 cups cooked quinoa, cooled
- 2 tbsps. freshly squeezed lemon juice
- ½ cup water
- 2 tbsps. coconut oil
- ½ tsp. sea salt

DIRECTIONS:
1. Add the asparagus and broccoli into a large bowl, combine together.
2. Stir in the quinoa.
3. Combine the lemon juice, water, coconut oil, and salt in a blender. Blend until the ingredients emulsify. Pour over the salad with the dressing. Stir to combine.
4. Place the salad in the refrigerator and chill for 15 minutes.
5. Serve cold.

VARIATIONS TIP:
When choosing asparagus, the thinner the spears, the milder the flavor. Also, white asparagus has a very mild taste.

Nutrition Info per Serving:
Calories: 364; Total Fat: 11.8 g; Carbohydrates: 53 g; Protein: 12.2 g; Fiber: 6.2 g

Thai-Style Vegetable Salad

Prep Time: 10 minutes, Cook Time: 0, Serves: 2

INGREDIENTS:
- 1 cup bean sprouts
- 4 cups chopped iceberg lettuce
- 1 zucchini, cut into thin strips or spirals
- 2 carrots, cut into thin slices or spirals
- 2 tbsps. chopped almonds
- 1 scallion, finely chopped
- 1 garlic clove
- Juice of 1 lime
- 1 packet stevia
- 1 tsp. tamarind paste
- ½ tsp. sea salt

DIRECTIONS:
1. Combine the bean sprouts, lettuce, zucchini, carrots, almonds and scallion in a large bowl.
2. Add the garlic, lime juice, stevia, tamarind and salt in a small food processor bowl. Blend to combine.
3. Pour over the vegetables with the dressing and mix thoroughly.
4. Evenly divide between two bowls and serve.

VARIATIONS TIP:
The bean sprouts called for here are the traditional ones. They are found in the produce section of your market. Alternatively, you can use the thinner alfalfa sprouts. Sprouts are a super alkaline food. Also, look for tamarind paste in the international food section of your market.

Nutrition Info per Serving:
Calories: 77; Total Fat: 3.2 g; Carbohydrates: 6.4 g; Protein: 2 g; Fiber: 5.5 g

Mango and Mixed Veggies Salad

Prep Time: 10 minutes, Cook Time: 0, Serves: 2

INGREDIENTS:

1 mango, peeled, destined, cubed
½ cup cherry tomatoes, halved
¼ of onion, chopped
½ of cucumber, deseeded, sliced
½ of green bell pepper, deseeded, sliced
¼ of key lime, juiced
⅓ tsp. salt
¼ tsp. cayenne pepper

DIRECTIONS:

1. Place the mango pieces in a medium bowl, add the tomatoes, onion, cucumber, and bell pepper and then drizzle with lime juice.
2. Season with the salt and cayenne pepper, toss until combined, and allow the salad to rest in the refrigerator for at least 20 minutes.
3. Serve immediately.

Nutrition Info per Serving:
Calories: 108; Fats: 0.5 g; Carb: 28.1 g; Protein: 1 g; Fiber: 3.3 g

Roasted Beet and Kale Salad with Lemon-Garlic Dressing

Prep Time: 10 minutes, Cook Time: 20 minutes, Serves: 1 or 2

INGREDIENTS:

FOR THE BEETS
4 small beets, peeled and cut into small cubes
1 tsp. avocado oil
⅛ tsp. garlic powder
¼ tsp. dried rosemary
Pinch sea salt
Pinch freshly ground black pepper
FOR THE KALE
2 cups bite-size stemmed curly kale pieces
⅛ tsp. sea salt
FOR THE DRESSING
2 tbsps. avocado oil
1 garlic clove, crushed
1 tbsp. brown rice syrup
1 tbsp. freshly squeezed lemon juice
Pinch sea salt
Pinch freshly ground black pepper

DIRECTIONS:

1. Preheat the oven to 400°F(205°C). Use parchment paper to line a baking pan.

TO PREPARE THE BEETS

2. Add the beets into a small bowl, toss with the avocado oil to coat. Sprinkle with the garlic powder, rosemary, salt, and pepper, and toss to coat. Place the beets onto the prepared baking pan and roast for 15 to 20 minutes, or until slightly crispy.

TO PREPARE THE KALE

3. While the beets are roasting, place the kale in a medium bowl, sprinkle with the salt, and use your hands to gently massage the kale, scrunching it for about 3 minutes, until it becomes soft and slightly limp. Transfer to a serving dish.

TO PREPARE THE DRESSING

4. Combine all of the dressing ingredients in a small bowl, whisk them together until well combined.

TO ASSEMBLE

5. Place the beets into the bowl with the kale, and drizzle with the dressing. Place on 1 large or 2 small plates and serve.

VARIATIONS TIP:

If you're short on time, just skip the roasting process and add the uncooked seasoned beets to your salad!

Nutrition Info per Serving:
Calories: 521; Total Fat: 33.53 g; Carbohydrates: 54.71 g; Protein: 7.18 g; Fiber: 11 g

Roasted Chickpea and Avocado Salad

Prep Time: 10 minutes, Cook Time: 20 minutes, Serves: 2

INGREDIENTS:

2 cups cooked chickpeas
1 tsp. onion powder
1 tsp. of sea salt
½ tsp. cayenne pepper
½ of cucumber, deseeded, sliced
2 avocados, peeled, pitted, cubed
1 medium white onion, peeled, diced
1 tbsp. olive oil
¼ cup chopped coriander
2 tbsps. hemp seeds, shelled
1 key lime, juiced

DIRECTIONS:

1. Preheat the oven to 425°F(220°C).
2. While the oven preheats, place the chickpeas and onions on a baking sheet, season with the onion powder, salt and pepper, drizzle with the oil and toss until combined.
3. Bake the chickpeas and onions for 20 minutes or until golden brown and crisp, allow them to cool for 10 minutes.
4. After baking, transfer the chickpeas to a bowl, stir in the avocado, coriander, hemp seeds and lime juice, mix well. Serve immediately.

Nutrition Info per Serving:
Calories: 208.3; Fats: 8 g; Carb: 30 g; Protein: 6.4 g; Fiber: 8 g

Vegetable Salad Lettuce Wrap

Prep Time: 10 minutes, Cook Time: 0, Serves: 1

INGREDIENTS:

- 4 leaves lettuce, iceberg or romaine
- 1 carrot, peeled and shredded
- ½ avocado, diced
- ⅓ cucumber, peeled and diced
- ½ tomato, diced
- 1 tbsp. chopped almonds

DIRECTIONS:

1. On a plate, lay out the lettuce leaves.
2. Fill each leaf with one-quarter each of the carrot, avocado, cucumber, tomato and almonds. Wrap each leaf around its filling.
3. Eat and enjoy.

VARIATIONS TIP:

Let the lettuce come to room temperature before filling to make it easier to fold.

Nutrition Info per Serving:
Calories: 189; Total Fat: 13.1 g; Carbohydrates: 17.8 g; Protein: 4.1 g; Fiber: 6.5 g

Cranberry, Brussel Sprouts and Quinoa Salad

Prep Time: 5 minutes, Cook Time: 0, Serves: 2

INGREDIENTS:

- 1 tbsp. key lime juice
- ½ of orange, juiced
- ½ tsp. orange zest
- 2 tbsps. dried cranberries
- ¼ cup quinoa, cooked
- ½ pound (227 g) Brussel sprouts, halved, diced, roasted
- 1 medium white onion, peeled, sliced caramelized
- ⅓ tsp. salt
- ⅛ tsp. cayenne pepper

DIRECTIONS:

1. Pour the lime juice and orange juice in a small bowl, then add the orange zest and stir until mixed.
2. Combine all of the remaining ingredients in a salad bowl, and drizzle with the lime-orange juice mixture, toss until mixed.
3. Serve immediately.

Nutrition Info per Serving:
Calories: 190; Fats: 12 g; Carb: 18 g; Protein: 5 g; Fiber: 3 g

Summer Veggies Salad

Prep Time: 15 minutes, Cook Time: 0, Serves: 4

INGREDIENTS:

- 2 cups cherry tomatoes, halved
- 4 cups chopped iceberg or romaine lettuce
- ½ cup shredded carrot
- 1 (14.5-ounce, 411 g) can whole green beans, drained
- 1 cucumber, peeled and sliced
- 1 scallion, sliced
- 2 radishes, thinly sliced

DIRECTIONS:

1. Combine the tomatoes, lettuce, carrot, green beans, cucumber, scallion and radishes in a large bowl.
2. Pour over with 2 tablespoons of your dressing of choice, toss well and serve immediately.

VARIATIONS TIP:

This salad can be made with any kind of lettuce. Experiment with mixed greens or some other variety you haven't tried before.

Nutrition Info per Serving:
Calories: 39; Total Fat: 0.3 g; Carbohydrates: 9 g; Protein: 1.6 g; Fiber: 2.1 g

Stick Salad

Prep Time: 10 minutes, Cook Time: 0, Serves: 2

INGREDIENTS:

- 1 zucchini, sliced into 8 pieces
- 1 yellow squash, sliced into 8 pieces
- 1 cucumber, sliced into 8 pieces
- 8 cherry tomatoes
- 8 cauliflower florets
- 8 steamed broccoli florets

DIRECTIONS:

1. Thread 1 zucchini slice, 1 yellow squash slice, 1 cucumber slice, 1 cherry tomato, 1 cauliflower floret and 1 broccoli floret on a wooden skewer. Set aside.
2. Repeat the process with all of the remaining ingredients.
3. Serve straight away.

VARIATIONS TIP:

To make this recipe thyroid friendly, leave off the tomatoes.

Nutrition Info per Serving:
Calories: 142; Total Fat: 1.5 g; Carbohydrates: 32.2 g; Protein: 7.8 g; Fiber: 8.9 g

Spinach and Strawberry Avocado Salad

Prep Time: 10 minutes, Cook Time: 0, Serves: 4

INGREDIENTS:
- 1 cup fresh strawberries, sliced
- ½ cup whole raw almonds
- 4 cups baby spinach
- ½ avocado, diced
- ¼ cup avocado salad dressing

DIRECTIONS:
1. Add all of the ingredients into a large bowl. Toss well to evenly coat the salad.
2. Serve immediately.

VARIATIONS TIP:
To keep the other half of the avocado from turning brown, leave the pit in and wrap it with plastic wrap before refrigerating.

Nutrition Info per Serving:
Calories: 117; Total Fat: 8.7 g; Carbohydrates: 8.3 g; Protein: 4 g; Fiber: 3.7 g

Romaine Lettuce and Onion Salad

Prep Time: 10 minutes, Cook Time: 10 minutes, Serves: 2

INGREDIENTS:
- 2 small heads of romaine lettuce, cut in half
- 2 tbsps. olive oil
- 1 tbsp. chopped red onion
- 1 tbsp. chopped basil
- ¼ tsp. onion powder
- ½ tbsp. agave syrup
- 1 tbsp. key lime juice
- ½ tsp. salt
- ¼ tsp. cayenne pepper

DIRECTIONS:
1. Heat a large skillet pan over medium heat, arrange with the lettuce heads, cut-side down, and then cook for 4 to 5 minutes per side until golden brown on both sides.
2. Transfer the lettuce heads to a plate and allow them to cool for 5 minutes.
3. While the lettuce heads cool, prepare the dressing, in a small bow, combine all of the remaining ingredients and stir until mixed.
4. Drizzle over the lettuce heads with the dressing and serve.

Nutrition Info per Serving:
Calories: 130; Fats: 2 g; Carb: 24 g; Protein: 2 g; Fiber: 4 g

Spring Salad with Walnuts

Prep Time: 5 minutes, Cook Time: 0, Serves: 2

INGREDIENTS:
- ½ key lime, juiced
- ½ tbsp. tahini butter
- ¼ tsp. salt
- ⅛ tsp. cayenne pepper
- ½ cup cherry tomatoes, halved
- 4 ounces (113 g) arugula
- ¼ cup basil leaves
- 2 tbsps. walnuts

DIRECTIONS:
1. Place the key lime juice in a small bowl, add the tahini butter, salt, and cayenne pepper and then whisk until combined.
2. Place the tomatoes, arugula and basil leaves in a medium bowl, pour in the dressing, and use your hands to massage.
3. Allow the salad to rest for 20 minutes, taste and adjust seasoning, top with the walnuts and serve.

Nutrition Info per Serving:
Calories: 87.3; Fats: 7 g; Carb: 6 g; Protein: 1.4 g; Fiber: 1.3 g

Spicy Wakame Pepper Salad with Sesame Seeds

Prep Time: 15 minutes, Cook Time: 0, Serves: 2

INGREDIENTS:
- 1 cup wakame stems
- ½ tsp. onion powder
- ½ tbsp. key lime juice
- ½ tbsp. agave syrup
- ½ tbsp. sesame oil
- ½ tbsp. chopped red bell pepper
- ½ tbsp. sesame seeds

DIRECTIONS:
1. In a bowl, add the wakame stems, pour in the water to cover, allow them to soak for 10 minutes, and then drain.
2. While the wakame stems soak, prepare the dressing, add the onion, lime juice, agave syrup and sesame oil in a small bowl, and whisk until blended.
3. In a large dish, add the drained wakame stems and bell pepper, pour in the dressing and toss until coated.
4. Sprinkle over the salad with the sesame seeds and serve.

Nutrition Info per Serving:
Calories: 106; Fats: 7.3 g; Carb: 8 g; Protein: 3 g; Fiber: 1.7 g

Chapter 6: Salads

Cabbage Almond Slaw

Prep Time: 10 minutes, Cook Time: 0, Serves: 4

INGREDIENTS:

- 2 cups shredded purple cabbage
- 2 cups shredded green cabbage
- ½ cup sliced, toasted almonds
- ½ tsp. sea salt
- ¼ cup lime juice

DIRECTIONS:

1. Add all of the ingredients except the dressing into a bowl, combine them together.
2. Pour the lime juice over the salad and mix well. Serve.

Nutrition Info per Serving:
Calories: 119; Total Fat: 5.3 g; Carbohydrates: 17.6 g; Protein: 3.9 g; Fiber: 2.6 g

Sea Vegetables Salad

Prep Time: 15 minutes, Cook Time: 0, Serves: 2

INGREDIENTS:

- 1 cup dried sea vegetables
- 1 ounce (28 g) dry seaweed
- 1 tsp. apple cider vinegar
- 1 tsp. spirulina
- 1 packet stevia
- 1 tsp. sesame seeds

DIRECTIONS:

1. According to the package directions to reconstitute the dried sea vegetables and seaweed.
2. At the same time, mix together the cider vinegar, spirulina, and stevia in a small bowl.
3. Drain the sea vegetables and seaweed. Squeeze any excess moisture from them and transfer them into a medium bowl. Add the spirulina mixture and toss to combine.
4. Place in the refrigerator to chill for 1 hour to blend the flavors.
5. Place the sesame seeds over and serve.

VARIATIONS TIP:

You can find sea vegetables and seaweed in a health food store (sometimes you can even find seaweed in your regular grocery store). You can also find sea vegetables online in the Resources section.

Nutrition Info per Serving:
Calories: 61; Total Fat: 0.2 g; Carbohydrates: 4.1 g; Protein: 2.3 g; Fiber: 6.5 g

Kale Tomato and Avocado Salad

Prep Time: 5 minutes, Cook Time: 0, Serves: 2

INGREDIENTS:

- 1 bundle of kale, cut into thin strips
- 1 tbsp. salt
- 12 cherry tomatoes, chopped
- 1 small white onion, peeled, chopped
- 1 avocado, peeled, pitted, sliced

DIRECTIONS:

1. Place the kale strips in a large bowl, sprinkle with the salt, and massage for 2 minutes.
2. Use a plastic wrap or its lid to cover the bowl, allow it to rest for at least 30 minutes, and stir in the tomatoes and onion until well combined.
3. Allow the salad to sit for 5 minutes, add the avocado slices, and serve.

Nutrition Info per Serving:
Calories: 143; Fats: 10.5 g; Carb: 12.4 g; Protein: 3 g; Fiber: 4.8 g

Wakame Lime Salad

Prep Time: 15 minutes, Cook Time: 0, Serves: 2

INGREDIENTS:

- 2 cups of wakame stems
- Spring water for soaking
- 1 tbsp. of sesame oil
- 1 tbsp. of agave syrup
- 1 tsp. of ginger
- 1 tsp. of onion powder
- 1 tbsp. key lime juice
- 2 tbsps. of diced red bell pepper
- 1 tbsp. of sesame seeds

DIRECTIONS:

1. In a medium bowl, add the wakame stems, and pour in the water to cover them.
2. Allow the wakame stems to soak for 8 to 10 minutes until soft, and drain the water.
3. Combine the sesame oil, agave syrup, ginger, onion powder and key lime juice in another bowl, and whisk them thoroughly.
4. On a plate, add the diced bell pepper and soaked wakame. Pour the dressing over the salad and toss well.
5. Sprinkle over with the sesame seeds.
6. Enjoy!

Nutrition Info per Serving:
Calories: 168; Total Fat: 9.91 g; Carbohydrates: 19.07 g; Protein: 4.33g; Fiber: 1.8 g

Amaranth Chickpea Salad

Prep Time: 5 minutes, Cook Time: 0, Serves: 2

INGREDIENTS:
- 2 tbsps. key lime juice
- ⅓ tsp. sea salt
- 1 cup cooked amaranth
- 1 small white onion, peeled, chopped
- ½ of cucumber, deseeded, chopped
- 1 cup cooked chickpeas
- ½ of medium red bell pepper, chopped
- ⅛ tsp. cayenne pepper

DIRECTIONS:
1. Place the lime juice in a small bowl, add the salt and stir until combined.
2. In a salad bowl, combine all of the remaining ingredients, drizzle with the lime juice mixture, toss until mixed, and serve.

Nutrition Info per Serving:
Calories: 214; Fats: 4.5 g; Carb: 37 g; Protein: 6.5 g; Fiber: 9 g

Fonio and Mixed Veggies Salad

Prep Time: 10 minutes, Cook Time: 5 minutes, Serves: 2

INGREDIENTS:
- 1 cup spring water
- ½ cup fonio
- 1 key lime, juiced
- 1 tbsp. grapeseed oil
- ⅓ tsp. salt
- ⅛ tsp. cayenne pepper
- ½ cup cooked chickpeas
- ¼ cup chopped cucumber
- ½ cup cherry tomatoes, halved
- ½ cup chopped red pepper

DIRECTIONS:
1. In a medium saucepan, add the water and bring to a boil over high heat.
2. Add the fonio, reduce the heat to low, cook for 1 minute, and then remove the pan from the heat.
3. Use its lid to cover the pan, allow the fonio to rest for 5 minutes, use a fork to fluff and then allow it to cool for 15 minutes.
4. Place the lime juice and oil in a salad bowl, then stir in the salt and cayenne pepper until combined.
5. Add the fonio and remaining ingredients, toss until mixed, and serve.

Nutrition Info per Serving:
Calories: 145; Fats: 3 g; Carb: 6 g; Protein: 6 g; Fiber: 5.5 g

Olive and Mixed Vegetable Salad

Prep Time: 15 minutes, Cook Time: 0, Serves: 2

INGREDIENTS:
- 6 rinsed lettuce leaves
- ½ chopped cucumber
- 5 halved mushrooms
- 10 olives
- 6 halved cherry (plum) tomatoes
- 1 tsp. of olive oil
- juice from ½ key lime
- pure sea salt, to taste

DIRECTIONS:
1. Tear the rinsed lettuce leaves into medium pieces, add into a medium salad bowl.
2. Place the chopped cucumber, mushroom halves, olives and cherry tomato halves in the bowl.
3. Combine together well.
4. Over the salad, pour with the olive oil and key lime juice.
5. Season with the pure sea salt. Mix well.
6. Enjoy!

Nutrition Info per Serving:
Calories: 183; Total Fat: 9.24 g; Carbohydrates: 26.71 g; Protein: 4.36 g; Fiber: 5.4 g

South of the Border Chopped Salad

Prep Time: 15 minutes, Cook Time: 0, Serves: 2

INGREDIENTS:
- 5 cups chopped romaine lettuce
- 1 avocado, diced
- ½ cup sprouted black beans
- 1 cup cherry tomatoes, halved
- ½ cup chopped fresh cilantro
- ¼ cup chopped almonds
- ½ cup salsa fresca

DIRECTIONS:
1. Combine all of the ingredients in a large bowl, toss them together to combine.
2. Evenly divide the salad between two bowls and serve.

VARIATIONS TIP:
Feel free to add any other vegetables you might like, such as shredded carrot or sliced jicama.

Nutrition Info per Serving:
Calories: 370; Total Fat: 16.9 g; Carbohydrates: 44.3 g; Protein: 15.3 g; Fiber: 14.1 g

Cucumber Arugula Detox Salad

Prep Time: 5 minutes, Cook Time: 0, Serves: 2

INGREDIENTS:

½ of cucumber, deseeded
4 ounces (113 g) arugula
1 tbsp. olive oil
1 tbsp. key lime juice
⅛ tsp. salt
⅛ tsp. cayenne pepper

DIRECTIONS:
1. Cut the cucumber into slices, place into a salad bowl, and add the arugula.
2. In a bowl, add the oil and lime juice, mix until combined, pour over the salad, and season with the salt and cayenne pepper.
3. Toss until combined and serve.

Nutrition Info per Serving:
Calories: 142; Fats: 12.5 g; Carb: 7.8 g; Protein: 1.6 g; Fiber: 1 g

Healthy Watercress Cucumber Salad

Prep Time: 10 minutes, Cook Time: 0, Serves: 2

INGREDIENTS:

2 tbsps. of olive oil
1 tbsp. key lime juice
½ of sliced cucumber
2 cups of torn watercress
cayenne powder, to taste
pure sea salt, to taste

DIRECTIONS:
1. In a salad bowl, add the olive oil and key lime juice. Mix them well to combine.
2. Slice the cucumber and place into the bowl.
3. Tear the watercress and add to the bowl.
4. On top of the vegetables, sprinkle with the cayenne powder and pure sea salt according to your liking.
5. Combine thoroughly.
6. Enjoy!

Nutrition Info per Serving:
Calories: 125; Total Fat: 13.54 g; Carbohydrates: 1.11 g; Protein: 0.83 g; Fiber: 0.2g

Orange Arugula Salad

Prep Time: 5 minutes, Cook Time: 0, Serves: 2

INGREDIENTS:

1 orange, zested, peeled, sliced
½ of avocado, peeled, pitted, sliced
4 slices of onion
4 ounces (113 g) arugula
2 tbsps. olive oil
1 tsp. agave syrup
2 tbsps. key lime juice
⅛ tsp. salt
⅛ tsp. cayenne pepper

DIRECTIONS:
1. Divide the oranges, avocado, onion, and arugula between two plates.
2. In a small bowl, add the oil, agave syrup, lime juice, salt and cayenne pepper, and stir until mixed.
3. Drizzle over the salad with the dressing, and serve.

Nutrition Info per Serving:
Calories: 265; Fats: 24 g; Carb: 11.6 g; Protein: 3.8 g; Fiber: 6.4 g

Avocado, Kale and Sprouts Salad

Prep Time: 5 minutes, Cook Time: 0, Serves: 2

INGREDIENTS:

1 key lime, juiced
½ of avocado, peeled, pitted, diced
2 cups kale leaves
1 cup cherry tomato
1 cup sprouts
Extra:
1 tsp. agave syrup
½ tbsp. olive oil
⅛ tsp. cayenne pepper

DIRECTIONS:
1. Place the lime juice in a small bowl, add the agave syrup and oil and then stir until mixed.
2. Add all of the remaining ingredients in a salad bowl, drizzle with the lime juice mixture and then toss until mixed.
3. Serve immediately.

Nutrition Info per Serving:
Calories: 179.2; Fats: 14.1 g; Carb: 13.5 g; Protein: 3.7 g; Fiber: 6.1 g

Watercress Avocado and Onion Salad

Prep Time: 10 minutes, Cook Time: 0, Serves: 2

INGREDIENTS:

1 sliced avocado
1 chopped seville orange
2 thin sliced red onions
4 cups of torn watercress
2 tbsps. of olive oil
cayenne powder, to taste
⅛ tsp. of pure sea salt
2 tbsps. of key lime juice
2 tsps. of agave syrup

DIRECTIONS:

1. Cut the avocado in half, peel, remove the seed, and slice it.
2. Peel the seville orange and cut it into medium cubes.
3. Remove the skin from the red onions and thinly slice.
4. In a salad bowl, add the avocado, onions, oranges and watercress.
5. In another bowl, combine the olive oil, cayenne powder, pure sea salt, key lime juice and agave syrup, mix together well.
6. Pour the dressing over the salad and toss well.
7. Enjoy!

Nutrition Info per Serving:
Calories: 358; Total Fat: 28.48 g; Carbohydrates: 28.08 g; Protein: 4.55 g; Fiber: 8.95 g

Grilled Romaine Lettuce with Lime Dressing

Prep Time: 15 minutes, Cook Time: 5 minutes, Serves: 2

INGREDIENTS:

4 heads of romaine lettuce
4 tbsps. of olive oil
1 tbsp. of minced fresh basil
1 tbsp. of diced red onion
1 tbsp. key lime juice
1 tbsp. of agave syrup
pure sea salt, to taste
cayenne powder, to taste
onion powder, to taste

DIRECTIONS:

1. Rinse the romaine heads well and cut them in half.
2. Put the Lettuce head halves on a grill. Or you can fry them on medium heat in a large nonstick pan. Don't use any oil while cooking.
3. Grill the lettuce heads until they are browned on both sides.
4. Remove the cooked Romaine Lettuce from the heat and let it cool before serving.
5. Prepare the dressing. In a small bowl, combine the olive oil, fresh basil, red onion, key lime juice, agave syrup, pure sea salt, onion powder and cayenne powder. Mix thoroughly.
6. Place the grilled romaine lettuce on a large serving plate and spoon over the salad with the dressing.
7. Enjoy immediately!

Nutrition Info per Serving:
Calories: 374; Total Fat: 28.14 g; Carbohydrates: 27.47 g; Protein: 9.98g; Fiber: 9.6 g

Spicy Vegetable and Squash "Noodle" Salad

Prep Time: 10 minutes, Cook Time: 0, Serves: 4

INGREDIENTS:

1 roasted spaghetti squash
1 red bell pepper, seeded and cut into strips
2 cups cooked broccoli florets
1 scallion, chopped
1 tbsp. sesame oil
1 tsp. sea salt
1 tsp. red pepper flakes
2 tbsps. toasted sesame seeds

DIRECTIONS:

1. Use a fork to remove the inside of the cooked squash in a large bowl to prepare the spaghetti squash "noodles".
2. Add the red bell pepper, broccoli, and scallion.
3. Combine the sesame oil, salt and red pepper flakes in a small bowl. Drizzle over the vegetables. Gently toss to combine.
4. Garnish with the sesame seeds and serve.

VARIATIONS TIP:
This recipe is great with shredded Chinese cabbage instead of spaghetti squash. But you'll need to let it sit in the dressing for an hour or so before serving for the cabbage to soften.

Nutrition Info per Serving:
Calories: 111; Total Fat: 6 g; Carbohydrates: 6.4 g; Protein: 2.5 g; Fiber: 2.5 g

Chapter 7: Soup and Stew

Squash and Onion Soup

Prep Time: 5 minutes, Cook Time: 35 minutes, Serves: 2

INGREDIENTS:

1 tbsp. grapeseed oil
2 large white onions, peeled, sliced
1 sprig of thyme
½ cup cubed squash
2 cups spring water
Extra:
½ tsp. salt
¼ tsp. cayenne pepper

DIRECTIONS:
1. Heat the oil in a medium pot over medium heat, add the onion and cook for 10 minutes.
2. Add the thyme sprig, reduce the heat to low and cook the onions for 15 to 20 minutes until soft, use its lid to cover the pan.
3. Stir in all of the remaining ingredients, mix well and simmer for 5 minutes.
4. Ladle the soup into bowls and serve.

Nutrition Info per Serving:
Calories: 76; Fats: 2.1 g; Carb: 13.1 g; Protein: 2.3 g; Fiber: 2.5 g

Avocado, Zucchini and Basil Soup with Pumpkin Seeds

Prep Time: 15 minutes, Cook Time: 0, Serves: 2

INGREDIENTS:

1 medium avocado
1 medium bell pepper
2 large zucchini, chopped
½ cup low-sodium vegetable broth
½ cup water
6 fresh basil leaves, plus 2 small leaves for garnish
2 tsps. chopped fresh rosemary
¼ cup chopped fennel
1 garlic clove, peeled, or 1 cube frozen garlic
⅛ tsp. sea salt
1½ tsps. hulled pumpkin seeds, toasted, for garnish

DIRECTIONS:
1. Combine all of the ingredients except the pumpkin seeds in a high-speed blender or food processor, blend until pureed.
2. Pour the soup into bowls. Garnish each bowl with the pumpkin seeds and a small basil leaf, and serve.

VARIATIONS TIP:
You can swap out the basil for 2 tablespoons fresh cilantro and use 2 small sprigs for the garnish. It adds an equally refreshing appeal.

Nutrition Info per Serving:
Calories: 224; Fat: 14 g; Carbohydrates: 24 g; Protein: 8 g; Fiber: 10 g; Sodium: 240 mg; Iron: 3 mg

Creamy Roasted Carrot and Tomato Soup

Prep Time: 15 minutes, Cook Time: 35 minutes, Serves: 2

INGREDIENTS:

1 tbsp. avocado oil
¾ cup chopped carrots
1 (15-ounce, 425 g) can no-sodium-added diced tomatoes, drained
¼ tsp. sea salt
½ cup low-sodium vegetable broth
1 cup water
2 tbsps. chopped fresh cilantro
1 tbsp. freshly squeezed lemon juice

DIRECTIONS:
1. Preheat the oven to 400°F(205°C).
2. Combine the oil, carrots, tomatoes, and salt in a glass baking dish, and mix well.
3. Bake the carrot-tomato mixture for 35 minutes, or until caramelized, then transfer to a food processor carefully.
4. Add the broth and water, and puree until smooth.
5. Garnish with the cilantro and season with the lemon juice, serve.

VARIATIONS TIP:
The baked tomato-carrot mixture makes a nice salsa-like garnish for baked fish or bean tacos, or is great served over wild rice or quinoa. Make a double batch, use half for the soup, and store the other half to use in other dishes throughout the week.

Nutrition Info per Serving:
Calories: 131; Fat: 7 g; Carbohydrates: 15 g; Protein: 2 g; Fiber: 4 g; Sodium: 259 mg; Iron: 2 mg

Garlic Coconut and Jalapeño Soup

Prep Time: 5 minutes, Cook Time: 5 minutes, Serves: 1 or 2

INGREDIENTS:

2 tbsps. avocado oil
3 garlic cloves, crushed
½ cup diced onions
¼ tsp. sea salt
1 tbsp. freshly squeezed lime juice
1 (13.5-ounce, 383 g) can full-fat coconut milk
½ to 1 jalapeño
2 tbsps. fresh cilantro leaves

DIRECTIONS:

1. Heat the avocado oil in a medium skillet over medium-high heat. Add the garlic, onion, and salt, and sauté for 3 to 5 minutes, or until the onions are soft.
2. Transfer the onion mixture into a blender, then add the lime juice, coconut milk, jalapeño, and cilantro, blend until creamy.
3. Pour into 1 large or 2 small bowls and serve.

VARIATIONS TIP:

A versatile soup, it can be enjoyed immediately out of the blender, chilled, or lightly warmed over low heat.

Nutrition Info per Serving:
Calories: 168; Fats: 14.29 g; Carb:9.73 g; Protein: 1.62 g; Fiber: 1.9 g

Garlic Ginger and Pear Soup

Prep Time: 10 minutes, Cook Time: 15 minutes, Serves: 1 or 2

INGREDIENTS:

2 tsps. avocado oil
2 garlic cloves, crushed
½ cup diced onions
¼ cup coconut milk (boxed)
1 cup vegetable broth
2 peeled and cubed pears
2 cups water
1-inch piece fresh ginger root, minced
¼ tsp. sea salt
Chopped scallions, for garnish (optional)
Sliced radishes, for garnish (optional)

DIRECTIONS:

1. Heat the avocado oil in a large skillet over medium-high heat. Add the garlic and onion, and sauté for 2 to 3 minutes, or until the onions are soft.
2. Add the coconut milk, vegetable broth, pears, water, ginger, and salt, and cook on medium-high heat for 8 to 10 minutes, or until the pears are soft. Turn off the heat and allow to cool.
3. Transfer the cooled soup to a blender, and blend until well combined. Adjust seasonings, if needed.
4. Pour into 1 large or 2 small bowls, garnish with the scallions and radishes (if using), and serve, or place the soup back on the stove top to lightly warm on low heat before serving.

VARIATIONS TIP:

You can enjoy this soup chilled, at room temperature, or lightly warmed on the stove top.

Nutrition Info per Serving:
Calories: 185; Fats: 12 g; Carb:20.6 g; Protein: 1.96 g; Fiber: 5.8 g

Garlic Onion and Kale Soup

Prep Time: 10 minutes, Cook Time: 20 minutes, Serves: 2 to 4

INGREDIENTS:

1 tbsp. avocado oil
2 cups thinly sliced yellow onions (3 medium)
1 tsp. unrefined whole cane sugar, such as Sucanat
2 garlic cloves, crushed
2 tbsps. coconut aminos
2 cups water
1 cup vegetable broth
½ tsp. dried thyme
½ tsp. sea salt
3 kale stalks, stemmed and cut into ribbons (about 2 cups)

DIRECTIONS:

1. Heat the avocado oil in a medium soup pot over medium-high heat. Add the onions and sauté for 3 to 5 minutes, or until the onions begin to get soft.
2. Add the sugar and continue to sauté for 8 to 10 minutes, or until the onions are slightly caramelized, stirring continuously.
3. Add the garlic, coconut aminos, water, vegetable broth, thyme, and salt. Lower the heat to medium-low, and simmer for 5 to 7 minutes. Adjust seasonings, if needed.
4. Add the kale and cook just long enough for the kale to wilt.
5. Turn off the heat, ladle into 2 large or 4 small bowls, and serve warm.

VARIATIONS TIP:

Yellow onions work best for this soup, but for variety, feel free to use a combination of 1 cup yellow onions and 1 cup red onions.

Nutrition Info per Serving:
Calories: 114; Fats: 5.18 g; Carb:15.55 g; Protein: 2.66 g; Fiber: 3.5 g

Chilled Zucchini Cucumber and Lime Soup

Prep Time: 15 minutes, Cook Time: 0, Serves: 1 or 2

INGREDIENTS:

½ zucchini, peeled
1 cucumber, peeled
1 tbsp. fresh cilantro leaves
1 tbsp. freshly squeezed lime juice
1 garlic clove, crushed
¼ tsp. sea salt

DIRECTIONS:

1. Combine all of the ingredients in a blender, blend them together until well combined. Add more salt, if needed.
2. Pour into 1 large or 2 small bowls and serve immediately, or place in the refrigerator to chill for 15 to 20 minutes before serving.

VARIATIONS TIP:
This recipe could also double as a healthy dip for freshly sliced veggies!

Nutrition Info per Serving:
Calories: 17; Fats: 0.19 g; Carb: 3.41 g; Protein: 0.81 g; Fiber: 0.8 g

Artichoke, Potato and Asparagus Soup

Prep Time: 15 minutes, Cook Time: 20 minutes, Serves: 4 cups

INGREDIENTS:

1 tbsp. avocado oil
2 garlic cloves, crushed
½ cup diced onion
8 stalks of asparagus, cut into bite-size pieces
1 cup cubed potatoes
2 cups vegetable broth
½ to ¾ tsp. sea salt
½ tsp. ground black pepper
1 can artichoke hearts, stemmed and halved
2 cups almond milk

DIRECTIONS:

1. Add the avocado oil, garlic and onion into a medium skillet, sauté over medium-high heat for 2 to 3 minutes, or until the onion is soft.
2. In a medium-size saucepan, add the sautéed mixture, asparagus, potatoes, vegetable broth, salt, and pepper; simmer over medium-high heat for 18 to 20 minutes, or until the potatoes are soft. Add extra vegetable broth, if necessary, to keep the liquid level between ½ to 1 inch over the contents in the saucepan. Turn off the heat and let cool.
3. Transfer the cooled soup mixture into a blender, then add the artichokes and almond milk, and blend until everything is well combined and the soup is smooth. Adjust seasonings to your preference and add extra vegetable broth or almond milk to thin it out, if you prefer.
4. Place the soup back in the saucepan and lightly warm on low heat before serving.

VARIATIONS TIP:
Substitute the almond milk with coconut milk—2 cups boxed coconut milk or one (13.5-ounce, 383 g) can of full-fat coconut milk—to make this a nut-free recipe.

Nutrition Info per Serving:
Calories: 157; Fats: 5.15 g; Carb: 26.29 g; Protein: 3.38 g; Fiber: 4 g

Creamy Mushroom Coconut Soup

Prep Time: 10 minutes, Cook Time: 20 minutes, Serves: 2 to 4

INGREDIENTS:

1 tbsp. avocado oil
1 garlic clove, crushed
1 cup diced onion
1 cup sliced shiitake mushrooms
1 cup sliced cremini mushrooms
¾ tsp. sea salt
½ tsp. freshly ground black pepper
1 (13.5-ounce, 383 g) can full-fat coconut milk
1 cup vegetable broth
½ tsp. dried thyme
1 tbsp. coconut aminos

DIRECTIONS:

1. Heat the avocado oil in a large soup pot over medium-high heat. Add the garlic, onion, mushrooms, salt, and pepper, and sauté until the onion is soft, about 2 to 3 minutes.
2. Add the coconut milk, vegetable broth, thyme, and coconut aminos to the pot. Lower the heat to medium-low, and simmer for about 15 minutes, stirring occasionally.
3. Adjust seasonings, if needed, ladle into 2 large or 4 small bowls, and serve warm.

VARIATIONS TIP:
The Tarragon Crackers here would go perfectly with this soup! See the tip here for more information on coconut aminos.

Nutrition Info per Serving:
Calories: 81; Fats: 4.9 g; Carb: 8.93 g; Protein: 1.23 g; Fiber: 1.8 g

Zucchini Chickpea and Kale Soup

Prep Time: 5 minutes, Cook Time: 25 minutes, Serves: 2

INGREDIENTS:
- 2 cups vegetable broth, homemade
- ½ of a medium white onion, peeled, diced
- ½ of a large zucchini, chopped
- ¾ tbsp. chopped thyme, fresh
- 1 ½ cup spring water
- ½ cup cooked, chickpeas
- 1 cup kale leaves
- 1 cup squash cubes
- ¾ tsp. salt
- ¾ tbsp. tarragon, fresh

DIRECTIONS:
1. Place a saucepan over medium-high heat, pour in the ¼ cup broth, add the onion, zucchini, and thyme and cook for 4 minutes.
2. Pour in the remaining broth and water, bring it to a boil, reduce the heat to low, and simmer for 10 to 15 minutes until tender.
3. Stir in the remaining ingredients, mix well, and continue to cook for 10 minutes or more until cooked.
4. Serve immediately.

Nutrition Info per Serving:
Calories: 184.5; Fats: 0.3 g; Carb: 31 g; Protein: 6.8 g; Fiber: 6 g

Creamy Coconut Squash Soup

Prep Time: 5 minutes, Cook Time: 25 minutes, Serves: 2

INGREDIENTS:
- 1 tbsp. grapeseed oil
- ½ of medium white onion, peeled, cubed
- 2 cups cubed squash
- 1 cup vegetable broth, homemade
- ½ cup soft-jelly coconut cream
- ⅛ tsp. cayenne pepper
- ⅛ tsp. sea salt
- ¼ cup basil leaves

DIRECTIONS:
1. Heat the oil in a medium saucepan over medium heat. When hot, add the onion, and cook for 5 minutes or until softened.
2. Add the squash, cook for 10 minutes until golden and begin to soften, add the vegetable broth and coconut cream, season with the pepper and salt, and bring the soup to a boil.
3. Reduce the heat to medium-low and simmer the soup for 10 minutes until the squash turns very soft.
4. Remove pan from heat, puree it with a stick blender until smooth, and then garnish with the basil.
5. Serve immediately.

Nutrition Info per Serving:
Calories: 183; Fats: 14.4 g; Carb: 13.4 g; Protein: 1.9 g; Fiber: 2.7 g

Creamy Mushroom Clams Chowder

Prep Time: 15 minutes, Cook Time: 30 minutes, Serves: 4

INGREDIENTS:
FOR THE MUSHROOM CLAMS
- 1 tsp. coconut oil
- ½ cup roughly chopped shiitake mushrooms
- ½ tsp. celery seed
- ¼ cup water

FOR THE SOUP BASE
- 3 medium carrots, peeled and chopped
- ½ medium onion, chopped
- 2 celery stalks, finely chopped
- 1 tsp. dried thyme
- 3 cups vegetable broth
- 1 sheet nori, finely crumbled

FOR THE CREAM BASE
- ¾ cup unsweetened almond milk
- 1 cup lightly steamed cauliflower
- ¼ tsp. sea salt

DIRECTIONS:
TO MAKE THE MUSHROOM CLAMS:
1. Add the coconut oil and mushrooms into a large pot, sauté over medium high heat for 3 minutes. Add the celery seed and water, stirring until the water is absorbed.
2. Turn off the heat and place the mushrooms onto a plate.

TO MAKE THE SOUP BASE:
3. Add the carrots, onion, celery, and thyme into the same pot, sauté over medium heat for about 5 minutes, or until the onion is softened. Add some of the broth, if needed.
4. Then add the nori and any remaining broth, bring to a boil.

TO MAKE THE CREAM BASE:
5. Add the almond milk, cauliflower, and salt in a blender or food processor, blend to combine. If the mixture is too thick, add some of the soup base to thin. Blend until smooth.

STEPS:
6. Combine the mushroom mix, the cream base and the soup base in the pot. Stir well to mix.
7. Heat for 5 minutes, or until warm, and serve.

Nutrition Info per Serving:
Calories: 97; Total Fat: 3.2 g; Carbohydrates: 10.8 g; Protein: 6.5 g; Fiber: 2.4 g

Chayote Mushroom Chickpea Stew

Prep Time: 10 minutes, Cook Time: 40 minutes, Serves: 2

INGREDIENTS:
½ tbsp. grapeseed oil
1 cup sliced mushrooms
⅓ cup diced white onions
⅓ cup hemp milk, homemade
2 cups spring water
⅓ cup vegetable broth, homemade
⅔ cup chayote squash cubes
⅓ tbsp. onion powder
⅔ tsp. sea salt
⅔ tsp. dried basil
⅓ tsp. crushed red pepper
½ cup chickpea flour

DIRECTIONS:
1. Heat the oil in a medium pot over medium-high heat, add the mushroom and onion, and then cook for 5 minutes.
2. Reduce the heat to medium, pour in the milk, 1 cup water, and broth, add the chayote, onion powder, salt, basil and pepper, stir until mixed, and bring it to a simmer, use the lid to cover the pan.
3. In a food processor, add the remaining water and the chickpea flour, pulse until blended, add to the pot and then stir until mixed.
4. Reduce the heat to low, simmer for 30 minutes, and serve.

Nutrition Info per Serving:
Calories: 173; Fats: 9 g; Carb: 24 g; Protein: 2 g; Fiber: 2 g

Chilled Berry Lemon and Mint Soup

Prep Time: 25 minutes, Cook Time: 0, Serves: 2

INGREDIENTS:
FOR THE SWEETENER
¼ cup water, plus more if desired
¼ cup unrefined whole cane sugar, such as Sucanat
FOR THE SOUP
1 tsp. freshly squeezed lemon juice
1 cup mixed berries (raspberries, blackberries, blueberries)
½ cup water
8 fresh mint leaves

DIRECTIONS:
TO PREPARE THE SWEETENER
1. Add the water and sugar into a small saucepan, heat over medium-low, stirring continuously for 1 to 2 minutes, until the sugar is dissolved. Allow to cool.
TO PREPARE THE SOUP
2. Transfer the cooled sugar water into a blender, then add the lemon juice, berries, water, and mint leaves, blend until well combined.
3. Place the mixture into the refrigerator and allow to chill for about 20 minutes, until completely chilled.
4. Ladle into 1 large or 2 small bowls and serve.

VARIATIONS TIP:
Save time and use frozen berries so you can enjoy the soup right away without having to wait for it to chill!

Nutrition Info per Serving:
Calories: 129; Fats: 0.51 g; Carb: 32.16 g; Protein: 1.35 g; Fiber: 2.3 g

Creamy Spinach Zucchini Soup

Prep Time: 15 minutes, Cook Time: 25 minutes, Serves: 4

INGREDIENTS:
2 tbsps. avocado oil
¼ tsp. dried thyme
¼ tsp. dried oregano
⅛ tsp. sea salt
1 large onion, chopped
2 large zucchini, peeled and chopped
1 cup water
1 cup low-sodium vegetable broth
1 cup baby spinach
6 large fresh basil leaves
⅓ cup cooked quinoa (optional)
Juice of 1 lemon

DIRECTIONS:
1. Heat the oil in a soup pot on medium heat for 1 minute, then add the thyme, oregano, and salt and cook for 30 seconds.
2. Add the onion, cover the pot and cook for 7 to 8 minutes, until softened, stirring regularly.
3. Stir in the zucchini. Cook for 12 minutes more, or until the zucchini is soft.
4. Add the water and broth, cook for another 3 minutes, until warmed.
5. Toss in the basil and spinach, cook until just wilted.
6. Pour the mixture into a food processor and process until pureed.
7. Stir in the quinoa (if using). Season with the lemon juice and serve.

VARIATIONS TIP:
If you suffer from GERD, replace the onions with an equal amount of chopped fennel. The fennel becomes soft and translucent just like the onion. It's a different flavor, but adds a similar textural appeal.

Nutrition Info per Serving:
Calories: 140; Fat: 11 g; Carbohydrates: 10 g; Protein: 3 g; Fiber: 3 g; Sodium: 201 mg; Iron: 1 mg

Garlic Parsnip Leek Soup

Prep Time: 15 minutes, Cook Time: 1 hour, 10 minutes, Serves: 4

INGREDIENTS:

Cooking spray
1 large onion, roughly chopped
5 garlic cloves, smashed
2 large celery stalks (with leaves), roughly chopped
2 large carrots, peeled and roughly chopped
1 parsnip, peeled and roughly chopped
1 leek, cleaned well and roughly chopped
2 bay leaves
9 cups water
2 tsps. sea salt

DIRECTIONS:

1. Use cooking spray to spray the bottom of a large stockpot. Add the onion to the pot and sauté over medium-low heat for about 5 minutes, stirring constantly.
2. Add the garlic, celery, carrots, parsnip, and leek to the pot. Sauté for another 3 minutes.
3. Add the bay leaves, water, and salt. Simmer for 1 hour.
4. Remove from the heat and allow to cool slightly. Strain out the vegetables, leaving only the broth.
5. To serve, return some of the vegetables if you wish and warm the soup to the desired temperature.

Nutrition Info per Serving:
Calories: 70; Total Fat: 0.03 g; Carbohydrates: 11.5 g; Protein: 1.8 g; Fiber: 2.2 g

Garlicky Broccoli and Potato Soup

Prep Time: 10 minutes, Cook Time: 25 minutes, Serves: 2 to 4

INGREDIENTS:

1 tbsp. avocado oil
2 garlic cloves, crushed
½ cup diced onion
1 (13.5-ounce, 383 g) can full-fat coconut milk
3 cups vegetable broth
3 cups bite-size broccoli florets
2 cups peeled and cubed potatoes
1 tsp. sea salt
1½ tsps. freshly ground black pepper

DIRECTIONS:

1. Heat the avocado oil in a large skillet over medium-high heat. Add the garlic and onion, and sauté for 2 to 3 minutes, or until the onions are soft.
2. Add the coconut milk, vegetable broth, broccoli, potatoes, salt, and pepper, and continue to cook for 18 to 20 minutes, or until the potatoes are soft. Turn off the heat and allow to cool.
3. Transfer the cooled soup into a blender, and blend until smooth.
4. Adjust the seasonings, if needed. Pour into 2 large or 4 small bowls and serve.

VARIATIONS TIP:
Sprinkle 1 or 2 teaspoons of nutritional yeast on top to give it a "cheesy" flavor!

Nutrition Info per Serving:
Calories: 165; Total Fat: 5.16 g; Carbohydrates: 27.36 g; Protein: 4.24 g; Fiber: 4.7 g

Lentil, Carrot and Potato Stew

Prep Time: 10 minutes, Cook Time: 30 minutes, Serves: 4

INGREDIENTS:

2 tbsps. avocado oil
2 garlic cloves, crushed
½ cup diced onion
1 to 1½ tsps. sea salt
1 tsp. freshly ground black pepper
2 carrots, sliced
1 cup dry lentils
1 celery stalk, diced
1 cup peeled and cubed potato
2 fresh oregano sprigs, chopped
2 fresh tarragon sprigs, chopped
5 cups vegetable broth, divided
1 (13.5-ounce, 383 g) can full-fat coconut milk

DIRECTIONS:

1. Heat the avocado oil in a large soup pot over medium-high heat. Add the garlic, onion, salt, and pepper, and sauté for 3 to 5 minutes, or until the onion is soft.
2. Stir in the carrots, lentils, celery, potato, oregano, tarragon, and 2½ cups of vegetable broth.
3. Bring to a boil, lower the heat to medium-low, and cook for 20 to 25 minutes, stirring frequently, adding additional vegetable broth a half cup at a time to make sure there is enough liquid for the potatoes and lentils to cook, until the potatoes and lentils are soft.
4. Turn off the heat, and stir in the coconut milk. Pour into 4 soup bowls and serve warm.

VARIATIONS TIP:
Want a brothy soup? Just omit the coconut milk, and you'll still enjoy the rustic flavors of this healthy stew.

Nutrition Info per Serving:
Calories: 211; Total Fat: 10.59 g; Carbohydrates: 24.77 g; Protein: 5.86 g; Fiber: 5.9 g

Watermelon Jalapeño Gazpacho

Prep Time: 5 minutes, Cook Time: 0, Serves: 1 or 2

INGREDIENTS:
- ¼ cup diced onion
- 2 cups cubed watermelon
- ½ to 1 jalapeño
- ¼ cup packed cilantro leaves
- 2 tbsps. freshly squeezed lime juice

DIRECTIONS:
1. Place the onion, watermelon, jalapeño and cilantro into a blender or food processor, add the lime juice that only long enough to break down the ingredients, pulse to combine, leaving them very finely diced and taking care to not overprocess.
2. Pour into 1 large or 2 small bowls and serve.

VARIATIONS TIP:
This recipe also doubles as a healthy salsa-type dip, but without tomatoes!

Nutrition Info per Serving:
Calories: 68; Total Fat: 0.31 g; Carbohydrates: 17.81 g; Protein: 1.55 g; Fiber: 1.3 g

Pumpkin Apple and Date Soup with Raisins

Prep Time: 15 minutes, Cook Time: 25 minutes, Serves: 2

INGREDIENTS:
- ½ cup chopped fennel
- 1 medium apple, cored and sliced
- 1 cup canned unsweetened pumpkin puree
- ¾ cup low-sodium vegetable broth
- 1½ cups water, divided
- 4 small dates, pitted
- ¼ tsp. ground cinnamon
- ¼ tsp. curry powder
- 2 tsps. grated fresh ginger, or 2 cubes frozen ginger
- ⅛ tsp. dried thyme
- ⅛ tsp. sea salt
- ⅛ tsp. ground cumin
- 2 tsps. fennel seeds, toasted, for garnish
- 4 tsps. raisins, for garnish

DIRECTIONS:
1. Mix the fennel, apples and ½ cup of water in a saucepan. Cover and cook on low for about 25 minutes, until the fennels and apples are softened.
2. Add the fennel-apple mixture and the remaining ingredients except the raisins and fennel seeds into a food processor. Process until pureed.
3. Pour the soup into two bowls and garnish each with 1 teaspoon of the toasted fennel seeds and 2 teaspoons of the raisins.
4. Serve immediately or allow to cool and serve at room temperature.

VARIATIONS TIP:
You can replace the pumpkin puree with 1 medium sweet potato, baked and peeled.

Nutrition Info per Serving:
Calories: 221; Fat: 5 g; Carbohydrates: 46 g; Protein: 6 g; Fiber: 11 g; Sodium: 260 mg; Iron: 4 mg

Squash and Mushroom Soup

Prep Time: 20 minutes, Cook Time: 45 minutes, Serves: 6-8

INGREDIENTS:
- 2 cups of chopped chayote squash
- 1-2 tbsps. of grape seed oil
- 1 cup of mashed onions
- 3 cups of sliced mushrooms
- 1 cup of aquafaba
- 6 cups of spring water
- 1 cup of homemade hempseed milk
- 1 tbsp. of onion powder
- 1 tsp. of cayenne powder
- 2 tsps. of basil
- 2 tsps. of pure sea salt
- 1 ½ cups of garbanzo bean flour

DIRECTIONS:
1. Peel the chayote squash and cut it into cubes.
2. In a large pot, add the grape seed oil, onions and mushrooms. Sauté on medium heat for 4 to 5 minutes.
3. Pour the aquafaba, 4 cups of spring water, and homemade hempseed milk in the pot.
4. Add the chayote squash and seasonings to the pot, stir and bring to a boil.
5. In a blender, add the garbanzo bean flour and 2 cups of spring water, and blend thoroughly for about 30 seconds until there are no lumps.
6. Add the blended mixture to the stockpot and cook on low heat for about 30 minutes. Stir occasionally.
7. Serve hot!

VARIATIONS TIP:
If you don't have prepared aquafaba, use vegetable broth instead. If you have neither, add one more cup of spring water.
You can serve this soup with our healthy crackers.

Nutrition Info per Serving:
Calories: 280; Total Fat: 8.01 g; Carbohydrates: 38.71 g; Protein: 15.15 g; Fiber: 7.1 g

Artichoke, Potato and Asparagus Soup, page 85

Creamy Roasted Carrot and Tomato Soup, page 83

Squash and Mushroom Soup, page 89

Creamy Onion Mushroom Soup, page 93

Mushroom Gravy with Walnuts

Prep Time: 5 minutes, Cook Time: 12 minutes, Serves: 2

INGREDIENTS:

1 tbsp. grapeseed oil
4 ounces (113 g) sliced mushrooms
¼ of onion, peeled, diced
¼ tsp. salt
⅛ tsp. cayenne pepper
¾ tbsp. spelt flour
¼ cup vegetable broth, homemade
½ cup walnut milk, homemade
½ tsp. dried thyme
1 tbsp. chopped walnuts

DIRECTIONS:

1. Heat the oil in a medium skillet pan over medium heat, add the mushrooms and onion, season with 1/16 teaspoon each of salt and cayenne pepper, and cook for 4 minutes until tender.
2. Add the spelt flour and stir until coated, cook for 1 minute, slowly whisk in the vegetable broth and milk, season with the remaining salt and cayenne pepper.
3. Reduce the heat to low, cook for 5 to 7 minutes until the sauce has thickened slightly and then stir in the thyme and walnuts.
4. Serve with the spelt flour bread.

Nutrition Info per Serving:
Calories: 65.3 Fats: 1.6 g; Carb: 9.6 g; Protein: 3.5 g; Fiber: 1 g

Easy Roasted Garlic Cauliflower Soup

Prep Time: 10 minutes, Cook Time: 35 minutes, Serves: 1 or 2

INGREDIENTS:

5 garlic cloves
4 cups bite-size cauliflower florets
1½ tbsps. avocado oil
¾ tsp. sea salt
½ tsp. freshly ground black pepper
1 cup vegetable broth, plus more if desired
1 cup almond milk

DIRECTIONS:

1. Preheat the oven to 450°F(235°C). Use parchment paper to line a baking sheet.
2. Add the garlic and cauliflower into a medium bowl, toss with the avocado oil to coat. Season with the salt and pepper, and toss again.
3. Place the vegetable mixture onto the prepared baking sheet, and roast for 30 minutes. Allow to cool then add to a high-speed blender.
4. Blend together the cooled vegetables, vegetable broth and almond milk until creamy and smooth. Adjust the salt and pepper, if needed, and add additional vegetable broth if you prefer a thinner consistency.
5. Pour into a medium saucepan, and warm it tightly on medium-low heat for 3 to 5 minutes.
6. Ladle into 1 large or 2 small bowls and serve warm.

VARIATIONS TIP:
Add some extra nutrients by garnishing your soup with some high-alkaline dulse flakes.

Nutrition Info per Serving:
Calories: 225; Fats: 12.66 g; Carb:26.35 g; Protein: 5.42 g; Fiber: 5.1 g

Spiced Tomato Bean and Bell Pepper Soup

Prep Time: 20 minutes, Cook Time: 1 hour 20 minutes, Serves: 6-8

INGREDIENTS:

2 tsps. of grape seed oil
½ cup of minced onions
½ cup of chopped red bell pepper
½ cup of chopped green bell pepper
1 chopped tomatillo
10 chopped plum tomatoes
3 cups of cooked garbanzo beans
2 tsps. of onion powder
1 tsp. of cayenne powder
1 tsp. of sweet basil
1 tsp. of oregano
½ tsp. of achiote
2 tsps. of pure sea salt
1 cup of spring water
Prepared sausage links

DIRECTIONS:

1. In a large pot, add the grape seed oil, onions, bell peppers and tomatillo.
2. Sauté on medium heat for 4 to 5 minutes.
3. Stir the tomatoes, garbanzo beans, seasonings and spring water to the stockpot.
4. Mix well and bring to a boil.
5. Cook on low heat for about 1 hour. Stir occasionally.
6. Cut the sausage links into slices and add them to the pot some minutes before the soup is fully cooked.
7. Serve hot!

VARIATIONS TIP:
If you prefer less spice, add only ½ teaspoon of Cayenne instead.

Nutrition Info per Serving:
Calories: 250; Total Fat: 5.06 g; Carbohydrates: 43.59 g; Protein: 10.29 g; Fiber: 7.7 g

Vegan "Beef" Stew

Prep Time: 10 minutes, Cook Time: 50 minutes, Serves: 4

INGREDIENTS:
- 1 tbsp. avocado oil
- 2 garlic cloves, crushed
- 1 cup onion, diced
- 1 tsp. sea salt
- 1 tsp. freshly ground black pepper
- 3 cups sliced carrot
- 3 cups vegetable broth, plus more if desired
- 1 large potato, cubed
- 2 cups water, plus more if desired
- 1 tsp. dried oregano
- 2 celery stalks, diced
- 1 dried bay leaf

DIRECTIONS:
1. Heat the avocado oil in a medium soup pot over medium heat. Add the garlic, onion, salt, and pepper, and sauté for 2 to 3 minutes, or until the onion is soft.
2. Stir in the carrot, vegetable broth, potato, water, oregano, celery and bay leaf. Bring to a boil, reduce the heat to medium-low, and cook for 30 to 45 minutes, or until the potatoes and carrots are soft.
3. Adjust the seasonings if needed, and if a soupier consistency is preferred, add additional vegetable broth and water, in half-cup increments.
4. Ladle into 4 soup bowls and serve warm.

Nutrition Info per Serving:
Calories: 129; Total Fat: 3.67 g; Carbohydrates: 22.51 g; Protein: 2.43 g; Fiber: 3 g

Kamut Squash and Chickpeas Soup

Prep Time: 5 minutes, Cook Time: 32 minutes, Serves: 2

INGREDIENTS:
- 6 tbsps. Kamut berries
- 1 cup spring water, boiling
- 1 tbsp. olive oil
- 1 cup chopped white onion
- ½ tbsp. chopped tarragon
- 1 tsp. chopped thyme
- 1 bay leaf
- 1 cup vegetable broth, homemade
- ¼ tsp. cayenne pepper
- ½ cup chopped squash
- ½ cup cooked chickpeas

DIRECTIONS:
1. In a small bowl, add the Kamut, pour in the boiling water, and allow it to stand for 30 minutes.
2. Heat the oil in a medium pot over medium heat, add the onion, stir in the tarragon and thyme and cook for 5 minutes until tender.
3. Drain the Kamut and transfer to the pot, add the bay leaves, pour in the vegetable broth, and bring to boil.
4. Use its lid to cover the pot, simmer for 20 to 30 minutes, then stir in the cayenne pepper and cook for 5 minutes.
5. Remove the bay leaf, add the squash and chickpeas, and cook for another 2 minutes.
6. Serve hot.

Nutrition Info per Serving:
Calories: 348.8; Fats: 8.8 g; Carb: 57.2 g; Protein: 11.3 g; Fiber: 7.8 g

Spiced Mixed Vegetable Soup

Prep Time: 20 minutes, Cook Time: 1 hour 20 minutes, Serves: 5-6

INGREDIENTS:
- 1 tbsp. of grape seed oil
- 1 cup of sliced white and red onions
- 1 ½ cups of chopped mushrooms
- 1 cup of sliced bell peppers
- 4 cups of spring water
- 4 cups of aquafaba
- 2 chopped plum tomatoes
- 1 cup of chopped kale
- ½ cup of mashed green onions
- 2 cups of chopped butternut Squash
- ½ tsp. of cayenne powder
- 1 tsp. of onion powder
- 1 tsp. of dill
- 1 tsp. of oregano
- 1 tsp. of basil
- 1 tsp. of savory
- 1 tsp. of sage
- 1 tsp. of pure sea salt

DIRECTIONS:
1. In a stockpot, add the grape seed oil, onions, mushrooms and peppers. Sauté over medium heat for about 5 minutes.
2. Add the spring water and aquafaba.
3. Add all of the remaining ingredients to the pot. Bring the mixture to a rolling boil.
4. Reduce the heat to low and cook for 1 to 2 hours.
5. Serve hot!

VARIATIONS TIP:
If you don't have prepared aquafaba, simply add 4 more cups of spring water.
If you prefer less spice, omit cayenne powder or add only ¼ teaspoon instead.
If you want to make vegetable broth, let it cool, strain the vegetables out, and serve it.

Nutrition Info per Serving:
Calories: 205; Total Fat: 5.02 g; Carbohydrates: 26.36 g; Protein: 15.32 g; Fiber: 3.2 g

Creamy Onion Mushroom Soup

Prep Time: 5 minutes, Cook Time: 20 minutes, Serves: 2

INGREDIENTS:
- 2 tsps. grapeseed oil
- 2 cups baby Bella mushrooms, diced
- ½ cup diced red onions
- ½ tsp. of sea salt
- ¼ tsp. cayenne pepper
- ½ tsp. soy sauce
- 1 cup vegetable broth
- 1 ½ cups soft-jelly coconut milk

DIRECTIONS:
1. Heat the oil in a medium saucepan over medium-high heat. When hot, add the mushrooms, onion, season with the salt and pepper, and cook for 3 to 4 minutes until the vegetables turn tender.
2. Add the soy sauce, pour in the broth and milk, stir until mixed and bring it to a boil.
3. Reduce the heat to medium-low and simmer the soup for 15 minutes until thickened to your desired level.
4. Serve immediately.

Nutrition Info per Serving:
Calories: 100; Fats: 2 g; Carb: 18 g; Protein: 2 g; Fiber: 2 g

Lemon Cashew Tarragon Soup

Prep Time: 10 minutes, Cook Time: 10 minutes, Serves: 1 or 2

INGREDIENTS:
- 1 tbsp. avocado oil
- 3 garlic cloves, crushed
- ½ cup diced onion
- ¼ plus ⅛ tsp. sea salt
- ¼ plus ⅛ tsp. freshly ground black pepper
- 1 tbsp. freshly squeezed lemon juice
- 1 (13.5-ounce, 383 g) can full-fat coconut milk
- 1 celery stalk
- ½ cup raw cashews
- 2 tbsps. chopped fresh tarragon

DIRECTIONS:
1. Heat the avocado oil in a medium skillet over medium-high heat. Add the garlic, onion, salt, and pepper, and sauté for 3 to 5 minutes, or until the onion is soft.
2. Transfer the onion mixture into a high-speed blender, then add the lemon juice, coconut milk, celery, cashews, and tarragon until smooth. Adjust seasonings, if needed.
3. Pour into 1 large or 2 small bowls and serve immediately, or pour into a medium saucepan and warm on low heat for 3 to 5 minutes before serving.

Nutrition Info per Serving:
Calories: 148; Total Fat: 10.55 g; Carbohydrates: 12.05 g; Protein: 3.17 g; Fiber: 2.3 g

Vegan Mushroom Chowder

Prep Time: 10 minutes, Cook Time: 40 minutes, Serves: 6-8

INGREDIENTS:
- 1 cup of aquafaba
- 7 cups of spring water
- ½ cup of chopped butternut squash
- 1 cup of mashed white onions
- ½ cup of medium diced kale
- 2 tsps. of dill
- ½ tsp. of Cayenne Powder
- 2 tsps. of Basil
- 1 tbsp. of Pure Sea Salt
- 1 ½ cups of cooked garbanzo beans
- 1 tbsp. of grape seed oil
- 1 cup of homemade hempseed milk
- 2 cups of garbanzo bean flour
- 1 ½ cups of chopped oyster mushrooms

DIRECTIONS:
1. In a large pot, pour in the aquafaba and 6 cups of spring water.
2. Add the chopped squash, mashed onions, diced kale, cooked garbanzo beans, and half of each seasoning to the pot.
3. Bring to a rolling boil and cook on medium heat for 10 minutes, stirring occasionally.
4. In another bowl, add the grape seed oil, hempseed milk, 1 cup of spring water and the rest of the seasonings, combine well and slowly whisk in the garbanzo bean flour.
5. Continue to add the flour, whisking constantly, until it is fully combined and there are no lumps.
6. Pour the mixture slowly into the pot with the vegetables and whisk to avoid lumps.
7. Add the chopped oyster mushrooms and cook on low heat for 10 minutes. Stir occasionally.
8. Serve hot.

VARIATIONS TIP:
If you don't have oyster mushrooms you may use any mushrooms you have on hand.
If you don't have homemade hempseed milk, you can substitute homemade walnut milk.
If you don't have prepared aquafaba, use vegetable broth instead. If you have neither, substitute one additional cup of spring water.

Nutrition Info per Serving:
Calories: 412; Total Fat: 8.06 g; Carbohydrates: 65.07 g; Protein: 22.74 g; Fiber: 12.7 g

Cucumber Avocado Gazpacho

Prep Time: 5 minutes, Cook Time: 0, Serves: 2

INGREDIENTS:
1 cucumber, deseeded, unpeeled, cold
1 avocado, peeled, pitted, cold
½ cup basil leaves, cold
½ of key lime, juiced
1 ½ tsp. sea salt
2 cups spring water, chilled

DIRECTIONS:
1. In the jar of a high-speed food processor or blender, add all of the ingredients, and pulse until smooth.
2. Tip the soup into a medium bowl and place in the refrigerator to chill for at least 1 hour.
3. Evenly pour the soup into two bowls, top with some more basil and serve.

Nutrition Info per Serving:
Calories: 190; Fats: 15 g; Carb: 15 g; Protein: 4 g; Fiber: 6 g

Creamy Cucumber Avocado Gazpacho

Prep Time: 10 minutes, Cook Time: 0, Serves: 2

INGREDIENTS:
1 cucumber
1 ripe avocado
juice from 1 key Lime
1 ¼ tsps. of Pure Sea
Salt
2 cups of Spring Water
2 handfuls of basil

DIRECTIONS:
1. Place the cucumber, avocado and key lime in a refrigerator, chill them until cold.
2. Peel the cucumber and remove the seeds, thinly slice some for garnish.
3. In a blender, combine all of the ingredients except the basil. And puree until smooth with some green specks.
4. Transfer the mixture into a pot with a lid. Then place in the refrigerator and allow it to chill.
5. After chilling, serve and garnish with the basil leaves and thinly sliced cucumber.
6. Enjoy!

Nutrition Info per Serving:
Calories: 178; Fats: 14.91 g; Carb:12.61 g; Protein: 2.71 g; Fiber: 7.5 g

Onion and Butternut Squash Soup

Prep Time: 5 minutes, Cook Time: 15 minutes, Serves: 2

INGREDIENTS:
1 cup spring water
⅔ tsp. sea salt
1 medium white onion, peeled, chopped
2 medium butternut squash, peeled, deseeded, chopped
2 cups soft-jelly coconut milk

DIRECTIONS:
1. Pour in the water in a large saucepan, bring it to a boil over medium-high heat.
2. Stir in the salt, and add the onion and squash, cook for 5 to 10 minutes until the vegetables turn tender.
3. Remove the pan from the heat, pour in the milk, and use an immersion blender to puree until smooth.
4. Serve immediately.

Nutrition Info per Serving:
Calories: 133.3; Fats: 4.8 g; Carb: 23.6 g; Protein: 2.1 g; Fiber: 1.3 g

Spicy Soursop and Kale Squash Soup

Prep Time: 5 minutes, Cook Time: 45 minutes, Serves: 2

INGREDIENTS:
2 Soursop leaves, rinsed, ripped in half
6 cups spring water
½ cup summer squash cubes
1 cup chopped kale
1 cup chayote squash cubes
½ cup zucchini cubes
½ cup wild rice
1 cup diced green bell peppers
½ cup diced white onions
2 tsps. sea salt
½ tbsp. basil
¼ tsp. cayenne pepper
½ tbsp. oregano

DIRECTIONS:
1. Place a medium pot over medium-high heat, add the soursop leaves, pour in 1 ½ cup water, and boil for 15 minutes, use lid to cover the pan.
2. Then remove the leaves from the broth, reduce the heat to medium, stir in all of the remaining ingredients to the pot, mix well, and cook for 30 minutes or more until done.
3. Serve immediately.

Nutrition Info per Serving:
Calories: 224; Fats: 5 g; Carb: 38.1 g; Protein: 5.8 g; Fiber: 3.4 g

Alkaline Zucchini Green Soup

Prep Time: 10 minutes, Cook Time: 10 minutes, Serves: 2

INGREDIENTS:
- 1 small zucchini, sliced
- 1 small white onion, peeled, sliced
- 2 cups leafy greens
- 1 medium green bell pepper, cored, sliced
- ¾ tsp. salt
- ¼ tsp. cayenne pepper
- 1 tsp. dried basil
- 2 ½ cups spring water

DIRECTIONS:
1. Place a medium pot over medium heat, add all of the ingredients, stir until mixed, and cook for 5 to 10 minutes until the vegetables turn tender-crisp.
2. Remove the pot from the heat, use an immersion blender to puree the soup and serve.

Nutrition Info per Serving:
Calories: 129; Fats: 0.2 g; Carb: 28 g; Protein: 1.1 g; Fiber: 4.5 g

Vegetable Spelt Noodles Soup

Prep Time: 5 minutes, Cook Time: 12 minutes, Serves: 2

INGREDIENTS:
- 1 tbsp. grapeseed oil
- ½ of onion, peeled, cubed
- ½ of green bell pepper, chopped
- ½ cup cherry tomatoes
- 4 ounces (113 g) sliced mushrooms, chopped
- ½ of zucchini, grated
- ¼ tsp. salt
- ⅛ tsp. cayenne pepper
- 2 cups spring water
- 1 pack of spelt noodles, cooked
- ¼ cup basil leaves
- ½ of key lime, juiced

DIRECTIONS:
1. Heat the oil in a medium saucepan over medium heat, add the onion and cook for 3 minutes or more until tender.
2. Stir in the bell pepper, cherry tomatoes, and mushrooms, mix well and continue to cook for 3 minutes until soft.
3. Add the grated zucchini, season with the salt, cayenne pepper, pour in the water, and bring the mixture to a boil.
4. Reduce the heat to low, add the cooked noodles and simmer the soup for 5 minutes.
5. After cooking, ladle the soup into two bowls, place the basil leaves on the top, drizzle with the lime juice and serve.

Nutrition Info per Serving:
Calories: 265; Fats: 2 g; Carb: 57 g; Protein: 4 g; Fiber: 13.6 g

Broccolini, Bok Choy and Rice Soup

Prep Time: 15 minutes, Cook Time: 10 minutes, Serves: 2

INGREDIENTS:
- 1 bunch broccolini, chopped roughly
- 1 cup chopped bok choy
- 3 cups vegetable broth
- ½ cup cooked brown rice

DIRECTIONS:
1. Add the broccolini, bok choy, vegetable broth and brown rice into a medium saucepan, bring to a simmer over medium heat, and cook for 10 minutes, or until the vegetables are cooked until tender.
2. Serve warm.

Nutrition Info per Serving:
Calories: 172; Total Fat: 3.5 g; Carbohydrates: 38.5 g; Protein: 11.7 g; Fiber: 2.7 g

Roasted Carrot Soup

Prep Time: 10 minutes, Cook Time: 30 minutes, Serves: 2 to 4

INGREDIENTS:
- 6 carrots
- 2 tbsps. avocado oil
- 2 garlic cloves, crushed
- 1 cup chopped onion
- 1 fennel bulb, cubed
- 1 tsp. sea salt
- 1 tsp. freshly ground black pepper
- 2 cups almond milk, plus more if desired

DIRECTIONS:
1. Preheat the oven to 400°F(205°C). Use parchment paper to line a baking sheet.
2. Cut the carrots into thirds, then cut each third in half. Place into a medium bowl.
3. Add the avocado oil, garlic, onion and fennel to the bowl, toss to coat. Season with the salt and pepper, and toss again.
4. Place the mixed vegetables onto the prepared baking sheet, and roast for 30 minutes.
5. After baking, remove from the oven and let the vegetables cool.
6. Place the roasted vegetables and almond milk in a high-speed blender, blend together until creamy and smooth. Adjust the seasonings, if needed, and add additional milk if you prefer a thinner consistency.
7. Pour into 2 large or 4 small bowls and serve.

VARIATIONS TIP:
This soup would work great as a sauce over spaghetti squash or even roasted cauliflower.

Nutrition Info per Serving:
Calories: 257; Total Fat: 11.86 g; Carbohydrates: 37.25 g; Protein: 3.76 g; Fiber: 7.4 g

Chapter 8: Dessert and Snack

Ginger Date Spice Pudding

Prep Time: 15 minutes, Cook Time: 0, Serves: 1

INGREDIENTS:
- 1½ tsps. apple cider vinegar
- 1¾ cups almond milk
- ½ cup coconut oil
- 1¼ cups pitted Medjool dates, quartered
- 1½ tsps. ginger
- 1½ tsps. cinnamon
- 1 vanilla bean, split lengthwise and seeds scraped out
- ¼ tsp. freshly grated whole nutmeg
- 1 tsp. sea salt

DIRECTIONS:
1. Combine the cider vinegar and almond milk in a medium bowl, allow to sit for 10 minutes until the milk curdles.
2. Add the remaining ingredients into a blender, top with the milk mixture. Process until smooth.
3. Place the pudding into an airtight container and chill in the refrigerator, or serve immediately.

VARIATIONS TIP:
If you're not familiar with whole nutmeg, it comes in glass jars and looks like nuts, and is commonly available in any grocery store's spice section.

Nutrition Info per Serving:
Calories: 304; Total Fat: 19.8 g; Carbohydrates: 32.8 g; Protein: 3.3 g; Fiber: 3.8 g

Dates, Spelt and Raisin Cookies

Prep Time: 10 minutes, Cook Time: 18 minutes, Serves: 2

INGREDIENTS:
- 1 cup spelt flour
- ½ cup dates, pitted
- 1/16 tsp. sea salt
- 1 ¾ tbsp. grapeseed oil
- ⅓ cup raisins
- 3 ½ tbsps. applesauce homemade or pureed apples
- ⅔ tbsp. spring water
- 2 tbsps. agave syrup

DIRECTIONS:
1. Preheat the oven to 350°F(180°C).
2. While the oven preheats, in a food processor, add the flour, dates and salt, pulse until well blended.
3. Transfer the flour mixture into a medium bowl, add all of the remaining ingredients, and stir until well mixed.
4. Divide the mixture into parts, each part about 2 tablespoons of the mixture, and then form each part into a ball.
5. Arrange the cookie balls on a cookie sheet lined with parchment sheet, use a fork to flatten it slightly and then bake for 18 minutes until done.
6. After baking, allow the cookies to cool for 10 minutes and serve.

Nutrition Info per Serving:
Calories: 149.2; Fats: 4 g; Carb: 55.3 g; Protein: 3 g; Fiber: 2.2 g

Almond and Sweet Potato Waffles

Prep Time: 15 minutes, Cook Time: 5 to 7 minutes, Serves: 4

INGREDIENTS:
- 2 tsps. baking powder
- 1¼ cups almond flour
- Dash nutmeg
- ½ tsp. sea salt
- Dash cinnamon
- ⅓ cup coconut oil
- 1½ cups unsweetened coconut milk
- 1 cup mashed sweet potato
- Cooking spray
- 1 cup unsweetened applesauce

DIRECTIONS:
1. Preheat the waffle iron.
2. Combine the baking powder, almond flour, nutmeg, salt and cinnamon in a large bowl.
3. Whisk together the coconut oil and coconut milk in a medium bowl until combined.
4. Place the liquid ingredients into the bowl with the dry ingredients. Whisk until combined.
5. Fold the sweet potatoes into the batter gently, not to over mix.
6. Use cooking spray to coat the waffle iron before making each waffle.
7. According to the directions indicated on the waffle iron to make the waffles.
8. Serve each waffle with ¼ cup of applesauce.

Nutrition Info per Serving:
Calories: 547; Total Fat: 25 g; Carbohydrates: 38 g; Protein: 14.6 g; Fiber: 16.9 g

Nondairy Sour Cashew Cream

Prep Time: 25 minutes, Cook Time: 0, Serves: 2

INGREDIENTS:

1 cup raw cashews
¼ cup freshly squeezed lemon juice
1 tbsp. apple cider vinegar
½ cup water, plus more if needed
½ tsp. sea salt

DIRECTIONS:

1. Place the cashews in a medium bowl, pour in enough room-temperature water to cover, soak for 15 to 20 minutes. Drain and rinse.
2. Add the soaked cashews and the remaining ingredients into a high-speed blender, blend them together until creamy and smooth. Add more water if needed, a little at a time, to get the consistency you prefer.
3. Place in an airtight glass container and store in the refrigerator.

VARIATIONS TIP:

If the sour cream thickens after refrigeration, add 1 tablespoon of water and stir well to thin it out.

Nutrition Info per Serving:
Calories: 89; Total Fat: 6.31 g; Carbohydrates: 7.27 g; Protein: 2.7 g; Fiber: 0.6 g

Spiced Flatbread

Prep Time: 10 minutes, Cook Time: 20 minutes, Serves: 6

INGREDIENTS:

2 cups of spelt flour
2 tsps. of oregano
2 tsps. of onion powder
2 tsps. of basil
¼ tsp. of cayenne
1 tbsp. of pure sea salt
2 tbsps. of grape seed oil
¾ cup of spring water

DIRECTIONS:

1. In a medium bowl, add the spelt flour and all the seasonings, and mix them well.
2. Add ½ cup of spring water and the grape seed oil, continue to mix.
3. Form the mixture into a dough ball. Add more spring water if it is too thick.
4. Prepare a place for rolling out the dough, and use the flour to cover.
5. Knead the dough for about 5 minutes until it achieves your desired consistency.
6. Divide the dough into 6 equal balls.
7. Roll out each ball into 4 inches in diameter circles.
8. Heat a non-stick pan. Add one flatbread and cook on medium heat.
9. Flip the flatbread every 2 to 3 minutes and cook until both sides appear small golden brown spots.
10. Continue to cook the rest of the pieces.
11. Serve.

VARIATIONS TIP:
You can adjust seasonings according to your liking.

Nutrition Info per Serving:
Calories: 202; Fat: 1.46 g; Carbohydrates: 42.16 g; Protein: 8.64 g; Fiber: 6.6 g

Sesame and Hemp Seed Oatmeal Cookies

Prep Time: 30 minutes, Cook Time: 0, Serves: 15 small cookies

INGREDIENTS:

3 tbsps. coconut oil, melted
½ cup quick rolled oats
⅔ cup cashew butter
¼ cup sesame seeds
¼ cup hemp seeds
3 tbsps. brown rice syrup
1 tsp. ground cinnamon
1 tsp. vanilla bean powder

DIRECTIONS:

1. Use parchment paper to line a baking sheet.
2. Add all of the ingredients into a medium bowl, stir them together until well combined.
3. Place the bowl in the refrigerator to chill for 5 to 10 minutes to allow the mixture to firm up.
4. Scoop a tablespoonful of dough at a time and use your hands to flatten into a disk. Use your fingertips to smooth the outer edges, and place on the prepared baking sheet. Repeat with the remaining dough.
5. Refrigerate the cookies until they firm up, about 20 minutes, and serve.
6. Place leftovers in an airtight container and store in the refrigerator; they will soften and lose their shape at room temperature.

VARIATIONS TIP:
Another fun way to make this recipe is to take the mixture (a tablespoon at a time) and roll it into the shape of a ball, and instead of a breakfast cookie, you'll have a healthy energy ball to start your day!

Nutrition Info per Serving:
Calories: 129; Fat: 9.06 g; Carbohydrates: 10.83 g; Protein: 3.04 g; Fiber: 1.7 g

Chapter 8: Dessert and Snack

Onion Rye Crackers

Prep Time: 10 minutes, Cook Time: 10 minutes, Serves: 2

INGREDIENTS:
- 1 cup rye flour
- 2 tbsps. grapeseed oil
- 1 tsp. onion powder
- ½ tsp. salt
- ½ tsp. dried basil
- ½ tsp. dried thyme
- 4 tbsps. spring water

DIRECTIONS:
1. Preheat the oven to 400°F (205°C).
2. While the oven preheats, in a food processor, add the flour, oil and all the seasonings, and pulse until combined.
3. Add the water, pulse until the dough comes together, and roll it into a ½-inch thick dough.
4. Cut out the cookies with a cookie cutter of the desired shape, arrange them on a large baking sheet and bake for 10 minutes until nicely browned.
5. Serve immediately.

Nutrition Info per Serving:
Calories: 81.2; Fats: 1.2 g; Carb: 16.4 g; Protein: 0.8 g; Fiber: 1.7 g

Santa's Ginger Coconut Snaps

Prep Time: 10 minutes, Cook Time: 10 to 15 minutes, Serves: 6

INGREDIENTS:
- ⅓ cup coconut flour
- ½ cup almond flour
- 2 tbsps. arrowroot powder
- ⅓ cup coconut sugar
- ½ tsp. baking soda
- ¼ tsp. sea salt
- ¼ tsp. cloves
- ½ tsp. ground ginger
- ½ tsp. cinnamon
- ¼ cup coconut oil
- 3 tbsps. ground flaxseed, soaked in 3 tbsps. warm water

DIRECTIONS:
1. Preheat the oven to 350°F (180°C).
2. Use parchment paper to line a baking sheet.
3. Add all of the ingredients except the coconut oil and flaxseed in a large bowl, mix them together.
4. Melt the coconut oil in a microwaveable bowl by microwaving on high for 30 seconds. Combine the oil with the flaxseed mixture. Add the coconut oil mixture to the bowl with the dry ingredients. Stir to combine. The dough will be stiff.
5. Scoop the dough by tablespoonfuls and use hand to roll into balls. Place the dough balls onto the prepared baking sheet and flatten into discs.
6. Put the sheet into the preheated oven and bake for 10 to 15 minutes, or until firm.
7. After baking, allow to cool before serving.

VARIATIONS TIP:
Don't use fresh ginger in this recipe. It won't mix in as well with the ingredients and you'll be left with chunks of strong ginger in the cookie.

Nutrition Info per Serving:
Calories: 174; Total Fat: 10.4 g; Carbohydrates: 17.2 g; Protein: 2.8 g; Fiber: 1.7 g

Spiced Chickpea French Fries

Prep Time: 20 minutes, Cook Time: 1 hour, 40 minutes, Serves: 4-8

INGREDIENTS:
- 4 cups of spring water
- 2 cups of chickpea flour
- ½ cup of diced green bell peppers
- ½ cup of minced onions
- 1 tbsp. of oregano
- 1 tsp. of cayenne
- 1 tbsp. of onion powder
- 1 tbsp. of pure sea salt
- 2 tbsps. of grape seed oil

DIRECTIONS:
1. In a large pot, add the spring water and bring to a boil.
2. Reduce the heat to medium and whisk in the chickpea flour.
3. Add the diced green bell peppers, minced onions, and seasonings to the pot. Cook for 10 minutes, until it thickens, stirring occasionally.
4. Use a piece of parchment paper to cover a baking sheet and use a little grape seed oil to grease.
5. Pour the batter on the sheet, use a spatula to spread, and cover with another lightly greased piece of parchment paper.
6. Place the baking sheet in the freezer for about 20 minutes.
7. Take out from the freezer and cut the batter into fry shaped pieces.
8. Preheat the oven to 400°F (205°C).
9. Use a piece of parchment paper to cover a baking sheet and lightly grease.
10. Arrange the french fries on the baking sheet.
11. Bake for about 20 minutes then flip them over and continue to bake for another 15 minutes until golden brown.
12. After baking, serve warm.

Nutrition Info per Serving:
Calories: 200; Total Fat: 3.27 g; Carbohydrates: 31.82 g; Protein: 22.02 g; Fiber: 12.7 g

Strawberry Spelt Sorbet

Prep Time: 10 minutes, Cook Time: 10 minutes (chill 4 hours), Serves: 4

INGREDIENTS:
1 ½ tsps. of spelt flour
½ cup of date sugar
2 cups of spring water
2 cups of strawberries

DIRECTIONS:
1. In a medium pot, add the spelt flour, date sugar and spring water, and boil on low heat for about 10 minutes, until it becomes thicken, like syrup.
2. Remove the pot from the heat and let it cool.
3. Then gently mix in the pureed strawberry.
4. Transfer this mixture into a container and freeze.
5. Cut it into pieces, and add the sorbet into a processor and process until smooth.
6. Return everything into the container and chill in the refrigerator for at least 4 hours.
7. Serve.

VARIATIONS TIP:
If you don't have fresh berries, you can use frozen ones.

Nutrition Info per Serving:
Calories: 74; Fats: 0.23 g; Carb: 18.4 g; Protein: 0.57 g; Fiber: 1.5 g

Garlic-Jicama Fries with Scallion Cashew Dip

Prep Time: 10 minutes, Cook Time: 40 minutes, Serves: 2

INGREDIENTS:
FOR THE JICAMA FRIES
½ jicama, peeled and cut into 32 (¼-inch-thick) sticks
1 tbsp. avocado oil
¼ tsp. garlic powder
¼ to ½ tsp. chipotle powder
¼ to ½ tsp. sea salt
¼ tsp. freshly ground black pepper
FOR THE SCALLION DIP
¾ cup roughly chopped scallions
1½ cups raw cashews
½ cup coconut milk (boxed)
1 tbsp. apple cider vinegar
1 tbsp. freshly squeezed lemon juice
¼ cup vegetable broth
1 garlic clove
½ tsp. sea salt

DIRECTIONS:
1. Preheat the oven to 400°F(205°C). Use parchment paper to line a baking sheet.
TO PREPARE THE JICAMA FRIES
2. Place the jicama sticks in a medium bowl, toss with the avocado oil to coat.
3. Add the garlic powder, chipotle powder, salt, and pepper, and toss again to coat. Adjust the seasonings, if needed.
4. Place the jicama sticks onto the prepared baking sheet and spread in a single layer.
5. Bake for 20 minutes, flip them over, and bake for another 15 to 20 minutes.
TO PREPARE THE SCALLION DIP
6. While the jicama sticks bake, add all of the scallion dip ingredients into a high-speed blender, blend them together until creamy and smooth. Adjust the seasonings, if needed, and serve.

VARIATIONS TIP:
The scallion dip can also double as a salad dressing: Just add a little extra coconut milk or vegetable broth to give it a thinner consistency.

Nutrition Info per Serving:
Calories: 277; Total Fat: 16.71 g; Carbohydrates: 28.72 g; Protein: 6.41 g; Fiber: 10.6 g

Easy Homemade Tortillas

Prep Time: 10 minutes, Cook Time: 20 minutes, Serves: 8

INGREDIENTS:
2 cups of spelt flour
1 tsp. of pure sea salt
½ cup of spring water

DIRECTIONS:
1. In a food processor, add the spelt flour and pure sea salt, mix for about 15 seconds.
2. Continue to blend, slowly add the grape seed oil until well incorporated.
3. Then slowly add the spring water while blending until a dough is formed.
4. Prepare a work surface and use a piece of parchment paper to cover it. Sprinkle with the flour.
5. Knead the dough for about 1 to 2 minutes until it achieves the right consistency.
6. Equally divide the dough into 8 balls.
7. Roll out each ball into a very thin circle.
8. Heat a non-stick pan, add one tortilla at a time, and cook on medium heat for about 30 to 60 seconds on each side.
9. Serve warm!

Nutrition Info per Serving:
Calories: 147; Fat: 1.06 g; Carbohydrates: 30.59 g; Protein: 6.35 g; Fiber: 4.7 g

Healthy Blueberry Muffins

Prep Time: 20 minutes, Cook Time: 1 hour, Serves: 3

INGREDIENTS:

grape seed oil
¾ cup of spelt flour
¾ cup of teff flour
¼ cup of sea moss gel (optional)
½ tsp. of pure sea salt
1 cup of coconut milk
⅓ cup of agave syrup
½ cup of blueberries

DIRECTIONS:
1. Preheat the oven to 365°F(185°C).
2. Use the oil to grease or line 6 standard muffin cups.
3. In a large bowl, add the spelt flour, teff, sea moss gel, pure sea salt, coconut milk and agave syrup. Mix them together.
4. Add the blueberries to the mixture and mix well.
5. Evenly divide muffin batter among the 6 muffin cups.
6. Bake for 30 minutes until golden brown.
7. After baking and serve the muffins!

Nutrition Info per Serving:
Calories: 313; Total Fat: 2 g; Carbohydrates: 67.1 g; Protein: 9.79 g; Fiber: 8.03 g

Frozen Cashew Butter Fudge

Prep Time: 10 minutes, Freeze 2 hours, Cook Time: 0, Serves: 16

INGREDIENTS:

¼ cup coconut oil (melted/liquid)
1 cup cashew butter
2 tbsps. brown rice syrup
Chia seeds,
unsweetened shredded coconut flakes, hemp seeds, and/or sesame seeds (optional toppings)

DIRECTIONS:
1. Add the coconut oil, cashew butter and brown rice syrup into a medium bowl, stir them together until well blended and smooth.
2. Evenly divide the mixture among 16 mini muffin cups with a spoon, filling each cup about three-quarters full.
3. Top with the chia seeds, unsweetened shredded coconut flakes, hemp seeds, or sesame seeds if desired.
4. Place the muffin cups in the freezer until they are hardened and firm, about 1 to 2 hours.
5. Store in the freezer until ready to serve (they will get soft and lose their shape at room temperature).

VARIATIONS TIP:
Add paper muffin cups to a regular muffin cup pan to help keep their shape, and then put the muffin cup pan on a flat baking sheet before putting in the freezer.

Nutrition Info per Serving:
Calories: 131; Fats: 11.34 g; Carb: 6.55 g; Protein: 2.82 g; Fiber: 0.34 g

Butternut Squash Pie

Prep Time: 20 minutes, Cook Time: 2 hour 30 minutes, Serves: 6-8

INGREDIENTS:

2 butternut squashes
¼ cup of spring water
¼ cup of agave syrup
¼ cup of date sugar
1 tsp. of pure sea salt
¼ cup of homemade hempseed milk
⅓ cup of grape seed oil
1 ¼ cups of spelt flour

DIRECTIONS:
FILLING:
1. Rinse the butternut squashes and peel.
2. Cut them in half and de-seed with a spoon.
3. Chop the squash into small chunks and place them into a medium pot.
4. Pour in the spring water to cover the squash and boil it for 20 to 25 minutes until cooked.
5. Drain and mash the cooked squash.
6. Add the agave syrup, date sugar, ⅛ teaspoon of the pure sea salt, and homemade hempseed milk, mix them thoroughly.

CRUST:

7. Preheat the oven to 350°F(180°C).
8. Place the grape seed oil, spelt flour, ½ teaspoon of the pure sea salt and spring water in a bowl, mix well.
9. Knead dough into a ball. Add more flour or water if needed. Let it rest for 5 minutes.
10. Spread out the spelt flour on a piece of parchment paper.
11. Use the rolling pin to roll out the dough on the paper, adding more flour to avoid sticking.
12. Put the dough into a pie plate and bake it in the oven for 10 minutes.
13. Take the crust out from the oven, add the pie filling, and bake for another 40 minutes.
14. After baking, take the pie out and allow it to cool for 30 minutes.
15. Serve.

Nutrition Info per Serving:
Calories: 123; Fats: 0.64 g; Carb: 28.07g; Protein: 2.86 g; Fiber: 2.03 g

Baked Spelt Biscuits

Prep Time: 10 minutes, Cook Time: 15 minutes, Serves: 2

INGREDIENTS:
1 cup spelt flour
½ tbsp. baking powder
½ tsp. salt
3 tbsps. walnut butter, homemade
6 tbsps. walnut milk, homemade

DIRECTIONS:
1. Preheat the oven to 450°F(235°C).
2. While the oven preheats, in a food processor, add the flour, baking powder, salt, and butter. Pulse until the mixture resembles crumbs.
3. Tip the mixture into a bowl, add the milk and stir until the dough comes together, then roll it into 1-inch thick dough.
4. Cut out biscuits with a cutter, arrange them on a baking sheet and bake for 12 to 15 minutes until golden brown.
5. Serve straight away.

Nutrition Info per Serving:
Calories: 240; Fats: 4 g; Carb: 56 g; Protein: 10 g; Fiber: 16 g

Easy Homemade Cashew and Almond Butters

Prep Time: 15 minutes, Cook Time: 0, Serves: 1 to 1½ cups

INGREDIENTS:

FOR CASHEW BUTTER
3 cups raw cashews
2 tbsps. coconut oil

FOR ALMOND BUTTER
3 cups raw almonds
3 tbsps. coconut oil
1 to 2 pinches sea salt

DIRECTIONS:
FOR CASHEW BUTTER
1. Place the cashews in a food processor, process on high for about 15 minutes, until they change to nut butter. Stop and scrape the sides every minute or so to help the processing along.
2. After about 8 minutes, the nuts should have a paste-like consistency. Add the coconut oil, and continue to process until creamy and smooth, about 7 to 8 minutes.
3. Place in an airtight container.

FOR ALMOND BUTTER
4. Place the almonds in a food processor, process on high for 20 minutes, until they change to nut butter. Stop and scrape the sides every minute or so to help the processing along. After about 10 minutes, the nuts should have a wet, crumbly texture.
5. Add the coconut oil and salt, and continue to process until creamy and smooth, about 10 minutes.
6. Place in an airtight container.

VARIATIONS TIP:
Glass mason jars are perfect for storing your nut butters.

Nutrition Info per Serving:
Calories: 539; Fats: 53.56 g; Carb: 13.24 g; Protein: 8.14 g; Fiber: 1.65 g

Vanilla Snickerdoodle Cookies

Prep Time: 10 minutes, Cook Time: 10 to 12 minutes, Serves: 6

INGREDIENTS:
⅓ cup coconut flour
½ cup almond flour
⅔ cup coconut sugar, divided
½ tsp. baking soda
2 tbsps. arrowroot powder
¼ tsp. sea salt
1 tsp. cinnamon
¼ cup coconut oil
1 vanilla bean, split lengthwise and seeds scraped out
3 tbsps. ground flaxseed, soaked in 3 tbsps. warm water

DIRECTIONS:
1. Preheat the oven to 350°F(180°C).
2. Use parchment paper to line a baking sheet.
3. Mix together the coconut flour, almond flour, ⅓ cup coconut sugar, baking soda, arrowroot, and salt in a large bowl.
4. Add the remaining ⅓ cup coconut sugar and the cinnamon in a small bowl. Stir to combine. Set aside.
5. Melt the coconut oil in a microwaveable bowl by microwaving on high for 30 seconds. Add the vanilla bean seeds and flaxseed mixture. Stir to combine.
6. Add the coconut oil mixture into the bowl with the dry ingredients. Stir to combine well. The dough will be stiff.
7. Use your hand to form the dough into 1-inch balls. Roll each dough ball into the reserved cinnamon sugar. Place them on the prepared baking sheet about 1½ inches apart.
8. Put the baking sheet in the oven and bake for 10 to 12 minutes, or until the tops are browned.
9. Allow to cool on a wire rack and serve.

Nutrition Info per Serving:
Calories: 174; Total Fat: 10.4 g; Carbohydrates: 17.2 g; Protein: 2.8 g; Fiber: 1.7 g

Vanilla Bean, Coconut and Cashew Truffles

Prep Time: 25 minutes, Cook Time: 0, Serves: 12 muffins

INGREDIENTS:

¼ cup coconut oil
2 cups unsweetened coconut flakes
2 tbsps. coconut flour
2 tbsps. cashew butter
¼ cup brown rice syrup
2 tsps. vanilla bean powder
⅛ tsp. sea salt

DIRECTIONS:

1. Combine all of the ingredients in a food processor, process until well combined. The mixture should be sticky.
2. Refrigerate the mixture until it firms up enough to form a ball shape, about 15 minutes.
3. Scoop a tablespoonful of the mixture at a time, and use your hands to roll into a small ball.
4. Place in the refrigerator until ready to serve (they will get soft and lose their shape at room temperature).

VARIATIONS TIP:

Dress up the truffles by rolling them in a small bowl of unsweetened shredded coconut flakes.

Nutrition Info per Serving:

Calories: 147; Total Fat: 10.1 g; Carbohydrates: 14.93 g; Protein: 1.03g; Fiber: 1.89 g

Peach Banana Muffin with Walnuts

Prep Time: 10 minutes, Cook Time: 15 minutes, Serves: 2

INGREDIENTS:

½ of peach, chopped
6 ½ tbsps. walnut milk, homemade
1 tsp. mashed burro banana
⅔ tsp. key lime juice
⅔ cup spelt flour
1/16 tsp. salt
2 ⅔ tbsp. date sugar
⅔ tbsps. chopped walnuts
Extra:
⅔ tbsp. spring water, warmed

DIRECTIONS:

1. Preheat the oven to 400°F(205°C).
2. Pour the milk in a medium bowl, and then whisk in the mashed burro banana and lime juice until well combined.
3. Place the flour in a separate medium bowl, stir in the salt and date sugar, mix well, whisk in the milk mixture until smooth, and then fold in the peach until mixed.
4. Use the oil to grease four silicone muffin cups, evenly fill them with the prepared batter and then sprinkle walnuts on top.
5. Bake the muffins for 10 to 15 minutes until the top is nicely golden brown, and when inserts the toothpick into each muffin comes out clean.
6. After baking, allow the muffins to cool for 10 minutes and serve.

Nutrition Info per Serving:

Calories: 76.1; Fats: 3.3 g; Carb: 14.3 g; Protein: 0.9 g; Fiber: 0.9 g

Vanilla Almond and Quinoa Muffins

Prep Time: 15 minutes, Cook Time: 15 to 18 minutes, Serves: 12

INGREDIENTS:

Cooking spray
¼ cup applesauce
1 cup vanilla almond milk
1 vanilla bean, split lengthwise and seeds scraped out
1 tbsp. ground flaxseed
¼ cup almond flour
1¼ cups coconut flour
1½ tsps. baking powder
½ tsp. sea salt
½ tsp. ground cinnamon
1¼ cups cooked quinoa

DIRECTIONS:

1. Preheat the oven to 350°F(180°C).
2. Use paper liners to line a muffin pan and cooking spray to spray the liners.
3. Add the applesauce, almond milk, vanilla bean seeds and flaxseed in a food processor. Blend until smooth.
4. Mix together the almond flour, coconut flour, baking powder, salt, and cinnamon in a medium bowl. Add these dry ingredients to the food processor and pulse until a batter forms.
5. Place the quinoa in the processor and mix until blended completely.
6. Use an ice cream scoop, scoop the batter into the lined muffin pan, filling each two-thirds full.
7. Put the pan in the preheated oven and bake for 15 to 18 minutes, or until a toothpick inserted comes out clean.
8. After baking, allow to cool and serve.

VARIATIONS TIP:

If you prefer your muffins a little bit sweeter, add a packet of stevia to the batter and mix well.

Nutrition Info per Serving:

Calories: 170; Total Fat: 6.1 g; Carbohydrates: 24.9 g; Protein: 4.5 g; Fiber: 2.3 g

Easy Roasted Okra Bites

Prep Time: 5 minutes, Cook Time: 20 minutes, Serves: 2

INGREDIENTS:
12 okra pods, cut into ¼-inch-thick slices
1 tsp. avocado oil
¼ tsp. freshly ground black pepper
½ tsp. sea salt

DIRECTIONS:
1. Preheat the oven to 450°F(235°C). Use parchment paper to line a baking sheet.
2. Place the okra in a medium bowl, toss with the avocado oil to coat. Season with pepper and salt, and toss again.
3. Transfer the seasoned okra onto the prepared baking sheet in a single layer, and roast for 15 to 20 minutes, flipping halfway through, not to overbake.
4. After baking, serve hot from the oven.

VARIATIONS TIP:
Sprinkle these over a salad for a healthy crouton-type topping.

Nutrition Info per Serving:
Calories: 45; Total Fat: 3.4 g; Carbohydrates: 5.54 g; Protein: 1.41 g; Fiber: 2.35g

Ginger Rhubarb Pumpkin Pie

Prep Time: 10 minutes, Cook Time: 30 minutes, Serves: 8

INGREDIENTS:
1 all-purpose pie crust
1 bunch rhubarb, trimmed and chopped
1 (8-ounce, 227 g) can pumpkin purée
1 tsp. cinnamon
1 tsp. ginger
1 tsp. nutmeg
1 tsp. freshly ground black pepper
1 tsp. chili powder
Dash sea salt
1 packet stevia

DIRECTIONS:
1. Preheat the oven to 350°F(180°C).
2. Line the prepared crust with an 8-inch pie plate.
3. Fill the water in a medium pot, and bring to a boil. Once the water boils, turn off the heat, add the rhubarb to the water, and allow to sit for 4 minutes. Drain the rhubarb.
4. Place the rhubarb and the remaining ingredients in a food processor, blend until smooth.
5. Pour the mixture over the pie crust. Use aluminum foil to cover.
6. Place the pan in the preheated oven and bake for 30 minutes.
7. After baking, allow to cool completely, and serve.

VARIATIONS TIP:
For an exotic presentation, bake this pie inside a scooped out pumpkin, omitting the crust.

Nutrition Info per Serving:
Calories: 148; Total Fat: 9.8 g; Carbohydrates: 38 g; Protein: 11.6 g; Fiber: 6.9 g

Baked Onion Rings

Prep Time: 20 minutes, Cook Time: 30 minutes, Serves: 8

INGREDIENTS:
½ cup of aquafaba
½ cup of homemade hempseed milk
2 tsps. of onion powder
1 tsp. of cayenne powder
2 tsps. of oregano
2 tsps. of pure sea salt
white onions or sweet onions
1 cup of spelt flour
3 tbsps. of grape seed oil

DIRECTIONS:
1. Preheat the oven to 450°F(235°C).
2. In a medium bowl, add the aquafaba and homemade hempseed milk and whisk them well.
3. Add 1 teaspoon of onion powder, ½ teaspoon of cayenne, 1 teaspoon of oregano, and 1 teaspoon of pure sea salt to the bowl and mix well.
4. Peel the onions, slice off the ends.
5. Cut the peeled onion into ¼ inch thick slices. Separate the onion slices into rings.
6. In a container with a lid, add the spelt flour, 1 teaspoon of onion powder, 1 teaspoon of oregano, ½ teaspoon of cayenne, and 1 teaspoon of pure sea salt. Shake all the dry ingredients well.
7. Use the grape seed oil to brush a baking sheet.
8. Place a few onion rings in the wet mixture.
9. Place the wet onion rings in the dry mixture and flip until coated on both sides.
10. Then transfer the coated onion rings on the baking sheet.
11. Repeat steps 8 through 10 until all onion rings are coated.
12. Lightly drizzle the grape seed oil over the rings.
13. Bake for about 10 to 15 minutes until golden brown.
14. After baking, allow them to cool before serving.

Nutrition Info per Serving:
Calories: 65; Total Fat: 0.84 g; Carbohydrates: 11.9g; Protein: 3.3 g; Fiber: 1.68 g

Amaranth and Chickpea Pancakes

Prep Time: 10 minutes, Cook Time: 6 minutes, Serves: 2

INGREDIENTS:

¼ cup blueberries
1 burro banana, peeled
½ cup amaranth greens
½ cup chickpea flour
½ cup spring water

Extra:
1 tbsp. walnut butter
1 tbsp. grapeseed oil
½ tsp. of sea salt
1 tbsp. agave syrup

DIRECTIONS:

1. Plug in a high-speed food processor or blender, place all of the ingredients except for the oil in its jar.
2. Use its lid to cover the blender jar, pulse for 40 to 60 seconds until smooth, then tip the mixture in a bowl and allow it to rest for 10 minutes.
3. When ready to cook, heat the oil in a large frying pan over medium-high heat.
4. Scoop the prepared batter into the hot pan into six portions, form each portion like a pancake and cook for 2 to 3 minutes per side until edges have cooked and firm.
5. Serve immediately.

Nutrition Info per Serving:
Calories: 144; Fats: 0.6 g; Carb: 31.6 g; Protein: 6 g; Fiber: 5.4 g

Thanksgiving Pumpkin Pudding

Prep Time: 10 minutes, Cook Time: 1 hour, Serves: 8

INGREDIENTS:

½ cup unsweetened coconut milk
1 (15-ounce, 425 g) can unsweetened pumpkin purée
½ tsp. nutmeg
1 tsp. cinnamon

¼ tsp. sea salt
½ cup apples, peeled, cored, and diced
½ cup raisins
Coconut whipped cream, for serving (optional)

DIRECTIONS:

1. Preheat the oven to 350°F(180°C).
2. Add the coconut milk, pumpkin, nutmeg, cinnamon, and salt in a food processor, blend until aerated.
3. Add the apples and raisins. Pulse just to combine. Pour the mixture into a 9-inch baking dish.
4. Bake for 60 minutes, or until the top cracks slightly.
5. After baking, serve warm with a dollop of coconut whipped cream (if using).

VARIATIONS TIP:

You can make your own pumpkin purée very easily by baking small "baking pumpkins" (not the Halloween carving kind). It's a good idea to scoop out the seeds first.

Nutrition Info per Serving:
Calories: 69; Total Fat: 0.6 g; Carbohydrates: 16.1 g; Protein: 1.4 g; Fiber: 2.2 g

Chia Seed – Cashew Cookies

Prep Time: 15 minutes, Cook Time: 10 minutes, Serves: 12

INGREDIENTS:

3 to 4 tbsps. coconut oil, divided, as needed
2 cups raw cashews
2 tbsps. chia seeds
2 tbsps. coconut flour

2 tbsps. freshly squeezed lime juice
¼ cup brown rice syrup
Pinch sea salt

DIRECTIONS:

1. Preheat the oven to 350°F(180°C). Use parchment paper to line a baking sheet.
2. Add the coconut oil and cashews into a food processor, process for about 10 minutes, until the cashews turn into cashew butter, and it will go through several different phases (cashews, cashew flour, cashew butter). Stop every 1 to 2 minutes to scrape the sides and make processing easier. Add another 1 tablespoon of coconut oil at a time, if needed to make creamier cashew butter, but don't exceed 4 tablespoons in total.
3. Place the cashew butter into a medium bowl, add the remaining ingredients, and stir until well combined.
4. Scoop a tablespoonful of dough at a time, use your hands to roll into a small ball. And use your palms to gently press the ball into a disk. Transfer to the prepared baking sheet. Repeat with the remaining cookie dough.
5. Bake for about 12 minutes, not to overbake.
6. After baking, allow to cool completely before removing the cookies from the pan or serving. They will be soft and crumbly right out of the oven but will get firmer after cooling.

VARIATIONS TIP:

Another fun variation of this cookie is to use freshly squeezed lemon juice. Just substitute the lime juice with the same amount of lemon juice.

Nutrition Info per Serving:
Calories: 66; Total Fat: 2.37 g; Carbohydrates: 10.83 g; Protein: 1.57 g; Fiber: 1.24 g

Blueberry Banana Sea Moss Pudding, page 113

Baked Onion Rings, page 105

Avocado Lime and Tomato Toast, page 112

Vanilla Snickerdoodle Cookies, page 103

Chapter 8: Dessert and Snack   107

No Baking Fig Almond Balls

Prep Time: 15 minutes, Cook Time: 0, Serves: 12

INGREDIENTS:
3 cups dried figs, stemmed
1 vanilla bean, split lengthwise and seeds scraped out
1 cup raw almonds
½ tsp. sea salt

DIRECTIONS:
1. Combine all of the ingredients in a food processor. Pulse until a dough forms.
2. Scoop the dough by tablespoonfuls and use hands to roll into balls.
3. Place in an airtight container and refrigerate for up to one week.

VARIATIONS TIP:
For a more elegant presentation, flatten each cookie ball and press an almond half into the center of each.

Nutrition Info per Serving:
Calories: 170; Total Fat: 4.4 g; Carbohydrates: 32.3 g; Protein: 3.6 g; Fiber: 5.1 g

Nut Cheesecake with Strawberry and Mango

Prep Time: 20 minutes, Cook Time: 0 (chill 4 hour 30 minutes), Serves: 8

INGREDIENTS:
FILLING:
5 to 6 dates
2 cups of brazil nuts
1 tbsp. of sea moss gel
¼ cup of agave syrup
¼ tsp. of pure sea salt
1 ½ cups of homemade walnut milk
2 tbsps. of lime juice

CRUST:
1 ½ cups of quartered dates
1 ½ cups of coconut flakes
¼ cup of agave syrup
¼ tsp. of pure sea salt
Toppings:
Sliced Strawberries
Sliced Mango

DIRECTIONS:
1. In a food processor, add all of the crust ingredients and blend for 30 seconds.
2. Use the parchment paper to cover a baking form and spread out the blended crust ingredients.
3. Place the sliced mango across the crust and freeze for 10 minutes.
4. In a blender, add all of the filling ingredients and blend until smooth.
5. Pour the filling over the crust, use foil or parchment paper to cover and allow it to stand for 3 to 4 hours in the refrigerator.
6. Then take out from the baking form and garnish with the strawberries and mango.
7. Serve!

Nutrition Info per Serving:
Calories: 480; Total Fat: 27.88 g; Carbohydrates: 57.89 g; Protein: 7.8 g; Fiber: 7.39 g

Self-Frosting Pineapple Carrot Cake

Prep Time: 15 minutes, Cook Time: 35 to 40 minutes, Serves: 8

INGREDIENTS:
Cooking spray
⅓ cup coconut oil plus 3 tbsps., melted, divided
½ cup grated carrot
1 ½ tsps. baking powder
1 ¼ cups almond flour
¼ tsp. sea salt
1 (8-ounce, 227 g) can crushed pineapple in juice, drained, juice reserved (about ¾ cup)
⅓ cup chopped almonds
½ cup flaked unsweetened coconut

DIRECTIONS:
1. Preheat the oven to 350°F(180°C).
2. Use cooking spray to coat an 8-inch round cake pan.
3. Combine ⅓ cup coconut oil and the carrot in a large bowl.
4. Sift together the baking powder, almond flour and salt in a medium bowl. Add these dry ingredients to the carrot-oil mixture, then add the reserved pineapple juice. Mix well after each addition.
5. In the prepared pan, spread with half of the batter. Place an even layer of the crushed pineapple over the batter. Place the remaining cake batter on the top.
6. Combine the almonds, coconut, and the remaining 3 tablespoons coconut oil in a small bowl. Evenly sprinkle the almond mixture over the cake.
7. Place the pan in the preheated oven and bake until a cake tester comes out clean, about 35 to 40 minutes.
8. After baking, flip the pan upside down onto a cake plate to reveal a perfectly formed cake!

VARIATIONS TIP:
If you don't have crushed pineapple on hand, you can use canned pineapple chunks or even rings by processing them in a food processor.

Nutrition Info per Serving:
Calories: 282; Total Fat: 26.6 g; Carbohydrates: 10.3 g; Protein: 4.8 g; Fiber: 3.2 g

Burro Banana Walnut Muffin

Prep Time: 10 minutes, Cook Time: 20 minutes, Serves: 2

INGREDIENTS:

¾ cup spelt flour
¼ tsp. of sea salt
6 tbsps. date sugar
1 burro banana, peeled, mashed
6 tbsps. walnut milk, homemade
½ tbsp. key lime juice
2 tbsps. grapeseed oil
¼ cup chopped walnuts
½ burro banana, peeled, cut into chunks

DIRECTIONS:

1. Preheat the oven to 400°F(205°C).
2. While the oven preheats, combine the flour, salt and sugar in a medium bowl, stir until mixed.
3. Then place the mashed burro banana in a separate bowl, add the milk, lime juice and oil, whisk until combined, and then combine with the flour mixture until smooth.
4. Fold in the walnuts and burro banana pieces, then evenly spoon the mixture into four muffin cups.
5. Bake the muffins for 15 to 20 minutes until firm and cooked, and then serve.

Nutrition Info per Serving:
Calories: 204.1; Fats: 8.5 g; Carb: 30 g; Protein: 3.3 g; Fiber: 1.4 g

Vegan Mushroom Chickpea Fritters

Prep Time: 10 minutes, Cook Time: 10 minutes, Serves: 2

INGREDIENTS:

200g mushrooms, chopped
1 medium green bell pepper, cored, chopped
2 medium white onions, peeled, chopped
1 tbsp. onion powder
1 tsp. of sea salt
⅛ tsp. cayenne pepper
1 tbsp. basil leaves, chopped
1 tbsp. oregano
1 cup chickpea flour
½ cup spring water
1 tbsp. grapeseed oil

DIRECTIONS:

1. Combine the mushrooms, bell pepper and onions in a large bowl, add all the seasonings, basil and oregano, stir until mixed, and then allow the mixture to rest for 5 minutes.
2. Add the chickpea flour, stir until mixed and then stir in the water until well combined and smooth.
3. Heat the oil in a large skillet pan over medium heat, ladle the vegetable mixture into portions, press down each portion, and cook for 3 to 4 minutes per side until cooked and golden brown.
4. Serve immediately.

Nutrition Info per Serving:
Calories: 281.5; Fats: 15.2 g; Carb: 26.2 g; Protein: 13.8 g; Fiber: 5 g

Flourless Cashew and Pumpkin Seed Cookies

Prep Time: 15 minutes, Cook Time: 10 minutes, Serves: 18 to 20 cookies

INGREDIENTS:

½ cup coconut oil
2 cups raw cashews
½ cup raw pumpkin seeds
½ cup almond flour
½ tsp. baking soda
2 tbsps. brown rice syrup
¼ tsp. sea salt

DIRECTIONS:

1. Preheat the oven to 350°F(180°C). Use parchment paper to line a baking sheet.
2. Add the coconut oil and raw cashews into a food processor, process for about 10 minutes, until the cashews turn into cashew butter, and it will go through several different stages (cashews, cashew flour, cashew butter). Stop every 1 to 2 minutes to scrape the sides and make processing easier. This should yield 1 cup of cashew butter.
3. Transfer the cashew butter to a medium bowl, add the pumpkin seeds, almond flour, baking soda, brown rice syrup, and salt, and stir until well combined.
4. Scoop a tablespoonful of dough at a time, use your hands to roll into a small ball. And use your palms to gently press the ball into a disk. Transfer to the prepared baking sheet. Repeat with the remaining cookie dough.
5. Bake for 10 to 12 minutes, not to overbake.
6. After baking, allow to cool completely before removing the cookies from the pan or serving. They will be soft and crumbly right out of the oven but will get firmer after cooling.
7. Place in an airtight container and store in the refrigerator to keep the coconut oil from melting.

VARIATIONS TIP:
Make sure you use homemade cashew butter, which has a different consistency than store-bought cashew butter; it will make a difference in this recipe.

Nutrition Info per Serving:
Calories: 96; Total Fat: 9.07 g; Carbohydrates: 3.32 g; Protein: 1.56 g; Fiber: 0.32 g

Coconut Cashew Almond and Date Bars

Prep Time: 10 minutes, Cook Time: 0, Serves: 6

INGREDIENTS:

- ½ cup raw almonds
- ½ cup raw cashews
- 8 small dates, pitted
- ¼ cup unsweetened finely shredded coconut
- ¼ cup flax meal

DIRECTIONS:

1. Combine all of the ingredients in a high-speed blender, blend until well combined.
2. Equally divide the mixture into 6 balls, each about 1½ inches in diameter. Mold each ball into a square or rectangle about ¼ inch thick.
3. Use plastic wrap to wrap each piece and store in the refrigerator for up to 1 week or freeze for up to 3 months.

VARIATIONS TIP:

Chop the dates by hand and mix all the ingredients together in a medium bowl for a simple trail mix instead. Divide evenly among 6 snack-size resealable plastic bags.

Nutrition Info per Serving:

Calories: 176; Fat: 12 g; Carbohydrates: 14 g; Protein: 5 g; Fiber: 4 g; Sodium: 4 mg; Iron: 1 mg

Herbed Almond Crackers

Prep Time: 15 minutes, Cook Time: 20 minutes, Serves: 6

INGREDIENTS:

- 1 tbsp. coconut oil
- 2 tbsps. flaxseed meal
- 4 tbsps. water
- 1½ tsps. fresh rosemary
- 1 cup almond flour
- ¾ tsp. finely chopped fresh thyme
- ¾ tsp. finely chopped fresh oregano
- 1 tbsp. sesame seeds (optional)
- ½ tsp. sea salt

DIRECTIONS:

1. Preheat the oven to 325°F(165°C).
2. Combine the coconut oil, flaxseed meal and water in a small bowl. Place in the refrigerator to chill for 10 minutes until the mixture thickens.
3. Combine the rosemary, almond flour, thyme, oregano and sesame seeds (if using) in a medium bowl. Stir in the flaxseed mixture, combining thoroughly.
4. Form the dough into a ball. Roll the dough to a ⅛-inch thickness on parchment paper. Sprinkle with the salt.
5. Transfer the parchment with the dough onto a baking sheet. Equally cut the dough into 24 crackers, not to cut through the parchment.
6. Place the baking sheet in the preheated oven. Bake for 20 minutes, make sure the crackers don't burn.
7. Remove from the oven and allow to cool and serve.

VARIATIONS TIP:

If you don't have flaxseed meal, grind flaxseeds in a clean coffee grinder or small food processor. When mixed with water, flaxseed acts as a thickener.

Nutrition Info per Serving:

Calories: 118; Total Fat: 4 g; Carbohydrates: 17.3 g; Protein: 2.9 g; Fiber: 1.6 g

Almond Tarragon Crackers

Prep Time: 10 minutes, Cook Time: 15 minutes, Serves: 60 small crackers

INGREDIENTS:

- 1 tbsp. ground flaxseed
- 3 tbsps. water
- 1 tbsp. avocado oil
- 2 cups almond flour
- 1 tbsp. fresh chopped tarragon
- ½ tsp. freshly ground black pepper
- ½ tsp. sea salt
- ¼ tsp. garlic powder

DIRECTIONS:

1. Preheat the oven to 350°F(180°C). Use parchment paper to line a baking sheet.
2. To prepare a flax egg, whisk together the flaxseed and water in a large bowl.
3. Add all of the remaining ingredients, and stir until well combined.
4. Transfer the mixture to the prepared baking sheet. Form the dough into a ball with your hands, then place another piece of parchment paper on the top of the ball.
5. Over the parchment paper, roll out the dough to about ¼-inch thickness with a rolling pin.
6. Cut the dough into 60 (1½-inch-by-1½-inch) squares with a knife or pizza cutter.
7. Bake for 12 to 14 minutes, or until the crackers are slightly golden on top. Then flip them over and bake for another one or two minutes.
8. Allow to cool and serve.

VARIATIONS TIP:

Substitute the tarragon with your favorite alkaline herb like oregano, scallions, dill, or thyme.

Nutrition Info per Serving:

Calories: 204; Total Fat: 19.73 g; Carbohydrates: 5.94 g; Protein: 3.09 g; Fiber: 3.7 g

Walnut Date Balls with Sesame Seeds

Prep Time: 5 minutes, Cook Time: 0, Serves: 2

INGREDIENTS:
- ½ cup dates, pitted
- ¼ cup walnuts
- ½ cup soft-jelly coconut, grated
- 2 tbsps. agave syrup
- ¼ tsp. of sea salt
- ¼ cup sesame seeds

DIRECTIONS:
1. Plug in a high-speed food processor or blender, combine all of the ingredients in its jar except for the sesame seeds.
2. Use its lid to cover the blender jar and pulse for 20 seconds until well combined.
3. Tip the mixture into a bowl, form it into even size balls and roll each ball into sesame seeds.
4. Serve immediately.

Nutrition Info per Serving:
Calories: 99.1; Fats: 5.3 g; Carb: 13.5 g; Protein: 2 g; Fiber: 2 g

Basic Pie Crust

Prep Time: 15 minutes, Cook Time: 0, Serves: 8

INGREDIENTS:
- 1 tbsp. coconut oil
- 1 cup almond flour
- ⅛ tsp. sea salt

DIRECTIONS:
1. Use parchment paper to line an 8-inch pie pan.
2. Add the coconut oil, almond flour and sea salt into a food processor, mix until a ball forms.
3. Place the dough ball in the middle of the parchment-lined pie plate. Put a second sheet of parchment paper on the top.
4. Evenly press the crust over the bottom and up the sides of the pan with your hands. Remove the top piece of parchment paper, but leave the one under the crust.
5. Pre-bake, if needed.

VARIATIONS TIP:
You can chill the dough before rolling out so it's easier to work with.

Nutrition Info per Serving:
Calories: 84; Total Fat: 7.6 g; Carbohydrates: 2.5 g; Protein: 2.5 g; Fiber: 1.4 g

Black Sapote and Nuts Pudding

Prep Time: 10 minutes, Cook Time: 0, Serves: 4

INGREDIENTS:
- 1 to 2 cups of black sapote
- 1 tbsp. of hemp seeds
- ¼ cup of agave syrup
- ½ cup of soaked brazil nuts (overnight or for at least 3 hours)
- ½ cup of spring water

DIRECTIONS:
1. Cut 1 to 2 cups of black sapote in half.
2. Remove all seeds and you should have 1 full cup of de-seeded fruit.
3. In a blender, add all of the ingredients and blend until smooth.
4. Serve and enjoy!

VARIATIONS TIP:
Store in the refrigerator if you don't use it immediately.

Nutrition Info per Serving:
Calories: 219; Fats: 12.55 g; Carb: 26.94 g; Protein: 3.49 g; Fiber: 3.83 g

Spelt Banana Walnut Pancakes

Prep Time: 10 minutes, Cook Time: 6 minutes, Serves: 2

INGREDIENTS:
- ¼ cup and 2 tbsps. walnut milk, homemade
- 1 ½ tsps. key lime juice
- ¼ cup mashed burro banana
- 1 ½ tsps. walnut butter, homemade
- ½ cup spelt flour
- ½ tsp. date sugar
- 1 tbsp. grapeseed oil

DIRECTIONS:
1. Pour the milk in a medium bowl, stir in the lime juice, allow it to rest for 5 minutes and then whisk in the mashed burro banana and butter until combined.
2. Add the flour in another medium bowl, stir in the sugar and then whisk in the milk mixture until smooth.
3. Heat the oil in a large skillet pan over medium-high heat. When hot, ladle in the batter in four portions, form each portion into a pancake and cook for 2 to 3 minutes per side until golden brown and cooked.
4. Serve immediately.

Nutrition Info per Serving:
Calories: 103.4; Fats: 1.6 g; Carb: 23.1 g; Protein: 7 g; Fiber: 3.5 g

Date Carrot Cake Cookies with Cashew Cream Frosting

Prep Time: 5 to 7 minutes (plus overnight soaking), Cook Time: 12 minutes, Serves: 12

INGREDIENTS:

FOR THE CARROT CAKE COOKIES
1 medium egg
¼ cup cashew butter
10 small dates, pitted
¼ cup almond meal
¼ cup unsweetened finely shredded coconut
1 tbsp. coconut oil
¼ tsp. ground cinnamon
¼ tsp. vanilla extract
⅛ tsp. sea salt
¼ cup brown rice flour
¾ cup rolled oats
½ tsp. baking soda
2 tbsps. shredded carrot
¼ cup golden raisins
3 tbsps. chopped walnuts
FOR THE CASHEW CREAM FROSTING
1 cup cashews, soaked in water overnight, then drained
8 small dates, pitted
¼ cup unsweetened shredded coconut
1 to 2 tsps. freshly squeezed lemon juice (optional)
½ cup water
⅛ tsp. sea salt
¼ tsp. vanilla extract

DIRECTIONS:

TO MAKE THE CARROT CAKE COOKIES
1. Preheat the oven to 375°F(190°C). Use parchment paper to line a baking sheet.
2. Add the egg, cashew butter, dates, almond meal, coconut oil, shredded coconut, cinnamon, vanilla and salt into a food processor. Blend until smooth and well combined.
3. Combine the brown rice flour, oats, and baking soda in a medium bowl. Add the wet ingredients and stir to combine well.
4. Fold in the carrot, raisins and walnuts.
5. Scoop the mixture into 1½-inch balls and arrange them on the prepared baking sheet, evenly spacing them. Bake for 12 minutes, or until a toothpick inserted into the center of a cookie comes out clean. Allow to cool completely.

TO MAKE THE CASHEW CREAM FROSTING
6. Combine all of the cashew cream frosting ingredients in a high-speed blender. Blend until well combined, with date specks sprinkled throughout.
7. Frost about 1 rounded teaspoon of the cashew cream frosting onto each cookie.

VARIATIONS TIP:

You can replace the egg by stirring together 1 tablespoon flax meal and 2 tablespoons water and letting the mixture stand until gelled and thickened. Use the flax mixture where the egg is called for in the recipe.

Nutrition Info per Serving:

Calories: 166; Fat: 9 g; Carbohydrates: 20 g; Protein: 4 g; Fiber: 3 g; Sodium: 100 mg; Iron: 1 mg

Avocado Lime and Tomato Toast

Prep Time: 5 minutes, Cook Time: 0, Serves: 2

INGREDIENTS:

1 avocado, peeled, pitted, mashed
2 tsps. key lime juice
2 slices of spelt bread, toasted
½ cup cherry tomato halves
½ tsp. salt

DIRECTIONS:

1. In a bowl, add the avocado and lime juice, and mash until smooth.
2. Evenly spread mashed avocado on top of each toast and then scatter the cherry tomatoes.
3. Sprinkle over the tomatoes with the salt and serve.

Nutrition Info per Serving:

Calories: 189; Fats: 11 g; Carb: 20 g; Protein: 3 g; Fiber: 5.4 g

Spicy Garlic Almonds

Prep Time: 5 minutes, Cook Time: 5 minutes, Serves: 1 cup

INGREDIENTS:

1 tsp. avocado oil
1 cup raw almonds
½ tsp. garlic powder
1 tsp. ground paprika
½ to ¾ tsp. sea salt

DIRECTIONS:

1. Heat the avocado oil in a large skillet over medium heat. Toss in the almonds, and combine gently until all the almonds are covered with the oil.
2. Add the garlic powder, paprika, and salt, gently tossing after each addition to make sure it is evenly distributed and all the almonds are covered. Adjust seasonings as needed. Continue to cook and tossing gently for about 5 minutes.
3. Turn off the heat and let cool and serve.

VARIATIONS TIP:

After you remove them from the stove top, toss the almonds with 1 to 2 tablespoons of nutritional yeast for a dairy-free "cheesy" flavor.

Nutrition Info per Serving:

Calories: 59; Total Fat: 5.41 g; Carbohydrates: 2.66 g; Protein: 0.84 g; Fiber: 1.1 g

Coconut Chocolate and Date Cookies

Prep Time: 30 minutes, Cook Time: 5 minutes, Serves: 12

INGREDIENTS:

FOR THE COOKIE BASE
1 cup dried shredded unsweetened coconut
2 pinches sea salt
1 cup raw almonds
1 packet stevia
2½ tbsps. coconut oil, melted

FOR THE COCONUT CARAMEL LAYER
½ cup dried shredded unsweetened coconut
2 tablespoons coconut oil, melted
8 Medjool dates
1 tablespoon water, plus additional as needed
Pinch sea salt

For the chocolate icing
4 tbsps. coconut oil, melted
4 tbsps. unsweetened Dutch-processed cocoa powder
1 packet stevia

DIRECTIONS:

TO MAKE THE COOKIE BASE
1. Use parchment paper to line a baking sheet.
2. Add the coconut into a food processor, blend for 60 seconds. Add the salt and almonds, blend until they are ground into a meal. Add the stevia and coconut oil, and blend until a dough forms.
3. Roll the dough between two sheets of wax paper to a ¼-inch thickness. Allow the dough to freeze for 10 minutes, or until firm.
4. Cut out 12 cookies with a round cookie cutter. Arrage each cookie base on the parchment-lined baking sheet.

TO MAKE THE COCONUT CARAMEL LAYER
5. Preheat the oven to 350°F(180°C).
6. Spread the coconut in an even layer on another baking sheet. Toast it in the preheated oven for 5 minutes, do not burn. Remove and cool.
7. Add the coconut oil, dates and water in a food processor. Blend to combine. Add the salt and more water, if needed. Continue to blend until the mixture resembles caramel. Add the toasted coconut and mix to combine.
8. Spread onto each cookie base. With an equal layer of the caramel-coconut mixture.

TO MAKE THE CHOCOLATE ICING
9. Mix together the coconut oil, cocoa powder and stevia in a small bowl.
10. Drizzle the icing over each of the 12 cookies with a spoon.
11. Place the cookies in the refrigerator to chill for 10 minutes to solidify the layers before eating.

VARIATIONS TIP:
Dutch-processing uses potassium carbonate to neutralize the high acidity of cocoa to a pH of 7. Look for Dutch-processed cocoa in your local market or under Resources.

Nutrition Info per Serving:
Calories: 180; Total Fat: 16.9 g; Carbohydrates: 7.4 g; Protein: 2.2 g; Fiber: 2.3 g

Blueberry Banana Sea Moss Pudding

Prep Time: 5 minutes, Cook Time: 0, Serves: 2

INGREDIENTS:

2 cups blueberries
2 burro bananas, peeled
6 tbsps. of sea moss gel
½ cup spring Water

DIRECTIONS:
1. Plug in a high-speed food processor or blender, add the blueberries, bananas and gel in its jar except for the water.
2. Use its lid to cover the blender jar, pulse until smooth, and slowly blend in the water until thickened to your desire level.
3. Serve immediately.

Nutrition Info per Serving:
Calories: 97.8; Fats: 0.5 g; Carb: 23.4 g; Protein: 0.7 g; Fiber: 2.8 g

Blueberry Coconut Spelt Pancakes

Prep Time: 10 minutes, Cook Time: 8 minutes, Serves: 2

INGREDIENTS:

1 cup spelt flour
2 tbsps. grapeseed oil
¼ cup agave syrup
⅛ tsp. sea moss
½ cup soft-jelly coconut milk
¼ cup spring water
¼ cup blueberries

DIRECTIONS:
1. Place the flour in a large bowl, add 1 tablespoon oil, agave syrup, and sea moss, stir until mixed.
2. Whisk in the milk and water until a smooth batter comes together, then fold in the berries.
3. Heat the remaining oil in a large skillet pan over medium heat. When hot, ladle in the batter, form into a pancake and then cook for 2 to 3 minutes per side until golden brown and cooked.
4. Serve immediately.

Nutrition Info per Serving:
Calories: 156; Fats: 3.6 g; Carb: 22.8 g; Protein: 8.4 g; Fiber: 3.3 g

Vanilla Orange Apple Pie

Prep Time: 10 minutes, Cook Time: 10 minutes, Serves: 4

INGREDIENTS:

4 golden delicious apples, peeled, cored, and sliced
1 vanilla bean, split lengthwise and seeds scraped out
¼ tsp. cinnamon
½ cup freshly squeezed orange juice
Unsweetened coconut milk, as needed (optional)

DIRECTIONS:

1. Combine the apples, vanilla bean seeds, cinnamon and orange juice in a large bowl, toss well.
2. Add the fruit mixture into a medium skillet, cook over medium heat for 10 minutes, or until the apples are soft and caramelized.
3. Evenly divide the mixture among four serving dishes, serve warm.
4. Place the coconut milk (if using) on the top.

VARIATIONS TIP:

You can use any kind of apples for this pie. Generally speaking, green apples keep their shape better than other kinds when cooked. But use your favorite here and enjoy.

Nutrition Info per Serving:
Calories: 109; Total Fat: 0.1 g; Carbohydrates: 28.5 g; Protein: 0.2 g; Fiber: 4.5 g

Zucchini Banana Bread Pancakes with Walnuts

Prep Time: 10 minutes, Cook Time: 8 minutes, Serves: 2

INGREDIENTS:

1 cup spelt flour
1 tbsp. date sugar
½ cup burro banana, mashed
1 cup walnut milk, homemade
½ cup grated zucchini
¼ cup chopped walnuts
1 tbsp. grapeseed oil

DIRECTIONS:

1. Place the flour in a medium bowl, add the date sugar, and stir until mixed.
2. Add the mashed burro banana and milk, whisk until smooth batter comes together, then fold in the zucchini and nuts until just mixed.
3. Heat the oil in a large skillet pan over medium-high heat, pour in the batter in portion and form each portion into a pancake.
4. Cook each pancake for 3 to 4 minutes per side and serve.

Nutrition Info per Serving:
Calories: 130; Fats: 4 g; Carb: 21 g; Protein: 3 g; Fiber: 3 g

Coconut and Date Energy Balls with Walnuts

Prep Time: 10 minutes, Cook Time: 0, Serves: 2

INGREDIENTS:

¼ cup walnuts
1 cup soft-jelly coconut, shredded
¼ cup blueberries
½ tsp. date sugar
¼ cup dried dates
½ tbsp. agave syrup

DIRECTIONS:

1. In a food processor, add the walnuts and pulse until the mixture resembles a fine powder.
2. Then add the coconut, berries, date sugar and dates, pulse until just mixed and then slowly blend in the agave syrup until the soft paste comes together.
3. Spoon the mixture into a medium bowl, place in the refrigerator to chill for at least 30 minutes and then roll the mixture into balls, 1 tablespoon of mixture per ball.
4. Roll the balls into some more coconut if desired and serve.

Nutrition Info per Serving:
Calories: 119; Fats: 8 g; Carb: 10 g; Protein: 2 g; Fiber: 1 g

Vegetarian Chickpea Mushroom Sausage Links

Prep Time: 10 minutes, Cook Time: 10 minutes, Serves: 2

INGREDIENTS:

2 cherry tomatoes
¼ cup chopped white onion
½ cup sliced mushrooms
¼ cup chickpea flour
1 cup cooked chickpeas

Extra:
1 tbsp. grapeseed oil
½ tsp. oregano
½ tsp. of sea salt
½ tsp. basil
½ tsp. cayenne powder
½ tsp. dill

DIRECTIONS:

1. In a food processor, add all of the ingredients except for the oil and chickpeas, and pulse until combined.

2. Add the chickpeas to the processor, blend again until well combined, and then spoon the mixture into a piping bag.
3. Heat the oil in a large skillet pan over medium-high heat, when hot, squeeze the chickpea mixture to make sausage links, and then cook for 3 to 4 minutes per side until nicely brown and cooked.
4. Serve immediately.

Nutrition Info per Serving:
Calories: 187.1; Fats: 7.4 g; Carb: 24.2 g; Protein: 7.3 g; Fiber: 6.3 g

Homemade Ravioli

Prep Time: 30 minutes, Cook Time: 1 hour, Serves: 5

INGREDIENTS:

FILLING:
2 cups of quartered mushrooms
1 quartered roma tomato
1 cup of diced green and red bell peppers
1 cup of chopped kale
⅓ cup of diced onions
2 tsps. of oregano
1 tbsp. of onion powder
1 tsp. of ginger
2 tsps. of dill
2 tsps. of basil
2 tsps. of thyme
1 tsp. of pure sea salt
½ tsp. of cayenne
1 cup of chickpea flour

CHEESE:
½ cup of soaked brazil nuts (overnight or for at least 3 hours)
½ tsp. of oregano
2 tsps. of onion powder
½ tsp. of cayenne powder
1 tsp. of pure sea salt
½ cup of spring water

DOUGH:
1 ½ cups of spelt flour
½ cup of chickpea flour
½ tsp. of oregano
½ tsp. of basil
1 tsp. of pure sea salt
3/4 cup of Spring Water

DIRECTIONS:
1. In a food processor, add all of the filling ingredients, except the Chickpea Flour, and blend for 30 to 40 seconds.
2. Then add Chickpea Flour to the mixture and blend until well combined.
3. Warm the grape seed oil in a skillet on high heat.
4. Reduce the heat to medium. Spread out the ravioli filling to the skillet and cook for 3 to 4 minutes on all sides.
5. Break up the filling and cook for another 3 minutes, then transfer it to a medium bowl.
6. In the food processor, add all of the cheese ingredients and blend until creamy. Add some spring water if it's too thick.
7. In a bowl, mix the filling with the cheese mixture.
8. In the food processor, place all of the dry ingredients for the dough and blend for 10 to 20 seconds. Add the spring water slowly while blending until dough can be shaped into a ball.
9. Spread the flour on the working space. Take ¼ of the dough and roll it out into a thin sheet.
10. Place rounded teaspoonfuls of filling and cheese 1 inch apart on one side of the dough. Fold the dough over and press together around the filling to seal. Use a pastry cutter or knife to cut it into individual ravioli.
11. Repeat steps 9 and 10 with the remaining dough and filling.
12. In a pot of, pour in the spring water and bring to a boil. Add a little pure sea salt and grape seed oil, then cook the ravioli for about 4 to 6 minutes.
13. Strain and serve immediately.

Nutrition Info per Serving:
Calories: 423; Fat: 12.67 g; Carbohydrates: 64.65 g; Protein: 18.5 g; Fiber:11.9 g

Zucchini Kale and Amaranth Patties

Prep Time: 10 minutes, Cook Time: 40 minutes, Serves: 2

INGREDIENTS:

1 tbsp. olive oil
½ of medium white onion, peeled, minced
1 medium zucchini, grated
1 ½ cups kale, chopped
½ cup amaranth, cooked
¼ cup chopped basil

Extra:
¼ cup chopped dill
2 tbsps. spelt flour
¼ tsp. cayenne pepper
½ tsp. salt
1 ½ tbsp. tahini
1 tbsp. key lime juice

DIRECTIONS:
1. Preheat the oven to 400°F(205°C).
2. While the oven preheats, heat the oil in a skillet pan over medium heat, when hot, add the onion and cook for 5 minutes until tender.
3. Stir in the zucchini, cook for 3 to 5 minutes until soft, then add the kale and cook for another 5 minutes until wilted.
4. Transfer the mixture into a bowl, and add all of the remaining ingredients, stir until mixed, then form the mixture into evenly sized patties.
5. On a baking sheet, arrange with patties, and bake for 15 minutes per side until golden brown and cooked.
6. After baking, serve immediately.

Nutrition Info per Serving:
Calories: 152; Fats: 3 g; Carb: 29 g; Protein: 7 g; Fiber: 6 g

Chickpea Flour Vegetable Quiche

Prep Time: 10 minutes, Cook Time: 15 minutes, Serves: 2

INGREDIENTS:

FOR THE BATTER
1 ½ tbsp. olive oil
1 ¼ cup chickpea flour
1 tsp. of sea salt
1 ½ cup spring water

FOR THE FILLING
½ cup chopped and cooked vegetables
½ tsp. dried oregano
½ tsp. dried basil

DIRECTIONS:
1. Preheat the oven to 500°F(260°C).
2. While the oven preheats, prepare the batter, combine all of the batter ingredients in a medium bowl, then whisk until smooth batter comes together.
3. Add the vegetables, oregano and basil into the batter and then stir until combined.
4. Grease the oil into six silicone muffin cups, evenly fill with the prepared batter and then bake for 10 to 15 minutes until firm and turn golden brown.
5. Serve immediately.

Nutrition Info per Serving:
Calories: 182; Fats: 6 g; Carb: 25.3 g; Protein: 8 g; Fiber: 7.2 g

Healthy Crackers with Sesame Seeds

Prep Time: 20 minutes, Cook Time: 30 minutes, Serves: 50 crackers

INGREDIENTS:

1 cup of spelt flour
½ cup of rye flour
2 tsps. of sesame seed
1 tsp. of agave syrup

1 tsp. of pure sea salt
¾ cup of spring water
2 tbsps. of grape seed oil

DIRECTIONS:
1. Preheat the oven to 350°F(180°C).
2. In a medium bowl, combine all of the ingredients except the oil and mix well.
3. Make a dough ball. Add more flour if it is too liquid.
4. Prepare a place for rolling out the dough and use a piece of parchment paper to cover.
5. Use the grape seed oil to lightly grease the paper and place the dough on it.
6. Use a rolling pin to roll out the dough, adding more flour to avoid sticking.
7. Cut the dough into squares with a shape cutter. If you don't have a shape cutter, you can use a pizza cutter.
8. Place the squares on a baking pan and use a fork or a skewer to poke holes in each square.
9. Use a little grape seed oil to brush the dough and sprinkle with more pure sea salt if needed.
10. Bake for 12 to 15 minutes or until the crackers are starting to become golden.
11. After baking, let cool before serving.

Nutrition Info per Serving:
Calories: 11; Total Fat: 0.25 g; Carbohydrates: 1.99 g; Protein: 0.39 g; Fiber: 0.31 g

Chapter 9: Smoothies

Fruit and Veggie Smoothie

Prep Time: 10 minutes, Cook Time: 0, Serves: 1

INGREDIENTS:
1 chopped pear
¼ avocado
½ chopped cucumber
1 handful of romaine
lettuce
date sugar (optional)
1 handful of watercress
½ cup of spring water

DIRECTIONS:
1. In the blender, combine all of the ingredients.
2. Blend for one minute until smooth.
3. Enjoy!

VARIATIONS TIP:
Peel and core Pears before using them.

Nutrition Info per Serving:
Calories: 263; Fat: 8.33 g; Carbohydrates: 48.23 g; Protein: 7.58 g; Fiber: 5.7 g

Pineapple Spinach Smoothie

Prep Time: 5 minutes, Cook Time: 0, Serves: 1

INGREDIENTS:
2 cups pineapple
1 cup spinach
2 tbsps. fresh mint leaves
1 cup unsweetened coconut water
Juice of ½ lime

DIRECTIONS:
1. Combine all of the ingredients in a blender.
2. Process until smooth.
3. Pour in a tall glass and serve immediately.

VARIATIONS TIP:
You can substitute key limes for a sweeter taste. These tiny limes are less tart than regular limes.

Nutrition Info per Serving:
Calories: 241; Total Fat: 1.5 g; Carbohydrates: 60.4 g; Protein: 2.6 g; Fiber: 5.3 g

Apple and Dandelion Green Smoothie

Prep Time: 5 minutes, Cook Time: 0, Serves: 2

INGREDIENTS:
1 apple, cored, deseeded
1 burro banana, peeled
1 cup dandelion greens
½ of cucumber, deseeded
½ tbsp. walnuts
Extra:
1 cup soft-jelly coconut milk
½ tsp. bromide plus powder

DIRECTIONS:
1. Plug in a high-speed food processor or blender, place all of the ingredients in its jar.
2. Use its lid to cover the blender jar and then pulse for 40 to 60 seconds until smooth.
3. After pulsing, pour the drink into two glasses and serve immediately.

Nutrition Info per Serving:
Calories: 317; Fats: 11 g; Carb: 42 g; Protein: 10 g; Fiber: 7 g

Cherry and Watermelon Smoothie

Prep Time: 5 minutes, Cook Time: 0, Serves: 1 or 2

INGREDIENTS:
10 pitted dark sweet cherries
2 cups cubed watermelon
1 tbsp. brown rice syrup
1 tbsp. freshly squeezed
lime juice
1 cup coconut milk (boxed)
5 to 7 ice cubes (optional)

DIRECTIONS:
1. Add all of the ingredients into a blender, blend them together until smooth.
2. Pour into 1 large or 2 small glasses and serve immediately.

VARIATIONS TIP:
If you prefer your smoothie a little sweeter, substitute the brown rice syrup with half a banana.

Nutrition Info per Serving:
Calories: 212; Fat: 1.12 g; Carbohydrates: 51.35 g; Protein: 4.55 g; Fiber: 5.7 g

Kale, Avocado and Banana Smoothie

Prep Time: 5 minutes, Cook Time: 0, Serves: 1 or 2

INGREDIENTS:

2 kale stalks, stemmed
½ avocado, roughly chopped
1½ cups almond milk
1 tbsp. hemp seeds
½ banana, roughly chopped

DIRECTIONS:

1. Combine all of the ingredients in a blender, blend them together until creamy and smooth.
2. Pour into 1 large or 2 small glasses and serve immediately.

VARIATIONS TIP:

Substitute the almond milk with coconut milk for a nut-free version.

Nutrition Info per Serving:
Calories: 230; Fat: 12.13 g; Carbohydrates: 30.19 g; Protein: 4.06 g; Fiber: 5.8 g

Pineapple Banana and Kale Smoothie

Prep Time: 5 minutes, Cook Time: 0, Serves: 1

INGREDIENTS:

1 cup fresh pineapple juice
1 medium banana, extra ripe
½ cup kale
½ cup ice cubes
1 packet stevia (optional)

DIRECTIONS:

1. Add all of the ingredients into a blender.
2. Process until smooth.
3. Pour in a tall glass and serve.

VARIATIONS TIP:

Stevia is an all-natural sweetener that comes from the leaf of the stevia plant. Make sure the kind you choose isn't mixed with lactose, which is a dairy product.

Nutrition Info per Serving:
Calories: 254; Total Fat: 0.03 g; Carbohydrates: 62.5 g; Protein: 3.1 g; Fiber: 4.5 g

Ginger Kale and Lemon Green Smoothie

Prep Time: 5 minutes, Cook Time: 0, Serves: 1 or 2

INGREDIENTS:

2 stalks kale, stemmed and roughly chopped
1½ cups coconut milk (boxed)
1 apple, cored and roughly chopped
2 stalks romaine lettuce, roughly chopped
½ celery stalk, roughly chopped
¼ - ½-inch piece of ginger root, peeled and chopped
1 tbsp. freshly squeezed lemon juice
5 to 7 ice cubes (optional)

DIRECTIONS:

1. Add all of the ingredients into a high-speed blender, blend them together until smooth.
2. Pour into 1 large or 2 small glasses and serve immediately.

VARIATIONS TIP:

To get the maximum benefits of lemon, use freshly squeezed as bottled lemon juice is typically pasteurized.

Nutrition Info per Serving:
Calories: 397; Fat: 5.14 g; Carbohydrates: 83.84 g; Protein: 19.95 g; Fiber: 36 g

Spinach Cucumber Liquid Guacamole

Prep Time: 10 minutes, Cook Time: 0, Serves: 1

INGREDIENTS:

1 cup spinach
½ avocado
1 cup fresh tomato juice
¼ cup cilantro
Pinch garlic powder
Pinch cayenne pepper
Pinch sea salt
½ cup diced cucumber
½ cup cherry tomatoes

DIRECTIONS:

1. Combine the spinach, avocado, tomato juice, cilantro, garlic powder, cayenne and salt in a blender.
2. Blend until smooth.
3. Add the cucumber and cherry tomatoes, and blend until small chunks remain.
4. Pour in a tall glass and serve.

VARIATIONS TIP:

If you're on the Thyroid-Support Plan, don't use this recipe. In fact, avoid any recipes in the book that contain tomatoes or tomato products.

Nutrition Info per Serving:
Calories: 274; Total Fat: 20.1 g; Carbohydrates: 24.8 g; Protein: 5.6 g; Fiber: 9.5 g

Blackberry, Banana and Avocado Smoothie

Prep Time: 5 minutes, Cook Time: 0, Serves: 1 or 2

INGREDIENTS:
- 1 cup blackberries
- 1½ cups coconut milk
- ½ banana, roughly chopped
- ½ avocado, roughly chopped

DIRECTIONS:
1. Add the blackberries, coconut milk, banana and avocado into a blender, blend them together until creamy and smooth.
2. Pour into 1 large or 2 small glasses and serve immediately.

VARIATIONS TIP:
You can substitute the blackberries with another alkaline fruit like blueberries, strawberries, or raspberries.

Nutrition Info per Serving:
Calories: 344; Fat: 16.35 g; Carbohydrates: 49.24 g; Protein: 7.25 g; Fiber: 19.9 g

Lettuce, Kale and Peach Protein Smoothie

Prep Time: 5 minutes, Cook Time: 0, Serves: 1 or 2

INGREDIENTS:
- 1 peach, roughly chopped
- ½ to 1 banana, roughly chopped
- 2 romaine lettuce leaves
- 1 kale stalk, stemmed
- 1½ cups coconut milk (boxed)
- 5 tbsps. pumpkin protein powder
- 5 to 7 ice cubes (optional)

DIRECTIONS:
1. Combine all of the ingredients in a blender, blend them together until smooth.
2. Pour into 1 large or 2 small glasses and serve immediately.

VARIATIONS TIP:
If you can't find 100 percent pumpkin protein powder, it's okay to omit it.

Nutrition Info per Serving:
Calories: 284; Fat: 4.98 g; Carbohydrates: 62.22 g; Protein: 7.03 g; Fiber: 12.6 g

Date Almond Raspberry Smoothie

Prep Time: 10 minutes, Cook Time: 0, Serves: 2

INGREDIENTS:
- 1¼ cups unsweetened almond milk
- ½ cup raspberries
- 2 small dates, pitted
- 1 medium banana (frozen is best), sliced
- 2 tbsps. sliced almonds
- 2 tbsps. unsweetened carob powder

DIRECTIONS:
1. Combine the almond milk, raspberries, dates, banana, almonds and carob powder in a high-speed blender, and blend until smooth and creamy.
2. Pour into two glasses and serve.

VARIATIONS TIP:
If you're really craving that chocolate flavor, swap out the carob for unsweetened cocoa powder.

Nutrition Info per Serving:
Calories: 208; Fat: 10 g; Carbohydrates: 32 g; Protein: 6 g; Fiber: 8 g; Sodium: 53 mg; Iron: 1 mg

Nutty Coconut Sea Moss Smoothie

Prep Time: 10 minutes, Cook Time: 0, Serves: 2

INGREDIENTS:
- 33 g sea moss, rinsed
- 1 tbsp. coconut nectar
- 1 cup walnut milk, unsweetened
- 2 cups spring water, warmed

Extra:
- ¼ cup dates

DIRECTIONS:
1. In a medium bowl, add the rinsed sea moss, fill in the water and allow it to soak for at least 4 hours until it thickened slightly.
2. Drain the soaked sea moss well and place into a food processor, pulse until the smooth paste comes together, and then place in the refrigerator to chill until required.
3. When ready to drink, place 8 tablespoons of sea moss paste in a food processor, then add the coconut nectar, milk, water and dates, pulse until smooth.
4. Evenly divide the drink between two glasses and serve immediately.

Nutrition Info per Serving:
Calories: 100.5; Fats: 0.1 g; Carb: 22.5 g; Protein: 1.7 g; Fiber: 3.5 g

Ginger Pear Green Sparkling Smoothie

Prep Time: 5 minutes, Cook Time: 0, Serves: 1

INGREDIENTS:
1 Asian pear, peeled and sliced
½ cup Chinese cabbage
1 cup unsweetened, lime-flavored sparkling water
1 packet stevia
1 tsp. grated fresh ginger
½ cup ice cubes

DIRECTIONS:
1. Combine all of the ingredients in the blender.
2. Cover the blender and process carefully until blended.
3. Pour in a tall glass and serve.

VARIATIONS TIP:
If you can't find lime-flavored sparkling water, use plain and add a squeeze or two of fresh lime juice.

Nutrition Info per Serving:
Calories: 85; Total Fat: 0.2 g; Carbohydrates: 22.3 g; Protein: 1 g; Fiber: 4.6 g

Homemade Chocolate Cherry Smoothie

Prep Time: 5 minutes, Cook Time: 0, Serves: 1

INGREDIENTS:
1 tsp. Dutch-processed cocoa powder
½ cup frozen dark cherries
¾ cup filtered water
1 packet stevia (optional)

DIRECTIONS:
1. Combine the cocoa powder, cherries, water and stevia (if using) in a blender.
2. Blend until smooth.
3. Pour in a tall glass and serve.

VARIATIONS TIP:
Several popular chocolate brands make a Dutch-processed cocoa, so look for it in your local market, or check the Resources section to buy it online.

Nutrition Info per Serving:
Calories: 60; Total Fat: 0.6 g; Carbohydrates: 13.2 g; Protein: 0.5 g; Fiber: 1.8 g

Avocado Blueberry Green Smoothie

Prep Time: 5 minutes, Cook Time: 0, Serves: 1 or 2

INGREDIENTS:
1 avocado, roughly chopped
1 cucumber, peeled and roughly chopped
1½ cups coconut milk (boxed)
1 cup fresh or frozen blueberries
½ to 1 banana, roughly chopped
5 to 7 ice cubes (optional)

DIRECTIONS:
1. Combine the avocado, cucumber, coconut milk, blueberries, banana and ice (if using) into a blender, blend them together until creamy and smooth.
2. Pour into 1 large or 2 small glasses and serve immediately.

VARIATIONS TIP:
Increase the greens in this smoothie by adding 1 stemmed kale leaf.

Nutrition Info per Serving:
Calories: 546; Fats: 31.69 g; Carb: 67.18 g; Protein: 9.09 g; Fiber: 24.6 g

Mango Kiwi and Cashew Smoothie

Prep Time: 5 minutes, Cook Time: 0, Serves: 1 or 2

INGREDIENTS:
½ cup chopped mango
1 kiwi, peeled and chopped
1½ cups coconut milk (boxed)
¼ cup raw cashews
5 to 7 ice cubes (optional)

DIRECTIONS:
1. Add the mango, kiwi, coconut milk, cashews and ice (if using) into a high-speed blender, blend them together until smooth.
2. Pour into 1 large or 2 small glasses and serve immediately.

VARIATIONS TIP:
For a fun summertime treat, use the mixture to make frozen ice pop treats in your favorite ice pop molds—just omit the ice cubes!

Nutrition Info per Serving:
Calories: 485; Fat: 21.51 g; Carbohydrates: 27.86 g; Protein: 44.77 g; Fiber: 5.5 g

Tropical Piña Smoothie

Prep Time: 5 minutes, Cook Time: 0, Serves: 1

INGREDIENTS:
2½ cups fresh pineapple chunks (or canned unsweetened)
½ cup unsweetened coconut milk
1 cup ice cubes

DIRECTIONS:
1. Combine the pineapple chunks, coconut milk and ice in a blender.
2. Process until smooth.
3. Pour in a tall glass and serve.

Nutrition Info per Serving:
Calories: 175; Total Fat: 3.2 g; Carbohydrates: 38.9 g; Protein: 1.7 g; Fiber: 3.8 g

Vanilla Coconut Ice Cream Sundae with Fruit

Prep Time: 15 minutes, Cook Time: 0, Serves: 4

INGREDIENTS:
1 vanilla bean, split lengthwise and seeds scraped out
1/2 cup coconut sugar
2 (13-ounce, 369 g) cans full-fat unsweetened coconut milk
⅛ tsp. sea salt
Toppings of choice (bananas, shredded unsweetened coconut, chopped almonds, strawberries)

DIRECTIONS:
1. Add the vanilla bean seeds, coconut sugar, coconut milk and salt in a blender, blend them together. Transfer the mixture to a freezer-safe bowl. Freeze overnight.
2. Put two scoops of the ice cream in a small bowl. Garnish with your favorite alkaline-friendly toppings. Serve immediately.

VARIATIONS TIP:
This recipe calls for a lot of sugar. If you prefer your dessert to be less sweet, you can adjust the amount. And, instead of freezing overnight, you can make this in your ice cream maker and process according to your machine's instructions.

Nutrition Info per Serving:
Calories: 306; Total Fat: 22.7 g; Carbohydrates: 30.8 g; Protein: 2.2 g; Fiber: 2.6 g

Avocado Cucumber Smoothie

Prep Time: 5 minutes, Cook Time: 0, Serves: 1

INGREDIENTS:
½ avocado
1 cup peeled and diced cucumber
½ cup ice cubes
½ cup cold water
Pinch sea salt
Pinch garlic powder

DIRECTIONS:
1. Combine all of the ingredients in a blender.
2. Process until desired consistency.
3. Pour in a tall glass and serve immediately.

VARIATIONS TIP:
Add a dash of cayenne pepper for a touch of heat.

Nutrition Info per Serving:
Calories: 221; Total Fat: 19.7 g; Carbohydrates: 12.4 g; Protein: 2.6 g; Fiber: 7.2 g

Homemade Gazpacho Smoothie

Prep Time: 15 minutes, Cook Time: 0, Serves: 1

INGREDIENTS:
½ celery stalk, chopped
¼ onion, chopped
1 medium tomato, chopped
½ carrot, peeled and chopped
2 cups spinach
½ cucumber, peeled and chopped
¼ cup fresh cilantro, stemmed
½ red bell pepper, seeded and chopped
¼ tsp. garlic powder
¼ tsp. cumin
Pinch sea salt
Fresh tomato juice, as needed

DIRECTIONS:
1. Combine all of the ingredients except the tomato juice in a blender.
2. Pulse until the desired consistency.
3. Slowly add the tomato juice if the mixture is too thick, until you have the desired consistency.
4. Pour in a tall glass and serve.

VARIATIONS TIP:
Because this is a cold smoothie, you can use frozen red bell peppers.

Nutrition Info per Serving:
Calories: 102; Total Fat: 0.8 g; Carbohydrates: 21.7 g; Protein: 4.9 g; Fiber: 6.3 g

Mixed Berry Banana Smoothie

Prep Time: 5 minutes, Cook Time: 0, Serves: 2

INGREDIENTS:
- 2 Burro Bananas
- 2 handfuls of Strawberries
- 2 handfuls of Blueberries
- 2 cups of Homemade Walnut Milk
- 1 cup of Water

DIRECTIONS:
1. In the blender, add all of the ingredients.
2. Blend until it becomes smooth and frothy.
3. Serve immediately!

VARIATIONS TIP:
If you don't have fresh berries or bananas, you can use frozen ones.

Nutrition Info per Serving:
Calories: 232; Fat: 5.26 g; Carbohydrates: 39.78 g; Protein: 9.43 g; Fiber: 3.3 g

Apple, Avocado and Pear Smoothie

Prep Time: 10 minutes, Cook Time: 0, Serves: 2

INGREDIENTS:
- 1 cup of chopped red apples
- 1 cup of cubed pears
- 2 medjool dates
- ⅓ of a medium avocado
- 1 cup of homemade walnut milk
- 1 tbsp. of hemp seeds
- 2 tbsps. of date syrup
- 1 handful of greens (optional)
- ½ cup of water
- 1 cup of ice

DIRECTIONS:
1. In a blender, combine all of the ingredients except the ice.
2. Blend until smooth.
3. Add the ice and blend once more.
4. Enjoy immediately.

Nutrition Info per Serving:
Calories: 469; Fats: 19.78 g; Carb: 72.61 g; Protein: 8.39 g; Fiber: 13.4 g

Spinach, Blueberry and Mango Smoothie

Prep Time: 15 minutes, Cook Time: 0, Serves: 2

INGREDIENTS:
- 1 small (6-inch) banana (best if frozen), chopped
- 1½ cups unsweetened almond milk
- ½ cup frozen wild blueberries
- ½ cup frozen mango chunks
- 1 cup loosely packed raw spinach
- 2 small dates, pitted
- 1 tbsp. almond meal or almond butter

DIRECTIONS:
1. Combine all of the ingredients in a high-speed blender.
2. Blend until smooth and creamy.
3. Pour into two glasses and serve immediately.

VARIATIONS TIP:
If you have fresh blueberries or mango, they're perfectly fine to use instead, as long as you have a frozen banana or a couple of ice cubes to make the smoothie thick, cool, and refreshing.

Nutrition Info per Serving:
Calories: 235; Fat: 12 g; Carbohydrates: 35 g; Protein: 6 g; Fiber: 5 g; Sodium: 73 mg; Iron: 2 mg

Vegan Dandelion Detox Smoothie

Prep Time: 10 minutes, Cook Time: 0, Serves: 2

INGREDIENTS:
- 1 large bunch of dandelion greens
- 3 chopped baby bananas
- ½ cup of blueberries
- 1 small bunch of watercress
- 6 medium dates
- 1 thumb of chopped ginger (optional)
- 1 tbsp. of burdock root powder
- 2 cups of coconut water
- ¼ cup of lime juice

DIRECTIONS:
1. In the blender, add all of the ingredients.
2. Blend for two minutes until smooth.
3. Enjoy!

VARIATIONS TIP:
If you don't have fresh berries, you can use frozen ones. If you don't have Coconut Water, you can substitute Spring Water.
Use this smoothie within three days. Store in a glass jar in the refrigerator.

Nutrition Info per Serving:
Calories: 397; Total Fat: 1.7 g; Carbohydrates: 98.24 g; Protein: 6.71 g; Fiber: 13.7 g

Nutty Strawberry Shake, page 130

Berry Peach Sea Moss Smoothie, page 126

Blackberry, Banana and Avocado Smoothie, page 120

Healthy Orange Banana Smoothie, page 125

Chapter 9: Smoothies

Peach, Orange and Kale Smoothie

Prep Time: 10 minutes, Cook Time: 0, Serves: 1

INGREDIENTS:

1 medium peach, peeled and sliced
1 orange, peeled and seeded
1 cup chopped kale
8 ounces (227 g) filtered water

DIRECTIONS:
1. Combine the peach, orange, kale and water in a blender.
2. Process until smooth.
3. Pour in a tall glass and serve immediately.

VARIATIONS TIP:

If you can't find a fresh peach, frozen will do. If the only peaches available are canned, drain and rinse before using.

Nutrition Info per Serving:
Calories: 158; Total Fat: 0.05 g; Carbohydrates: 38 g; Protein: 4.6 g; Fiber: 6.9 g

Papaya, Mango and Raspberry Smoothie

Prep Time: 5 minutes, Cook Time: 0, Serves: 1

INGREDIENTS:

½ medium papaya, seeds removed and chopped
¾ cup frozen mango pieces
¼ cup raspberries

DIRECTIONS:
1. Combine the papaya, mango and raspberries in a blender.
2. Blend until smooth.
3. Pour in a tall glass and serve immediately.

VARIATIONS TIP:

You can find frozen mango alongside other frozen fruits in your local market. Add water, as needed, if the smoothie is too thick after it is blended.

Nutrition Info per Serving:
Calories: 153; Total Fat: 0.06 g; Carbohydrates: 39.7 g; Protein: 2.1 g; Fiber: 6.7 g

Banana, Raspberry and Lime Smoothie

Prep Time: 5 minutes, Cook Time: 0, Serves: 1 or 2

INGREDIENTS:

½ banana
1 cup raspberries
1½ cups coconut milk (boxed)
1 tsp. freshly squeezed lime juice
5 to 7 ice cubes (optional)
Fresh mint leaves, for garnish (optional)

DIRECTIONS:
1. Add the banana, raspberries, coconut milk, lime juice and ice (if using) into a blender, blend them together until well combined and smooth.
2. Pour into 1 or 2 glasses, garnish with the mint leaves (if using) and serve.

VARIATIONS TIP:

Increase the nutritional profile of this smoothie by adding 2 scoops of pumpkin protein powder.

Nutrition Info per Serving:
Calories: 355; Fat: 1.23 g; Carbohydrates: 87.05 g; Protein: 5.38 g; Fiber: 14 g

Healthy Orange Banana Smoothie

Prep Time: 10 minutes, Cook Time: 0, Serves: 1

INGREDIENTS:

1 medium frozen banana, cut into chunks
6 ounces (170 g) freshly squeezed orange juice
1 vanilla bean, split lengthwise and seeds scraped out
1 ounce (28 g) unsweetened coconut milk
1 packet stevia (optional)

DIRECTIONS:
1. Combine the banana, orange juice, vanilla bean seeds, coconut milk, and stevia (if using) in a blender.
2. Blend until smooth.
3. Pour in a tall glass and serve immediately.

VARIATIONS TIP:

If freshly squeezed orange juice isn't available, you can use the kind in a carton. Just make sure it's organic and doesn't have any added sugar. Avoid the kind that comes from concentrate that is rehydrated.

Nutrition Info per Serving:
Calories: 182; Total Fat: 0.3 g; Carbohydrates: 44 g; Protein: 2.3 g; Fiber: 3.8 g

Kale Detox Smoothie

Prep Time: 10 minutes, Cook Time: 0, Serves: 2

INGREDIENTS:
1 cup of chopped cucumbers
1 cubed apple
2 handfuls of kale
¼ cup of lime juice
1 tbsp. of sea moss gel
1 thumb of chopped ginger (optional)
2 cups of coconut water

DIRECTIONS:
1. In the blender, combine all of the ingredients.
2. Blender it until it becomes smooth and frothy.
3. Serve.

VARIATIONS TIP:
Peel and core Apples before using them.
If you don't have Coconut Water, you can substitute Spring Water.
Use this smoothie within three days. Store in a glass jar in the refrigerator.

Nutrition Info per Serving:
Calories: 117; Fat: 0.91 g; Carbohydrates: 26.98 g; Protein: 3.17 g; Fiber: 6 g

Berry Peach Sea Moss Smoothie

Prep Time: 10 minutes, Cook Time: 0, Serves: 1

INGREDIENTS:
½ cup of strawberries
½ cup of blueberries
½ cup of cherries
½ cup of quartered peaches
1 tbsp. of sea moss gel
1 tbsp. of agave syrup
1 cup of coconut milk
1 tbsp. of hemp seeds

DIRECTIONS:
1. In the blender, add all of the ingredients.
2. Mix until it becomes smooth and frothy.
3. Enjoy!

VARIATIONS TIP:
If you don't have fresh berries, you can use frozen ones.
If you don't have Coconut Milk, you can substitute Spring Water.
Add extra ¼ cup of Coconut Milk or Spring Water if the smoothie is too thick.

Nutrition Info per Serving:
Calories: 308; Fat: 5.91 g; Carbohydrates: 63.06 g; Protein: 5.65 g; Fiber: 8.2 g

Hemp Seed and Banana Chard Smoothie

Prep Time: 5 minutes, Cook Time: 0, Serves: 1 or 2

INGREDIENTS:
½ to 1 banana, roughly chopped
½ cup chopped rainbow or red chard
1½ cups coconut milk
(boxed)
2 tbsps. hemp seeds
2 tbsps. almond butter
5 to 7 ice cubes (optional)

DIRECTIONS:
1. Combine the banana, chard, coconut milk, hemp seeds, almond butter and ice (if using) into a blender, blend them together until creamy and smooth.
2. Pour into 1 large or 2 small glasses and serve immediately.

VARIATIONS TIP:
Substitute the chard with kale.

Nutrition Info per Serving:
Calories: 212; Total Fat: 13.86 g; Carbohydrates: 18.51 g; Protein: 6.95 g; Fiber: 5.3 g

Kiwi, Blueberry and Hemp Seed Smoothie

Prep Time: 5 minutes, Cook Time: 0, Serves: 1 or 2

INGREDIENTS:
1 kiwi, peeled and chopped
1 cup fresh or frozen blueberries
1½ cups almond milk
2 tbsps. hemp seeds
5 to 7 ice cubes (optional)

DIRECTIONS:
1. Add the kiwi, blueberries, almond milk. hemp seeds and ice (if using) into a blender, blend them together until smooth.
2. Pour into 1 large or 2 small glasses and serve immediately.

VARIATIONS TIP:
Make this a nut-free recipe by substituting the almond milk with coconut milk.

Nutrition Info per Serving:
Calories: 371; Fat: 14.5 g; Carbohydrates: 59.13 g; Protein: 6.56 g; Fiber: 7.1 g

Sunshine Fruit Smoothie

Prep Time: 10 minutes, Cook Time: 0, Serves: 2

INGREDIENTS:
1 cup of raspberries
1 chopped seville orange
1 cup of diced mango
½ chopped burro banana or 1 baby banana
1 cup of water

DIRECTIONS:
1. In the blender, add all of the ingredients.
2. Blend until it becomes smooth.
3. Enjoy!

Nutrition Info per Serving:
Calories: 239; Total Fat: 1.83 g; Carbohydrates: 70.43 g; Protein: 4.75 g; Fiber: 15.2 g

Spinach Peach Green Smoothie

Prep Time: 5 minutes, Cook Time: 0, Serves: 1

INGREDIENTS:
1 cup frozen sliced peaches
1 cup spinach
1 cup unsweetened coconut milk

DIRECTIONS:
1. Combine the peaches, spinach and coconut milk in a blender.
2. Blend until smooth.
3. Pour in a tall glass and serve.

Nutrition Info per Serving:
Calories: 230; Total Fat: 6 g; Carbohydrates: 43.5 g; Protein: 4.9 g; Fiber: 5.8 g

Recovery Strawberry and Watermelon Smoothie

Prep Time: 5 minutes, Cook Time: 0, Serves: 1

INGREDIENTS:
1 cup of strawberries
1 cup of watermelon chunks
1 tbsp. of date syrup
1 cup of coconut water

DIRECTIONS:
1. In the blender, add all of the ingredients.
2. Blend until smooth.
3. Enjoy immediately!

Nutrition Info per Serving:
Calories: 200; Total Fat: 1.19 g; Carbohydrates: 48.48 g; Protein: 3.63 g; Fiber: 6.1 g

Nutty Mixed Berry Smoothie

Prep Time: 5 minutes, Cook Time: 0, Serves: 2

INGREDIENTS:
¼ cup strawberries
¼ cup blackberries
¼ cup blueberries
¼ cup raspberries
2 tbsps. walnuts

Extra:
1 tbsp. of bromide plus powder
⅔ cup spring water

DIRECTIONS:
1. Plug in a high-speed food processor or blender, and combine the berries, walnuts, bromide and water in its jar.
2. Use its lid to cover the blender jar and then pulse for 40 to 60 seconds until smooth.
3. After pulsing, evenly pour the drink into two glasses and serve immediately.

Nutrition Info per Serving:
Calories: 180; Fats: 8 g; Carb: 25 g; Protein: 4 g; Fiber: 5 g

Triple Berry Protein Coconut Smoothie

Prep Time: 5 minutes, Cook Time: 0, Serves: 1 or 2

INGREDIENTS:
⅓ cup blueberries
⅓ cup raspberries
⅓ cup blackberries
1½ cups coconut milk
(boxed)
3 tbsps. 100% pumpkin protein powder

DIRECTIONS:
1. Combine all of the ingredients in a blender, blend them together until well combined and smooth.
2. Pour into 1 or 2 glasses and serve immediately.

VARIATIONS TIP:
If you'd like a sweeter smoothie, just add ½ banana.

Nutrition Info per Serving:
Calories: 355; Total Fat: 3.34 g; Carbohydrates: 82.89 g; Protein: 5.92 g; Fiber: 13.5 g

Sweet Peach Smoothie

Prep Time: 10 minutes, Cook Time: 0, Serves: 1

INGREDIENTS:
- 2 quartered peaches
- ½ cup of red currants
- 1 cup of coconut milk
- 1 tbsp. of agave syrup
- 1 tsp. of bromide plus powder
- ½ cup of ice

DIRECTIONS:
1. In a blender, add all of the ingredients except the ice.
2. Blend until smooth.
3. Add the ice and blend again.
4. Enjoy!

Nutrition Info per Serving:
Calories: 237; Total Fat: 1.4 g; Carbohydrates: 55.79 g; Protein: 5.25 g; Fiber: 9.6 g

Breakfast Quinoa Melon Smoothie

Prep Time: 10 minutes, Cook Time: 0, Serves: 1

INGREDIENTS:
- ½ cup of cooked quinoa or amaranth
- 1 cup of cubed melon or papaya
- 1 cup of homemade walnut milk
- 1 tsp. of bromide plus powder
- 1 tbsp. of date sugar or 1 date

DIRECTIONS:
1. In the blender, add all of the ingredients.
2. Blend until it becomes smooth and frothy.
3. Enjoy immediately!

Nutrition Info per Serving:
Calories: 339; Fat: 7.11 g; Carbohydrates: 57.13 g; Protein: 14.21 g; Fiber: 4.2 g

Banana Mango Smoothie

Prep Time: 5 minutes, Cook Time: 0, Serves: 2

INGREDIENTS:
- 2 fresh chopped Mangos
- 3 frozen quartered Burro Bananas

DIRECTIONS:
1. In the blender, add all of the ingredients.
2. Blend for one minute until smooth.
3. Serve immediately!

VARIATIONS TIP:
If you don't have frozen Mango, you can add extra fresh Mango.

Nutrition Info per Serving:
Calories: 257; Fat: 1.21 g; Carbohydrates: 65.14 g; Protein: 3.28 g; Fiber: 7.2 g

Apple and Berries Smoothie

Prep Time: 5 minutes, Cook Time: 0, Serves: 2

INGREDIENTS:
- 1 cup mixed berries
- 1 apple, cored, diced
- 2 cups greens
- 1 cup hemp milk, homemade

DIRECTIONS:
1. Plug in a high-speed food processor or blender, combine the berries, apple, greens and milk in its jar.
2. Use its lid to cover the blender jar and then pulse for 40 to 60 seconds until smooth.
3. Pour the drink into two glasses and serve immediately.

Nutrition Info per Serving:
Calories: 136.5; Fats: 2.9 g; Carb: 23.4 g; Protein 7.1 g; Fiber: 8.1 g

Apple Pie Sea Moss Smoothie

Prep Time: 5 minutes, Cook Time: 0, Serves: 2

INGREDIENTS:
- 2 cups of fresh apple juice
- 1 tbsp. of sea moss gel
- 1 tbsp. of ginger (optional)
- 1 pinch of clove powder
- 2 cups of ice

DIRECTIONS:
1. In the blender, combine all of the ingredients except the ice.
2. Blend for one minute until smooth.
3. Add the ice and blend it one more time.
4. Enjoy immediately.

Nutrition Info per Serving:
Calories: 119; Fats: 0.35 g; Carb: 29.05 g; Protein: 0.42 g; Fiber: 0.6 g

Nutty Vanilla Banana Smoothie

Prep Time: 10 minutes, Cook Time: 0, Serves: 1

INGREDIENTS:
1 cup filtered water
¼ cup raw almonds
1 medium banana, peeled
¼ tsp. nutmeg
1 whole vanilla bean, split lengthwise and seeds scraped out
½ tsp. cinnamon
½ cup ice cubes

DIRECTIONS:
1. Add all of the ingredients in a blender.
2. Blend until smooth.
3. Pour in a tall glass and serve.

Nutrition Info per Serving:
Calories: 254; Total Fat: 12.1 g; Carbohydrates: 33.4 g; Protein: 6.3 g; Fiber: 7.2 g

Irish Walnuts Moss Milkshake

Prep Time: 5 minutes, Cook Time: 0, Serves: 2

INGREDIENTS:
1 mason jar sea moss gel
½ cup walnuts
1 burro banana, peeled
½ cup hemp milk, homemade
2 tbsps. date sugar

DIRECTIONS:
1. Take out a jar of prepared sea moss gel.
2. Plug in a high-speed food processor or blender and add all the walnuts, banana, milk and sugar in the jar.
3. Use its lid to cover the blender jar and then pulse for 40 to 60 seconds until smooth.
4. Pour the drink into two glasses and then serve.

Nutrition Info per Serving:
Calories: 241; Fats: 14.55 g; Carb: 25.9 g; Protein 6.74 g; Fiber: 3.5 g

Zucchini, Avocado and Dandelion Green Smoothie

Prep Time: 5 minutes, Cook Time: 0, Serves: 2

INGREDIENTS:
1 cup dandelion greens
3 tbsps. hemp seeds
⅓ cup diced zucchini
¼ of a large avocado, peeled, pitted
1 ¼ cup walnut milk, homemade

DIRECTIONS:
1. Plug in a high-speed food processor or blender, and place the dandelion greens, hemp seeds, zucchini, avocado and milk in its jar.
2. Use its lid to cover the blender jar and then pulse for 40 to 60 seconds until smooth.
3. After pulsing, evenly divide the drink between two glasses and serve immediately.

Nutrition Info per Serving:
Calories: 165; Fats: 6.8 g; Carb: 17.3 g; Protein: 8.5 g; Fiber: 5.5 g

Nutty Strawberry Shake

Prep Time: 5 minutes, Cook Time: 10 minutes, Serves: 2

INGREDIENTS:

½ cup Brazil nuts, soaked
1 cup strawberries
⅓ cup Irish moss gel
1 tbsp. agave syrup
1 ½ cups spring water

DIRECTIONS:

1. Plug in a high-speed food processor or blender, and then add the nuts, strawberries, gel, syrup and water in its jar.
2. Use its lid to cover the blender jar and then pulse for 40 to 60 seconds until smooth.
3. After pulsing, pour the drink into two glasses and serve immediately.

Nutrition Info per Serving:
Calories: 137; Fats: 5 g; Carb: 22 g; Protein: 1 g; Fiber: 2 g

Apple Banana Sea Moss Delight

Prep Time: 5 minutes, Cook Time: 0, Serves: 2

INGREDIENTS:

1 mason jar sea moss gel
1 Apple, chopped
½ banana, peeled
½ cup walnut milk, homemade

DIRECTIONS:

1. Take out a jar of prepared sea moss gel.
2. Plug in a high-speed food processor or blender, then place all of the ingredients in the jar.
3. Use its lid to cover the blender jar and then pulse for 40 to 60 seconds until smooth.
4. Pour the drink into two glasses and serve immediately.

Nutrition Info per Serving:
Calories: 209; Fats: 2.92 g; Carb: 44.55 g; Protein 5.17 g; Fiber: 5.9 g

Warm Garlic Ginger and Lemon Smoothie

Prep Time: 10 minutes, Cook Time: 0, Serves: 1

INGREDIENTS:

½ tsp. sesame oil
¼ tsp. grated fresh ginger
Juice of 1 lemon
1 garlic clove, peeled
1 cup warm water
¼ tsp. sea salt

DIRECTIONS:

1. Combine all of the ingredients in a blender.
2. Pulse until the desired consistency.
3. Pour in a tall glass and serve immediately.

VARIATIONS TIP:
Keep a container of reconstituted lemon juice in your refrigerator. It's perfect for times when you don't have fresh lemons on hand.

Nutrition Info per Serving:
Calories: 36; Total Fat: 2.43 g; Carbohydrates: 4.39 g; Protein: 0.37 g; Fiber: 0.2 g

Chapter 10: Fruit

Apple Slices with Peanut Butter and Granola

Prep Time: 5 minutes, Cook Time: 0, Serves: 4

INGREDIENTS:
2 medium apples, cored and sliced
¼ cup peanut butter
½ cup maple oat flax granola

DIRECTIONS:
1. On each apple slice, spread with a bit of peanut butter evenly.
2. Dip the peanut butter–coated side of each slice into the granola and then serve.

VARIATIONS TIP:
If you don't have granola on hand, you can make a muesli mixture to use in its place by combining 2 tablespoons gluten-free rolled oats, 1 tablespoon raisins, and 1 tablespoon sliced almonds.

Nutrition Info per Serving:
Calories: 200; Fat: 12 g; Carbohydrates: 19 g; Protein: 5 g; Fiber: 4 g; Sodium: 195 mg; Iron: 1 mg

Baked Garlicky Almond Avocado Fries

Prep Time: 10 minutes, Cook Time: 15 minutes, Serves: 16 fries

INGREDIENTS:
2 tbsps. nutritional yeast
¼ to ½ tsp. garlic powder
½ cup almond flour
¼ to ½ tsp. sea salt
¼ to ½ tsp. ground paprika, plus more for sprinkling
2 avocados, slightly underripe
½ cup almond milk

DIRECTIONS:
1. Preheat the oven to 420°F(218°C). Use parchment paper to line a baking sheet.
2. Add all of the ingredients except the avocados and almond milk into a small bowl, stir them together until well combined.
3. Cut the avocados in half and pit them, and quarter each half from pole to pole. Peel off the skin.
4. In another small bowl, add the almond milk.
5. First dip an avocado slice into the milk and then the coating mixture, tossing it gently to make sure it is completely covered, and arrange on the prepared baking sheet. Repeat with the remaining avocado slices.
6. Bake for 15 to 17 minutes, not to overcook or burn them.
7. After baking, take out from the oven, sprinkle with extra paprika, and serve.

Nutrition Info per Serving:
Calories: 50; Fats: 3.91 g; Carb: 3.35 g; Protein: 1.2 g; Fiber: 1.9 g

Nutty Banana Berry Chia Pudding

Prep Time: 2 hours, plus overnight chilling, Cook Time: 0, Serves: 2

INGREDIENTS:
4 tbsps. chia seeds
1 cup unsweetened almond milk
2 tbsps. wild frozen blueberries
½ medium banana, sliced
2 tbsps. sliced almonds
3 tsps. raisins

DIRECTIONS:
1. Divide the chia seeds and almond milk between two 8-ounce glass jars with tight-fitting lids or repurposed jam jars, seal tightly, and shake well.
2. Place in the refrigerator to chill for 2 hours, or until the mixture thickens.
3. Place 1 tablespoon of the blueberries, half the banana slices, 1 tablespoon of the almonds, and 1½ teaspoons of the raisins on the top of each pudding.
4. Tightly seal the jars and store in the refrigerator overnight. Enjoy one the following morning. Keep the remaining jar in the refrigerator for up to 4 days.

VARIATIONS TIP:
If you have a nut allergy, swap the almonds for pumpkin seeds.

Nutrition Info per Serving:
Calories: 273; Fat: 15 g; Carbohydrates: 29 g; Protein: 8 g; Fiber: 10 g; Sodium: 98 mg; Iron: 4 mg

Baked Raisins Stuffed Apples

Prep Time: 10 minutes, Cook Time: 15 minutes, Serves: 2

INGREDIENTS:
- 2 apples, tops removed and reserved
- 1 tsp. cinnamon
- ¼ cup raisins
- 1 packet stevia

DIRECTIONS:
1. Preheat the oven to 350°F(180°C).
2. Scoop out the insides of the apples with a spoon and place the contents into a medium bowl, discarding the core and seeds. Leave enough apple inside the skin so you have a shell and the skin is not pierced.
3. Add the cinnamon, raisins, and stevia in the medium bowl, mix together with the scooped-out apple pieces.
4. Evenly spoon the apple mixture back into the apple shells. Use a reserved top to cover each apple.
5. Arrange the apples in a baking pan and bake for 15 minutes, or until the apples are soft.
6. After baking, allow the apples to cool slightly and serve warm.

VARIATIONS TIP:
There are two kinds of raisins, brown and golden. Brown raisins come from red grapes and golden ones come from green grapes. Use both for an extra serving of micronutrients.

Nutrition Info per Serving:
Calories: 95; Carbohydrates: 25.1 g; Fiber: 4.1 g

Baked Peach Coconut Cobbler

Prep Time: 15 minutes, Cook Time: 15 minutes, Serves: 6

INGREDIENTS:
- Cooking spray
- 1 packet stevia
- 2 pounds (907 g) peaches, peeled and roughly chopped
- ¼ tsp. cinnamon
- 1 vanilla bean, split lengthwise and seeds scraped out
- ½ cup shredded unsweetened coconut
- 1½ cups raw almonds
- 1 tbsp. coconut oil, melted
- ¼ tsp. sea salt

DIRECTIONS:
1. Preheat the oven to 350°F(180°C).
2. Use cooking spray to coat a 9-inch baking dish.
3. Combine the stevia, peaches, cinnamon and vanilla bean in a large saucepan, stir over medium heat until the mixture comes to a boil. Remove from the heat.
4. Combine the coconut, almonds, coconut oil, and salt in a food processor. Pulse until a sticky, crumbly mixture forms.
5. Place the peaches onto the prepared baking dish. Place the almond-coconut mixture on the top.
6. Bake for 15 minutes, or until the top is lightly golden. Serve warm.

VARIATIONS TIP:
To peel peaches quickly, dunk each one in boiling water (using tongs) for about 30 seconds. The skin should peel right off.

Nutrition Info per Serving:
Calories: 240; Total Fat: 16.8 g; Carbohydrates: 20.8 g; Protein: 6.6 g; Fiber: 5.8 g

Baked Vanilla Fruit Granola

Prep Time: 10 minutes, Cook Time: 15 minutes, Serves: 4

INGREDIENTS:
- 1 cup slivered almonds
- ½ cup flaxseed
- 1 cup flaked unsweetened coconut
- ½ teaspoon cinnamon
- ¼ teaspoon ginger
- ½ cup raisins
- 1 vanilla bean, split lengthwise and seeds scraped out
- ¼ cup coconut oil
- ¼ teaspoon nutmeg
- ¼ teaspoon sea salt
- ½ cup unsweetened dried pineapple tidbits

DIRECTIONS:
1. Preheat the oven to 350°F(180°C).
2. Add all of the ingredients except the dried pineapple tidbits in a medium bowl, toss until well combined.
3. Evenly spread the mixture on a baking sheet and place it into the preheated oven. Bake for 15 minutes, until golden brown, stirring occasionally.
4. Remove from the oven and allow to cool, without stirring.
5. Once cooled, add the pineapple tidbits and stir well.
6. Keep in an airtight container.

VARIATIONS TIP:
This granola will keep in an airtight container for a week or so. Or make an extra batch, and freeze it to have on hand for months!

Nutrition Info per Serving:
Calories: 182; Total Fat: 0.3 g; Carbohydrates: 44 g; Protein: 2.3 g; Fiber: 3.8 g

Watermelon Greens Salad with Basil Vinaigrette

Prep Time: 10 minutes, Cook Time: 0, Serves: 1 or 2

INGREDIENTS:
- ¼ cup avocado oil
- ½ cup fresh basil leaves, plus 8 fresh basil leaves, chopped
- 1 garlic clove
- ¼ cup apple cider vinegar
- ¼ tsp. sea salt
- 2 to 4 cups mixed salad greens
- 2 cups cubed watermelon

DIRECTIONS:
1. Add all of the ingredients except the mixed salad greens and watermelon into a blender, blend them together until well combined.
2. On 1 large or 2 small plates, add the salad greens. Place the cubed watermelon on the top, drizzle with the vinaigrette, garnish with the chopped basil, and serve.

VARIATIONS TIP:
This is also great as a light snack, without the salad greens. Just fill a bowl with cubed watermelon and chopped basil, and drizzle with the vinaigrette.

Nutrition Info per Serving:
Calories: 313; Fat: 27.66 g; Carbohydrates: 17.4 g; Protein: 1.91 g; Fiber: 1.8 g

Homemade Apple Butter

Prep Time: 10 minutes, Cook Time: 3 hours, Serves: 24

INGREDIENTS:
- 2 cups fresh apple juice
- 4 pounds (1.8 kg) apples, peeled, cored, and chopped
- 1 tbsp. freshly squeezed lemon juice
- 1 vanilla bean, split lengthwise and seeds scraped out
- 1 tsp. cinnamon
- 2 packets stevia
- Pinch ground cloves

DIRECTIONS:
1. Combine the apple juice, apples and lemon juice in a large pot. Bring to a simmer and cook for 1 hour, until soft. Remove from the heat and allow to cool slightly.
2. Purée the apples with an immersion blender (or your regular blender in batches) until smooth.
3. Add the vanilla bean seeds, cinnamon, stevia and cloves to the apples. Return the pot to the heat and cook for another 2 hours, stirring frequently.
4. Cool the apple butter. Place into an airtight container and refrigerate.

VARIATIONS TIP:
You can use apple cider in place of apple juice for this recipe, but choose some with no added sugar. Also, do not use the cinnamon or spices in this recipe if you do.

Nutrition Info per Serving:
Calories: 49; Total Fat: 0.2 g; Carbohydrates: 12.9 g; Protein: 0.2 g; Fiber: 1.9 g

Sweet Blueberry and Chia Seed Vanilla Cobbler

Prep Time: 5 minutes, Cook Time: 45 minutes, Serves: 2 to 4

INGREDIENTS:
FOR THE BLUEBERRIES
- 2 tbsps. unrefined whole cane sugar, such as Sucanat
- 2 cups blueberries
- 1 tbsp. chia seeds

FOR THE TOPPING
- ½ cup oat flour
- ½ cup almond flour
- 2 tbsps. coconut oil (melted/liquid)
- 4 tbsps. coconut milk (boxed)
- 1½ tsps. baking powder
- 1 tsp. vanilla bean powder
- 2 tbsps. unrefined whole cane sugar, such as Sucanat
- ¼ tsp. sea salt

DIRECTIONS:
1. Preheat the oven to 350°F(180°C).

TO PREPARE THE BLUEBERRIES

2. Add the sugar, blueberries and chia seeds into a medium bowl, stir them together. Transfer the mixture to a 9-inch oval ovenproof baking dish or four (4-ounce) ramekin bowls.

TO PREPARE THE TOPPING

3. Combine all of the topping ingredients in a medium bowl, stir them together until well combined.

TO ASSEMBLE

4. Drop the topping over the blueberry mixture, a tablespoonful at a time. You can leave the topping as "dollops" or evenly spread it over the top of the blueberry mixture for a full crust.
5. Bake until the topping is slightly golden and cooked through, about 45 minutes.
6. After baking, serve warm.

Nutrition Info per Serving:
Calories: 303; Fat: 12.55 g; Carbohydrates: 48.93 g; Protein: 3.38 g; Fiber: 3.9 g

Almond and Coconut Stuffed Dates

Prep Time: 5 minutes, Cook Time: 0, Serves: 1

INGREDIENTS:

4 small dates, pitted
4 tsps. unsweetened finely shredded coconut
4 whole raw almonds

DIRECTIONS:
1. Use a small paring knife to slice each date open lengthwise.
2. Press into the center of each date with 1 teaspoon of the coconut.
3. In the center of the coconut, add an almond.
4. Sprinkle over the dates with any remaining coconut, and serve immediately.

VARIATIONS TIP:
To add some variety, swap each almond for a cashew (or use 4 or 5 hulled pumpkin seeds per date).

Nutrition Info per Serving:
Calories: 159; Fat: 7 g; Carbohydrates: 25 g; Protein: 2 g; Fiber: 4 g; Sodium: 2 mg; Iron: 1 mg

Sweet Thumbprint Cookies with Blueberry–Chia Seed Jam

Prep Time: 25 minutes, Cook Time: 10 minutes, Serves: 8 cookies

INGREDIENTS:

3 tbsps. coconut oil, melted
1¼ cups almond flour
1 to 2 pinches sea salt
1½ tbsps. brown rice syrup
Blueberry chia seed fruit jam

DIRECTIONS:
1. Preheat the oven to 375°F(190°C). Use parchment paper to line a baking sheet.
2. Add the coconut oil, almond flour, salt and brown rice syrup in a medium bowl, stir them together until well combined. The mixture should be very wet. Place in the refrigerator to chill for 10 to 15 minutes, or until firm.
3. Scoop a tablespoonful of dough at a time and use your hands to flatten into a disk, and use your fingertips to smooth the outer edges. Press your thumb in the center to make the "thumbprint" indention, and put on the prepared baking sheet. Repeat with the remaining dough.
4. Bake for about 10 minutes, not overbake.
5. After baking, take the cookies out of the oven, and after they cool a bit, repeat the "thumbprint" indention process, if necessary. Let cool completely before removing from the pan or adding the chia seed fruit topping.
6. Fill the blueberry chia seed fruit jam into the thumbprint indentions and serve.

VARIATIONS TIP:
Make several batches of the cookies, and fill each batch with a different chia seed jam flavor for a colorful presentation or party theme!

Nutrition Info per Serving:
Calories: 56; Fat: 5.23 g; Carbohydrates: 3 g; Protein: 0.06 g; Fiber: 0.1 g

Baked Oatmeal Stuffed Apple Crumble

Prep Time: 5 minutes, Cook Time: 20 to 25 minutes, Serves: 4

INGREDIENTS:

4 small apples
¼ cup gluten-free rolled oats
3 or 4 small dates, pitted
¼ cup unsweetened shredded coconut
1 tsp. maple syrup
⅛ tsp. ground cinnamon
1 tsp. coconut oil
⅛ tsp. vanilla extract
⅛ tsp. sea salt

DIRECTIONS:
1. Preheat the oven to 400°F(205°C).
2. Core each apple, but leave the bottom intact to form a cup. Place each apple on an 8-inch square of aluminum foil.
3. Combine the oats and the remaining ingredients in a high-speed blender or food processor, blend until well combined.
4. Fill 2 tablespoons of the oat mixture into each apple.
5. Wrap the foil around each apple, leaving a few the top exposed, and arrange the apples on a baking sheet. Bake until the apples are soft and the filling is golden, about 20 to 25 minutes.

VARIATIONS TIP:
If it's difficult to core the apple while retaining its shape, simply slice it, layer the slices in the foil, and top with the crumble. Wrap with the foil similarly to expose only the crumble to keep the apple inside moist.

Nutrition Info per Serving:
Calories: 162; Fat: 5 g; Carbohydrates: 32 g; Protein: 1 g; Fiber: 6 g; Sodium: 75 mg; Iron: 1 mg

Baked Grapefruit and Coconut

Prep Time: 15 minutes, Cook Time: 15 minutes, Serves: 1

INGREDIENTS:
1 grapefruit, halved
2 tbsps. grated unsweetened coconut

DIRECTIONS:
1. Preheat the oven to 350°F(180°C).
2. On a foil-lined baking pan, add the grapefruit halves. Place 1 tablespoon of coconut on top of each half.
3. Put the pan in the preheated oven and bake until the coconut is browned, about 15 minutes.
4. Transfer the grapefruit halves onto a plate, and use a spoon to eat.

VARIATIONS TIP:
Ruby Red is a variety of grapefruit that tends to be sweeter than other kinds. If you're not a big grapefruit fan, try Ruby Red first.

Nutrition Info per Serving:
Calories: 86; Total Fat: 0.07 g; Carbohydrates: 11.9 g; Protein: 1.2 g; Fiber: 2.3 g

Vanilla Apple Pie Crumble

Prep Time: 10 minutes, Cook Time: 25 minutes, Serves: 6

INGREDIENTS:
FOR THE APPLE FILLING
1 tbsp. brown rice syrup
1 Braeburn apple, diced small
⅛ tsp. freshly squeezed lemon juice
½ tsp. ground cinnamon
FOR THE CRUMBLE
3 tbsps. water
1 tbsp. ground flaxseed
1 tbsp. avocado oil
½ cup unrefined whole cane sugar, such as Sucanat
2 cups almond flour
⅛ tsp. vanilla bean powder
½ tsp. ground cinnamon
Pinch sea salt

DIRECTIONS:
1. Preheat the oven to 350°F(180°C). Use parchment paper to line a 9-by-5-inch loaf pan.
2. TO PREPARE THE APPLE FILLING
3. Add the brown rice syrup, apple, lemon juice and cinnamon into a small bowl, stir them together until well combined. Set aside.
4. TO PREPARE THE CRUMBLE
5. Stir together the water and flaxseed to make a flax egg in a small bowl.
6. Add the flax egg, avocado oil, sugar, almond flour, vanilla bean powder, cinnamon, and salt into a medium bowl, stir them together until well combined.
7. Press half the crumble mixture firmly into the bottom of the prepared loaf pan.
8. Evenly spread the apple filling over the crust. Sprinkle over the apple mixture with the remaining crumble.
9. Bake for 20 to 25 minutes and serve.

Nutrition Info per Serving:
Calories: 86; Fat: 3.29 g; Carbohydrates: 14.65 g; Protein: 0.48 g; Fiber: 1 g

Chia Seed and Strawberry Overnight Oats Parfait

Prep Time: 10 minutes, Cook Time: 0, Serves: 1 or 2

INGREDIENTS:
FOR THE STRAWBERRY MIXTURE
1 tsp. chia seeds
1 cup diced strawberries
1 to 2 tsps. brown rice syrup
FOR THE OAT MIXTURE
1 cup coconut milk (boxed)
1 cup quick rolled oats
1 tbsp. brown rice syrup
⅛ tbsp. vanilla bean powder

DIRECTIONS:
TO PREPARE THE STRAWBERRY MIXTURE
1. Add the chia seeds, strawberries and rice syrup into a small bowl, stir them together until well combined.
TO PREPARE THE OAT MIXTURE
2. Stir together the coconut milk, oats, brown rice syrup, and vanilla bean powder in a small bowl until well combined.
3. In the bottom of 1 large glass mason jar or 2 small jars, add half the oat mixture, and layer over the oat mixture with half of the strawberry mixture. Repeat with the remaining oat and strawberry mixtures.
4. Cover the mason jar(s), and place in the refrigerator to chill overnight.
5. Uncover and serve.

VARIATIONS TIP:
Substitute the strawberries with your favorite alkaline fruit like mango, pineapple, or kiwi, and feel free to use almond milk instead of coconut milk if you don't need a nut-free version.

Nutrition Info per Serving:
Calories: 461; Fats: 27.27 g; Carb: 52.09 g; Protein: 8.26 g; Fiber: 5.9 g

Mixed Berry Chia Seed Coconut Pudding

Prep Time: 5 minutes, plus 1 hour to chill, Cook Time: 0, Serves: 1

INGREDIENTS:
½ cup mixed berries (raspberries, blackberries, blueberries), plus more (optional) for topping
1 cup coconut milk
2 tbsps. chia seeds
1 to 2 tbsps. unrefined whole cane sugar, such as Sucanat (boxed)

DIRECTIONS:
1. Combine the berries, coconut milk, chia seeds, and sugar in a mason jar, adjusting the sugar to your preference.
2. Tightly seal the jar, and shake vigorously until well mixed.
3. Place in the refrigerator for about 1 hour, or until the pudding thickens to your preference.
4. Stir, place the extra mixed berries (if using) on the top, and enjoy.

VARIATIONS TIP:
This is a versatile recipe. Substitute the mixed berries with your favorite alkaline fruit, like strawberries, mango, bananas, or kiwi.

Nutrition Info per Serving:
Calories: 219; Fat: 2.75 g; Carbohydrates: 47.65 g; Protein: 3.55 g; Fiber: 6.8 g

Banana Walnut Muffins

Prep Time: 20 minutes, Cook Time: 1 hour, Serves: 6

INGREDIENTS:
DRY INGREDIENTS:
½ tsp. of pure sea salt
1 ½ cups of spell or teff flour
¾ cup of date syrup
WET INGREDIENTS:
¼ cup of grape seed oil
¾ cup of homemade walnut milk
1 tbsp. key lime juice
2 medium pureed burro bananas
FILLING INGREDIENTS:
1 chopped burro banana
½ cup of chopped walnuts (plus extra for decorating)

DIRECTIONS:
1. Preheat the oven to 400°F(205°C).
2. Grease 12 cups or line with cupcake liners and place on a muffin tray.
3. In a large bowl, add all of the dry ingredients and mix them thoroughly.
4. In a smaller bowl, combine all of the wet ingredients and mix well with the pureed bananas.
5. In a large container, mix the dry ingredients and the wet ingredients, not to over mix.
6. Gently fold in the filling ingredients.
7. Pour the muffin batter into the 12 prepared muffin cups and garnish with some extra walnuts.
8. Bake for 22 to 26 minutes until golden brown.
9. After baking, let the muffins cool for 10 minutes.
10. Serve.

Nutrition Info per Serving:
Calories: 419; Total Fat: 7.3 g; Carbohydrates: 82.93 g; Protein: 10.14 g; Fiber: 5.8 g

Pear Nachos and Almond Butter Drizzle with Almond

Prep Time: 5 minutes, Cook Time: 0, Serves: 1

INGREDIENTS:
1 pear, unpeeled and sliced
2 tbsps. almond butter
2 to 3 tsps. unrefined whole cane sugar, such as Sucanat
⅛ tsp. ground cinnamon
⅛ tsp. vanilla bean powder
1 to 2 tbsp. water, if needed
1 tbsp. slivered almonds
1 to 2 tsps. hemp seeds
1 to 2 tsps. unsweetened shredded coconut flakes

DIRECTIONS:
1. On a serving platter, arrange with the pear slices.
2. To prepare the drizzle, combine the almon butter, sugar, cinnamon and vanilla bean powder in a small bowl, stir them together until well combined. Depending on the thickness of the almond butter, to thin it out, you may need to add 1 to 2 tablespoons of water, but only add enough to make it thin enough to drizzle.
3. Drizzle over the sliced pears with the almond butter mixture; garnish with the almonds, hemp seeds and coconut flakes; and serve. Use any extra drizzle to dip the pear slices in.

VARIATIONS TIP:
Swap out the pear with an apple for a sweeter dessert.

Nutrition Info per Serving:
Calories: 300; Fat: 20.64 g; Carbohydrates: 26.03 g; Protein: 8.25 g; Fiber: 8.4 g

Vanilla Apple Pie Crumble, page 136

Mixed Berry Chia Seed Coconut Pudding, page 137

Quick Blueberry-Banana Ice Cream, page 141

Baked Garlicky Almond Avocado Fries, page 132

Winter Warm Fruit Compote

Prep Time: 10 minutes, Cook Time: 10 minutes, Serves: 4

INGREDIENTS:

1 apple, peeled, cored, and diced
½ cup figs, stemmed and quartered
1 orange, peeled and sectioned
¼ cup dark cherries
½ cup dried plums (prunes), halved
1 cup filtered water
1 tsp. grated fresh ginger
1 vanilla bean, split lengthwise and seeds scraped out
½ tsp. cloves
½ tsp. cinnamon
1 packet stevia (optional)

DIRECTIONS:

1. Place all of the ingredients in a medium saucepan.
2. Bring to a simmer over medium heat and cook for 10 minutes, or until the fruit is tender but not too soft, stirring occasionally. Remove from the heat.
3. After cooking, allow to stand for 30 minutes to meld the flavors.
4. Reheat if needed, evenly spoon into four bowls and serve warm.

VARIATIONS TIP:
This is also delicious served cold.

Nutrition Info per Serving:
Calories: 102; Total Fat: 0.4 g; Carbohydrates: 26 g; Protein: 1 g; Fiber: 4.2 g

Blackberry Lime Jam

Prep Time: 10 minutes, Cook Time: 10 minutes, Serves: 1

INGREDIENTS:

¾ cup of blackberries
3 tbsps. of agave syrup
1 tbsp. of key lime juice
¼ cup of sea moss gel + extra 2 tbsps.

DIRECTIONS:

1. In a medium pot, add the rinsed blackberries and cook on medium heat, and stir until the liquid appears.
2. Once berries soften, chop up any large pieces with a immersion blender. If you don't have a blender put the mixture in a food processor, mix it well, then place back to the pot.
3. Add the agave syrup, key lime juice and sea moss gel to the blended mixture. Boil on medium heat and stir well until it becomes thick.
4. Remove from the heat and allow it to cool for 10 minutes.
5. Serve it with bread pieces or the Flatbread.

VARIATIONS TIP:
If you don't have Sea Moss Gel, you can omit it.
Store this Blackberry Jam in a mason jar with a lid in the refrigerator for 2 to 3 weeks.
Don't store at room temperature!

Nutrition Info per Serving:
Calories: 376; Total Fat: 0.47 g; Carbohydrates: 98.33 g; Protein: 3.15 g; Fiber: 6.8 g

Fresh Fruit with Vanilla Cashew and Lemon Cream

Prep Time: 25 minutes, Cook Time: 0, Serves: 4

INGREDIENTS:

Room-temperature water, for soaking
1 cup raw cashews
2 tbsps. brown rice syrup
2 tbsps. unrefined whole cane sugar, such as Sucanat
1 (13.5-ounce, 383 g) can coconut milk
1 tsp. freshly squeezed lemon juice
¼ tsp. ground cinnamon
2 tsps. vanilla bean powder
¼ tsp. sea salt
4 cups alkaline fruit, such as raspberries, blackberries, blueberries, strawberries, mango, pineapple, or cantaloupe

DIRECTIONS:

1. Place the cashews in a medium bowl, pour in enough room-temperature water to cover, allow to soak for 15 to 20 minutes. Drain and rinse the cashews.
2. Combine the soaked cashews and the remaining ingredients except the fruit in a high-speed blender, blend them together until creamy and smooth. Add more sugar, if needed.
3. In each of 4 serving bowls, add 1 cup of fruit, drizzle each bowl of fruit with ½ cup of cream, and serve.

VARIATIONS TIP:
Soaking the cashews softens them, making blending easier. Store any remaining cashew cream in an airtight container in the refrigerator. Add unsweetened shredded coconut flakes over the fruit and cream to make an ambrosia-style dessert.

Nutrition Info per Serving:
Calories: 219; Fats: 3.31 g; Carb: 48.66 g; Protein: 2.98 g; Fiber: 3.4 g

Chapter 10: Fruit

Chilled Mango Lime Pepper Slaw

Prep Time: 10 minutes, Cook Time: 15 minutes, Serves: 1

INGREDIENTS:
- 1 cup sliced bell pepper
- 1 mango, peeled and cut into bite-size pieces
- 1 cup sliced jicama
- Juice of 1 lime
- 1 tbsp. chili powder

DIRECTIONS:
1. Combine bell pepper, mango, and jicama in a small bowl.
2. Top the vegetables, squeeze with the lime juice. Sprinkle with the chili powder.
3. Place in the refrigerator to chill for 15 minutes to allow flavors to blend and enjoy.

VARIATIONS TIP:
If you're feeling lazy, skip the skewers and add the lime juice and chili powder straight onto mango that has been pitted and scored.

Nutrition Info per Serving:
Calories: 201; Total Fat: 1.3 g; Carbohydrates: 50 g; Protein: 2.8 g; Fiber: 5 g

Sweet Chia Seed Fruit Jam

Prep Time: 5 minutes, Cook Time: 0, Serves: 1 cup

INGREDIENTS:
- ¼ cup chia seeds
- 1½ cups alkaline fruit (chopped mango, blueberries, chopped strawberries, blackberries, etc.)
- 1 to 2 tbsps. unrefined whole cane sugar, such as Sucanat

DIRECTIONS:
1. Add the chia seeds, fruit and sugar into a food processor, process them together until well blended. Adjust the sweetener, if needed.
2. Place extra chia jam in an airtight container and store in the refrigerator.

VARIATIONS TIP:
Glass mason jars are excellent to use for storing your chia seed jam.

Nutrition Info per Serving:
Calories: 231; Fat: 6.41 g; Carbohydrates: 40.86 g; Protein: 2.96 g; Fiber: 2.9 g

Banana Almond Spilts with Cherry

Prep Time: 10 minutes, Cook Time: 0, Serves: 1

INGREDIENTS:
- 1 large banana, peeled and halved lengthwise
- 2 scoops coconut ice cream
- 1 tbsp. toasted, chopped almonds
- 2 tbsps. toasted, shredded, unsweetened coconut
- ¼ cup coconut whipped cream
- 1 dark cherry, stem on

DIRECTIONS:
1. Place the banana in a single-serving dish. Add the ice cream between the banana halves.
2. Place the almonds, coconut, and whipped cream on the top.
3. Crown with the cherry on top and serve.

VARIATIONS TIP:
Other ideas for toppings include fruit preserves, almond butter, and fresh strawberries.

Nutrition Info per Serving:
Calories: 393; Total Fat: 21.6 g; Carbohydrates: 47.6 g; Protein: 6.6 g; Fiber: 6.6 g

Vanilla Banana and Cashew Cream

Prep Time: 10 minutes, Cook Time: 0, Serves: 6

INGREDIENTS:
- 1 cup cashews, soaked in 2 cups water overnight, then drained
- 4 ripe medium bananas, sliced and frozen
- 1 tbsp. unsweetened carob powder, ground cinnamon, or unsweetened cocoa powder
- ½ cup water
- ⅛ tsp. sea salt
- ½ tsp. vanilla extract

DIRECTIONS:
1. Combine all of the ingredients in a high-speed blender.
2. Blend until smooth and creamy. And serve immediately.

VARIATIONS TIP:
Try this with nut butter instead. Simply replace the cashews with 3 tablespoons of your choice of nut butter.

Nutrition Info per Serving:
Calories: 200; Fat: 10 g; Carbohydrates: 25 g; Protein: 5 g; Fiber: 3 g; Sodium: 53 mg; Iron: 2 mg

Quick Blueberry-Banana Ice Cream

Prep Time: 5 minutes, Cook Time: 0, Serves: 2

INGREDIENTS:
1 cup blueberries
2 bananas, sliced and frozen

DIRECTIONS:
1. Combine the blueberries and frozen bananas in a food processor, process until the mixture reaches a soft serve–type consistency.
2. Serve immediately.

VARIATIONS TIP:
Always keep at least two sliced bananas in your freezer at all times so you can make this recipe at a moment's notice!

Nutrition Info per Serving:
Calories: 185; Fat: 0.69 g; Carbohydrates: 46.74 g; Protein: 1.71 g; Fiber: 4.2 g

Banana Veggies Fries

Prep Time: 5 minutes, Cook Time: 10 minutes, Serves: 2

INGREDIENTS:
2 tsps. grapeseed oil
4 baby burro bananas, peeled, cut in squares
½ of a medium onion, peeled, chopped
½ of medium green bell pepper, cored, chopped
¼ tsp. salt
¼ tsp. cayenne pepper

DIRECTIONS:
1. Heat the oil in a medium skillet pan over medium-low heat, add the burro banana pieces and cook for 3 minutes or until beginning to brown.
2. Then turn the burro banana pieces, stir in all of the remaining ingredients, mix well and continue to cook for 5 to 7 minutes, until the onions have caramelized.
3. Serve immediately.

Nutrition Info per Serving:
Calories: 130.5; Fats: 6.5 g; Carb: 20 g; Protein: 1 g; Fiber: 3 g

Summer Fruit Vanilla Pops

Prep Time: 5 minutes, Cook Time: 0 (freeze 2 hours), Serves: 6

INGREDIENTS:
1 packet stevia
1 (13-ounce, 369 g) can unsweetened coconut milk
1 vanilla bean, split lengthwise and seeds scraped out
1½ cups chopped fresh fruit

DIRECTIONS:
1. Mix together the stevia, coconut milk, and vanilla bean seeds in a small bowl.
2. Divide the chopped fruit evenly among the ice pop molds. They will be partially filled.
3. Pour over the fruit with the coconut milk mixture, gently shaking each mold to settle the milk.
4. Insert the ice pop handles into the molds. Freeze for about 2 hours, until completely frozen.

VARIATIONS TIP:
If you don't have ice pop molds, get some! Until then, though, you make these in ice cube trays and cover with plastic wrap. Stick toothpicks in the middle before freezing.

Nutrition Info per Serving:
Calories: 163; Total Fat: 14.1 g; Carbohydrates: 7.1 g; Protein: 2.5 g; Fiber: 4.2 g

Coconut Banana Candy Coins

Prep Time: 5 minutes, Cook Time: 5 minutes, Serves: 1

INGREDIENTS:
Pinch sea salt
2 tbsps. shredded unsweetened coconut
2 tbsps. coconut oil
1 banana, peeled and sliced into ¼-inch-thick slices

DIRECTIONS:
1. Combine the salt and coconut on a plate.
2. Melt the coconut oil in a medium pan over medium heat.
3. Press each banana slice into the coconut mixture until coated.
4. Transfer each slice into the heated coconut oil. Sauté for 2 minutes, flip, and continue to cook for 2 to 3 minutes on the second side.
5. After cooking, allow to cool slightly and serve warm.

VARIATIONS TIP:
Try this recipe with plantains, the less sweet cousin of the banana. The coins will be slightly firmer and less sweet than those made with bananas.

Nutrition Info per Serving:
Calories: 171; Total Fat: 6.3 g; Carbohydrates: 28.4 g; Protein: 1.5 g; Fiber: 4.4 g

Kale and Almond Stuffed Avocados

Prep Time: 10 minutes, Cook Time: 0, Serves: 1 or 2

INGREDIENTS:

1 tbsp. avocado oil
½ cup chopped Lacinato kale
½ cup almonds
1 garlic clove
½ jalapeño
2 tbsps. nutritional yeast
1 tbsp. freshly squeezed lemon juice
1 tbsp. apple cider vinegar
¼ tsp. sea salt
1 avocado, halved and pitted

DIRECTIONS:

1. Combine all of the ingredients except the avocado in a food processor, pulse them together until everything is well combined, the almonds are in small pieces, and it has a chunky texture, not to overprocess.
2. In the center of each avocado half, add half of the stuffing mixture and serve.

VARIATIONS TIP:

If you have extra time, you can enjoy this as a warm breakfast by baking the avocado in the oven: Just add the stuffed avocado to a baking pan lined with parchment paper and bake at 425°F(220°C) for 5 to 10 minutes, or until the avocado is soft.

Nutrition Info per Serving:
Calories: 272; Fats: 22.14 g; Carb: 15.63 g; Protein: 6.9 g; Fiber: 8.3 g

Spiced Party Mix

Prep Time: 15 minutes, Cook Time: 10 minutes, Serves: 6

INGREDIENTS:

Cooking spray
½ cup flaked unsweetened coconut
1 cup raisins
1 cup raw almonds
½ cup roasted peas
½ cup pumpkin seeds
1 cup dried pineapple pieces
1 tsp. chili powder
1 tsp. ground ginger
2 tbsps. garlic powder
2 tbsps. onion powder
1 tsp. sea salt
1 tbsp. coconut oil

DIRECTIONS:

1. Preheat the oven to 425°F(220°C).
2. Use cooking spray to coat a large baking pan.
3. Combine all of the remaining ingredients in a medium bowl.
4. In the baking pan, spread the mix in an even layer.
5. Bake for 10 minutes in the preheated oven, being careful that it doesn't burn.
6. After baking, remove from the oven and allow to cool before serving.

VARIATIONS TIP:

You can get dried, roasted peas in the Asian food section of your local market. Try the wasabi flavored ones to make it spicy!

Nutrition Info per Serving:
Calories: 227; Total Fat: 12.7 g; Carbohydrates: 27.9 g; Protein: 5.1 g; Fiber: 4.1 g

Blackberry Banana Bars

Prep Time: 20 minutes, Cook Time: 1 hour 20 minutes, Serves: 4

INGREDIENTS:

3 burro bananas or 4 baby bananas
½ cup of grape seed oil
¼ cup of agave syrup
1 cup of spelt flour
2 cups of quinoa flakes
1 cup of prepared blackberry jam

DIRECTIONS:

1. Preheat the oven to 350°F(180°C).
2. Peel Bananas and use a fork to mash them in a large bowl.
3. Add the grape seed oil and agave syrup, and mix well.
4. Add the spelt flour and quinoa flakes. Knead the dough until it becomes sticky to your fingers.
5. Use the parchment paper to cover a 9x9-inch baking pan.
6. Take ⅔ of the dough and use your fingers to smooth it out over the parchment pan.
7. Spread the blackberry jam over the dough.
8. Crumble the remainder dough and sprinkle them over the top.
9. Bake for 20 minutes.
10. Remove from the oven and allow it to cool for 10 to 15 minutes.
11. Cut into small pieces and serve.

VARIATIONS TIP:

You can keep this Blackberry Bar in the refrigerator for 5 to 6 days or in the freezer up to 3 months.

Nutrition Info per Serving:
Calories: 427; Total Fat: 3.22 g; Carbohydrates: 92.81 g; Protein: 12.06 g; Fiber: 11.2 g

Avocado, Banana and Strawberry Ice Cream

Prep Time: 10 minutes, Cook Time: 0 (chill 5-6 hours), Serves: 5

INGREDIENTS:

5 quartered baby bananas
1 cup strawberries
½ avocado, chopped
1 tbsp. of agave syrup
¼ cup of homemade walnut milk

DIRECTIONS:
1. In a blender, add all of the ingredients and blend them well.
2. Taste, and add extra milk if it is too thick, or if you want it sweeter, add more agave syrup.
3. Transfer it into a container with a lid and allow to freeze for at least 5 to 6 hours.
4. Enjoy!

Nutrition Info per Serving:
Calories: 128; Total Fat: 3.55 g; Carbohydrates: 25.12 g; Protein: 1.88 g; Fiber: 4 g

Cream Berry Peach Parfait

Prep Time: 10 minutes, Cook Time: 0, Serves: 2

INGREDIENTS:

¼ cup sliced strawberries
1 cup coconut whipped cream
¼ cup blackberries
¼ cup sliced raspberries
¼ cup sliced peaches

DIRECTIONS:
1. Place 2 tablespoons strawberries in a large clear glass, add 2 tablespoons whipped cream on the top. Then cover with 2 tablespoons blackberries and another 2 tablespoons whipped cream. Continue to add 2 tablespoons raspberries and 2 tablespoons whipped cream. Finish with 2 tablespoons peaches and 2 tablespoons whipped cream.
2. For the second glass, repeat the steps with the remaining ingredients.
3. Serve immediately.

VARIATIONS TIP:
Feel free to swap in any fruits you like. Get bold and layer in things like pumpkin or sweet potato!

Nutrition Info per Serving:
Calories: 120; Total Fat: 10 g; Carbohydrates: 4 g; Protein: 1.7 g; Fiber: 6.3 g

Lemon Blueberry and Banana Soft Serve

Prep Time: 5 minutes, Cook Time: 0, Serves: 2

INGREDIENTS:

1 cup frozen wild blueberries
1 small ripe banana
1 tsp. freshly squeezed lemon juice

DIRECTIONS:
1. Add the blueberries, banana and lemon juice in a high-speed blender or food processor.
2. Blend until creamy and smooth.
3. Serve immediately.

VARIATIONS TIP:
You can enjoy one serving now and freeze the rest. Use it as a base for a smoothie by adding 1 cup unsweetened almond milk and ½ cup fresh or frozen fruit.

Nutrition Info per Serving:
Calories: 81; Fat: 1 g; Carbohydrates: 20 g; Protein: 1 g; Fiber: 3 g; Sodium: 3 mg; Iron: 1 mg

Chapter 11: Bowl

Barbecued Broccoli Rice and Pineapple Bowl

Prep Time: 10 minutes, Cook Time: 5 minutes, Serves: 1

INGREDIENTS:
½ cup cooked brown rice
1 cup steamed broccoli
2 tbsps. homemade barbecue sauce
¼ cup packed-in-juice pineapple chunks, drained, liquid reserved

DIRECTIONS:
1. Layer the brown rice, broccoli, and pineapple in a medium bowl.
2. Combine the barbecue sauce and the reserved pineapple juice in a small saucepan, whisk them together and cook over medium heat for about 5 minutes, until thickened and bubbly.
3. Pour over the rice and broccoli and serve.

VARIATIONS TIP:
The sauce will keep for a few days in the refrigerator, or you can freeze it and it will last for months.

Nutrition Info per Serving:
Calories: 223; Total Fat: 1.6 g; Carbohydrates: 47.6 g; Protein: 3.6 g; Fiber: 4.6 g

Arugula, Zucchini and Pesto Grain Bowl

Prep Time: 15 minutes, Cook Time: 0, Serves: 4

INGREDIENTS:
4 cups arugula
4 cups zucchini noodles (spiralized or thinly sliced)
2 cups cooked quinoa
½ cup vegan spinach-basil pesto
½ cup sliced cherry tomatoes or drained canned low-sodium diced tomatoes
4 tbsps. hulled pumpkin seeds

DIRECTIONS:
1. Evenly divide the arugula among four bowls.
2. Layer 1 cup of the zucchini noodles, ½ cup of the quinoa, 2 tablespoons of the pesto, and 2 tablespoons of the tomatoes in each bowl.
3. Top each with 1 tablespoon of the pumpkin seeds, and serve.

VARIATIONS TIP:
If you have a tomato allergy or GERD, replace the tomatoes with an equal amount of reheated cooked carrots.

Nutrition Info per Serving:
Calories: 245; Fat: 13 g; Carbohydrates: 24 g; Protein: 9 g; Fiber: 5 g; Sodium: 34 mg; Iron: 3 mg

Chickpea, Mushroom and Zucchini Bowl

Prep Time: 5 minutes, Cook Time: 10 minutes, Serves: 2

INGREDIENTS:
1 tbsp. grapeseed oil
¼ of white onion, peeled, chopped
¼ of red bell pepper, cored, chopped
4 small oyster mushrooms, destemmed, diced
⅓ tsp. sea salt
¼ tsp. cayenne pepper
1 ½ cup cooked chickpeas
1 tsp. dried basil
1 tsp. dried oregano
2 ½ cups vegetable broth, homemade
2 zucchinis, spiralized

DIRECTIONS:
1. Heat the oil in a medium pot over medium-high heat, add the onion, red bell pepper, and mushrooms, season with salt and cayenne pepper, and cook for 5 minutes until tender.
2. Reduce the heat to medium-low, add all of the remaining ingredients except for the zucchini noodles, stir until mixed, and simmer the soup for 15 to 20 minutes.
3. Then add the zucchini noodles into the pan, stir until mixed, and cook for 1 minute or more until thoroughly warmed. Serve immediately.

Nutrition Info per Serving:
Calories: 242; Fats: 9 g; Carb: 34 g; Protein: 10 g; Fiber: 9 g

Bell Pepper, Zucchini and Mushroom Bowl

Prep Time: 5 minutes, Cook Time: 8 minutes, Serves: 2

INGREDIENTS:

- 1 tbsp. grapeseed oil
- ½ of medium red bell pepper, sliced
- ½ of medium green bell pepper, sliced
- ½ of medium white onion, peeled, sliced
- ½ cup sliced mushrooms
- 2 zucchini, spiralized
- ⅓ tsp. salt
- ⅛ tsp. cayenne pepper

DIRECTIONS:

1. Heat the oil in a large skillet pan over medium-high heat, when hot, add the bell peppers, onion and mushrooms, and cook for 3 to 5 minutes until tender-crisp.
2. Stir in the zucchini noodles, toss until mixed, and cook for 2 minutes until warm, season with the salt and cayenne pepper.
3. Serve immediately.

Nutrition Info per Serving:
Calories: 168; Fats: 2 g; Carb: 36 g; Protein: 0.9 g; Fiber: 6 g

Black Bean Quinoa and Vegetable Bowl

Prep Time: 15 minutes, Cook Time: 0, Serves: 4

INGREDIENTS:

- 1 to 2 tsps. taco spice blend
- 1 cup canned black beans, drained and rinsed
- 4 cups chopped Tuscan kale
- Sea salt
- 1 cup sliced mushrooms
- ½ cup shredded carrots
- 1 cup cooked quinoa
- 1 medium avocado, sliced
- ¼ cup simple hummus
- Juice of ½ medium lime
- 1 to 3 tbsps. warm water
- 8 tsps. pico de gallo
- 3 tbsps. shelled pistachios
- 4 tsps. chopped fresh cilantro

DIRECTIONS:

1. Combine the taco spice blend and black beans in a small bowl.
2. In a large bowl, add the kale and lightly season with the salt. Massage the kale until softened slightly with your hands. Evenly divide the kale, bean mixture, mushrooms, carrots, quinoa, and avocado among four bowls.
3. Mix the hummus with the lime juice in a small bowl, then add the warm water, 1 tablespoon at a time, until it has thinned to a dressing consistency. Drizzle over each veggie bowl with 1 tablespoon of the dressing.
4. Evenly garnish each bowl with the pico de gallo, pistachios, and cilantro, and serve.

VARIATIONS TIP:
If you know you won't be serving all four bowls, store the undressed ingredients and the dressing in separate airtight containers in the refrigerator for up to 4 days.

Nutrition Info per Serving:
Calories: 290; Fat: 12 g; Carbohydrates: 47 g; Protein: 12 g; Fiber: 12 g; Sodium: 508 mg; Iron: 4 mg

Indian Curried Quinoa Vegetable Bowl

Prep Time: 10 minutes, Cook Time: 5 minutes, Serves: 1

INGREDIENTS:

- 1 cup cooked quinoa, warmed
- ½ cup cooked cauliflower florets
- 1 large carrot, peeled, sliced, and steamed
- ⅛ cup chickpeas
- ½ cup coconut milk
- ¼ cup sliced mushrooms
- ½ tsp. ground ginger
- 1 tbsp. yellow curry powder
- 1 tsp. sea salt
- 1 tbsp. tomato paste

DIRECTIONS:

1. Layer the quinoa, cauliflower, carrot, and chickpeas in a medium bowl.
2. Combine the coconut milk, mushrooms, ginger, curry powder, salt, and tomato paste in a small saucepan, cook over medium heat, whisk until the mixture simmers. Cook for 5 minutes and then allow to cool slightly.
3. Pour over the quinoa mixture with the sauce and serve immediately.

VARIATIONS TIP:
For a change of pace, add some eggplant, too. Just remember that doing so will make this unsuitable for those on the Thyroid-Support Plan.

Nutrition Info per Serving:
Calories: 469; Total Fat: 0.2 g; Carbohydrates: 26.1 g; Protein: 5.4 g; Fiber: 13.5 g

Creamy Banana Bowl with Strawberry and Almond

Prep Time: 10 minutes, Cook Time: 0, Serves: 1

INGREDIENTS:
2 bananas, peeled, sliced, and frozen
2 tbsps. coconut milk
2 tbsps. grated unsweetened coconut
2 tbsps. fruit-sweetened-only strawberry jam
2 tbsps. chopped toasted almonds
¼ cup coconut whipped cream

DIRECTIONS:
1. Place the frozen bananas in a food processor, then add the coconut milk and blend until they're the consistency of ice cream. Transfer to a single-serving bowl.
2. Place the coconut, jam, toasted almonds, and whipped cream over the bananas.
3. Serve immediately.

VARIATIONS TIP:
You can add other fruits as you like. Frozen cherries are a great addition, as are fresh strawberries.

Nutrition Info per Serving:
Calories: 454; Total Fat: 19.2 g; Carbohydrates: 69.4 g; Protein: 6.9 g; Fiber: 9.6 g

Coconut, Raspberry and Avocado Smoothie Bowl

Prep Time: 15 minutes, Cook Time: 0, Serves: 2

INGREDIENTS:
1 cup raspberries, plus more (optional) for topping
1½ cups coconut milk (boxed)
1 avocado, roughly chopped
3 tbsps. unrefined whole cane sugar, such as Sucanat, divided
1 tsp. unsweetened shredded coconut
1 tsp. chia seeds
Mixed berries, for topping (optional)

DIRECTIONS:
1. Combine the raspberries, coconut milk, avocado, and 2 tablespoons of sugar in a blender, blend until smooth and creamy.
2. Pour the mixture into 2 serving bowls, sprinkle the extra raspberries (if using), the remaining 1 tablespoon of the sugar, shredded coconut, chia seeds, and mixed berries (if using) over the top, and serve.

VARIATIONS TIP:
Smoothie bowls are customizable! Substitute the raspberries with blackberries, blueberries, or mango. You can even add or change the toppings, too—try hemp seeds, sunflower seeds, or other alkaline fruits.

Nutrition Info per Serving:
Calories: 245; Fats: 15.65 g; Carb: 26.64 g; Protein: 4.15 g; Fiber: 12.9 g

Lentil and Pasta Bowl with Basil Cider Dressing

Prep Time: 15 minutes, Cook Time: 0, Serves: 1 or 2

INGREDIENTS:
FOR THE DRESSING
⅓ cup avocado oil
2 tbsps. apple cider vinegar
½ tsp. dried oregano
2 tbsps. water
2 small fresh basil leaves, chopped
¼ to ½ tsp. sea salt
¼ tsp. ground black pepper
FOR ASSEMBLING
1 cup cooked lentils
1 cup cooked green lentil elbow pasta
¼ cup thinly sliced onion
½ cup unpeeled chopped cucumber
5 to 10 small basil leaves, for garnish (optional)

DIRECTIONS:
TO PREPARE THE DRESSING
1. Combine all of the dressing ingredients in a small bowl, whisk them together until everything is well combined. Adjust the seasonings to your preference.
TO ASSEMBLE
2. In a serving bowl, add the cooked lentils and pasta, gently toss them together so they are evenly distributed. Place the onions and cucumbers on the top, drizzle with the dressing, and garnish with the basil leaves (if using).
3. Transfer to 1 large or 2 small plates and serve.

VARIATIONS TIP:
Add some variety to this recipe by switching the elbow pasta to either 100-percent red or 100-percent green lentil rotini, penne, or mini fettuccine pasta.

Nutrition Info per Serving:
Calories: 566; Fats: 36.81 g; Carb: 44 g; Protein: 18.29 g; Fiber: 16.35g

Quick Frozen Banana and Protein Breakfast Bowl

Prep Time: 5 minutes, plus overnight to freeze, Cook Time: 0, Serves: 1

INGREDIENTS:
- 2 bananas
- 4 tbsps. pumpkin seed protein powder
- Chia seeds,
- unsweetened shredded coconut flakes or hemp seeds for topping (optional)

DIRECTIONS:
1. Peel and slice two bananas, place in a freezer-safe container, and freeze overnight.
2. Place the frozen bananas in a food processor, process until they become smooth and creamy with a soft-serve ice cream consistency.
3. Add the pumpkin protein powder to the processor, and process just long enough to mix it in completely.
4. Pour into a serving dish, place the chia seeds, coconut flakes or hemp seeds(if using), and serve.

VARIATIONS TIP:
Always keep frozen sliced bananas in your freezer so you can make this recipe at a moment's notice.

Nutrition Info per Serving:
Calories: 395; Fats: 16.88 g; Carb: 57.77 g; Protein: 12.47 g; Fiber: 8.4 g

Quinoa Eggplant and Tomato Bowl

Prep Time: 5 minutes, Cook Time: 10 minutes, Serves: 1

INGREDIENTS:
- 1 (14.5-ounce, 411 g) can tomatoes, whole, diced, or crushed, undrained
- 1 medium onion, diced
- 4 garlic cloves, minced
- ½ cup sliced zucchini
- ½ tsp. chopped fresh oregano
- ⅓ cup fresh chopped basil
- 2 tbsps. freshly squeezed lemon juice
- 1 cup cooked quinoa, warmed
- ½ cup eggplant, peeled, diced, cooked, and rewarmed

DIRECTIONS:
1. Drain 2 tablespoons of liquid from the tomatoes, then place it to a medium saucepan, add the onion and sauté over medium heat for 5 minutes, or until translucent.
2. Add the tomatoes with their remaining juices, garlic, zucchini, oregano and basil. Stir to combine. Simmer for 5 minutes. Remove from the heat and stir in the lemon juice.
3. Layer the quinoa and the eggplant in a single-serving bowl. Place the tomato mixture on the top.
4. Serve warm.

VARIATIONS TIP:
Make a double batch and combine the ingredients in a pot with 2 cups of vegetable broth to make a hearty Italian soup. Warm over medium heat and serve hot.

Nutrition Info per Serving:
Calories: 390; Total Fat: 5.4 g; Carbohydrates: 71.5 g; Protein: 14.5 g; Fiber: 10.8 g

Southern Collard Green and Okra Bowl

Prep Time: 10 minutes, Cook Time: 40 minutes, Serves: 1

INGREDIENTS:
- ¼ cup vegetable broth, divided
- ¼ sweet onion, chopped
- 1 garlic clove, finely chopped
- 4 ounces (113 g) canned diced tomatoes
- ½ tsp. sea salt, divided
- 1 cup collard greens
- 1 sliced okra, fresh or frozen
- 1 sweet potato, peeled and cut into bite-size pieces
- ¼ cup almond milk

DIRECTIONS:
1. Heat 2 tablespoons vegetable broth in a large saucepan over medium heat, Add the onion and sauté for 5 minutes, or until translucent.
2. Add the garlic, tomatoes, ¼ teaspoon salt, collard greens, the remaining 2 tablespoons broth and okra. Simmer for 30 to 35 minutes, or until tender.
3. While the greens cook, cook the sweet potato pieces in a medium pot of boiling water for 10 minutes, or until tender. Drain and transfer into a medium bowl. Add the remaining ¼ teaspoon salt and almond milk. Mash the sweet potatoes with an electric mixer.
4. Transfer the warm mashed sweet potato to a bowl. Place the collard greens and okra mixture on the top. Finish with any tomato sauce left in the pan.

VARIATIONS TIP:
If you're concerned that the okra will be slimy, use the frozen kind.

Nutrition Info per Serving:
Calories: 201; Total Fat: 2.7 g; Carbohydrates: 37.5 g; Protein: 9 g; Fiber: 7.3 g

Bell Pepper, Zucchini and Mushroom Bowl, page 146

Mashed Potato Bowl with Green Peas, page 151

Pineapple and Coconut Oatmeal Bowl with Pumpkin Seeds, page 150

Sautéed Broccoli Carrot Bowl, page 151

Chapter 11: Bowl 149

Healthy Spiced Mushroom Bowl

Prep Time: 5 minutes, Cook Time: 10 minutes, Serves: 2

INGREDIENTS:
½ tbsp. grapeseed oil
6 tsps. spice mix
1 medium onion, peeled, sliced
¾ cup vegetable broth, homemade
8 cherry tomatoes, chopped
¼ tsp. salt
6 tbsps. soft-jelly coconut milk
¼ tsp. cayenne pepper
¾ cup tomato sauce, alkaline
1 ½ cup sliced mushrooms

DIRECTIONS:
1. Heat the oil in a large skillet pan over medium heat, add the onion, and then cook for 5 minutes until golden brown.
2. Place the spice mix in the pan, then add all of the remaining ingredients except for the mushrooms, stir until mixed, and bring the mixture to a simmer.
3. Stir in the mushrooms, reduce the heat to medium-low, and cook for 10 to 15 minutes until cooked.
4. Serve immediately.

Nutrition Info per Serving:
Calories: 186; Fats: 3.4 g; Carb: 36.7 g; Protein: 2.1 g; Fiber: 3.5 g

Pineapple and Coconut Oatmeal Bowl with Pumpkin Seeds

Prep Time: 10 minutes, Cook Time: 5 minutes, Serves: 2

INGREDIENTS:
FOR THE OATMEAL
1 (13.5-ounce, 383 g) can full-fat coconut milk
1 cup quick rolled oats
2 tbsps. unrefined whole cane sugar, such as Sucanat
FOR ASSEMBLING
¼ cup unsweetened coconut flakes
½ cup cubed pineapple
1 tbsp. pumpkin seeds, chopped
1 tbsp. chia seeds

DIRECTIONS:
TO MAKE THE OATMEAL
1. Add the coconut milk, oats and sugar into a small saucepan, cook over medium-low heat for 3 to 5 minutes, or until the oats are soft; adjust the sugar to your preference.
TO ASSEMBLE
2. Transfer the oatmeal to 2 serving bowls, place the coconut flakes, cubed pineapple, and pumpkin and chia seeds on the top, and serve.

Nutrition Info per Serving:
Calories: 318; Fats: 8 g; Carb: 55.48 g; Protein: 7.93 g; Fiber: 7.35 g

Wild Rice and Broccoli Bowl with Roasted Garlic Cashew Sauce

Prep Time: 10 minutes, Cook Time: 20 minutes, Serves: 1

INGREDIENTS:
FOR THE ROASTED BROCCOLI AND GARLIC
6 garlic cloves, peeled
1 cup bite-size broccoli florets
1 tsp. avocado oil
Pinch garlic powder
Pinch sea salt
Pinch black pepper
FOR THE DRESSING
6 roasted garlic cloves (from above)
1 cup raw cashews
½ tsp. avocado oil
1 cup water
¼ tsp. garlic powder
½ tsp. apple cider vinegar
¼ to ½ tsp. sea salt
Pinch freshly ground black pepper
FOR ASSEMBLING
1 cup cooked wild rice
2 tbsps. diced onion
¼ cup slivered almonds
½ cup chopped collard greens

DIRECTIONS:
1. Preheat the oven to 400°F(205°C). Use parchment paper to line a baking sheet.
TO PREPARE THE ROASTED BROCCOLI AND GARLIC
2. Add the garlic and broccoli into a small bowl, toss with the avocado oil to coat. Season with the garlic powder, salt and pepper, and transfer to the prepared baking sheet.
3. Roast the broccoli and garlic for 15 to 20 minutes, or until the broccoli gets soft and slightly crispy.
TO PREPARE THE DRESSING
4. Combine all of the dressing ingredients in a high-speed blender, blend them together until creamy and smooth. Adjust the seasonings, if needed.
TO ASSEMBLE
5. Stir together the cooked rice with the roasted broccoli, onion, almond slivers, and collard greens in a serving bowl. Stir in the dressing and serve.

VARIATIONS TIP:
Substitute the collard greens with chopped kale or your favorite alkaline leafy green.

Nutrition Info per Serving:
Calories: 677; Fats: 21.06 g; Carb: 110.52 g; Protein: 21.69 g; Fiber: 13.1 g

Sautéed Broccoli Carrot Bowl

Prep Time: 15 minutes, Cook Time: 10 minutes, Serves: 1

INGREDIENTS:
- 2 garlic cloves, finely minced
- 1 carrot, peeled and sliced
- ½ cup bite-size broccoli florets
- 2 cups vegetable broth

DIRECTIONS:
1. Add the garlic, carrot, broccoli and broth into a medium saucepan, cook over medium heat for 10 minutes, or until the vegetables reach a desired level of tenderness.
2. Pour into a bowl, and serve warm.

VARIATIONS TIP:
Add other vegetables to boost the healing properties. If you're going to use spinach, though, add it no more than 5 minutes before serving.

Nutrition Info per Serving:
Calories: 126; Total Fat: 2.9 g; Carbohydrates: 12.8 g; Protein: 11.8 g; Fiber: 2.8 g

Shredded Squash Tomato Bowl

Prep Time: 15 minutes, Cook Time: 2 minutes, Serves: 2

INGREDIENTS:
- 2 cups cooked, shredded spaghetti squash
- 1 cup chopped fresh tomatoes
- 1 cup sun-dried tomato sauce

DIRECTIONS:
1. In a bowl big enough for two people, layer the spaghetti squash and tomatoes. Pour the sun-dried tomato sauce over the top.
2. Warm the bowl in the microwave for 2 minutes on high, or until heated through.
3. Use two forks to serve.

VARIATIONS TIP:
Feel free to layer in any additional vegetables that you like. Mushrooms, spinach, or even broccoli would be good.

Nutrition Info per Serving:
Calories: 153; Total Fat: 4.1 g; Carbohydrates: 27.1 g; Protein: 3.5 g; Fiber: 4.2 g

Red Quinoa Cherry Bowl

Prep Time: 10 minutes, Cook Time: 2 minutes, Serves: 1

INGREDIENTS:
- 1 cup cooked red quinoa
- ½ cup roasted, diced red peppers
- ½ cup dark red cherries, pitted and sliced
- ½ cup coconut milk
- ¾ tsp. red curry paste

DIRECTIONS:
1. Layer the quinoa, red peppers, and cherries in a single-serving bowl.
2. Add the coconut milk and curry paste into a blender, mix them together. Pour over the layered quinoa, peppers, and cherries with the liquid.
3. Microwave on high for about 2 minutes, or until warm.

VARIATIONS TIP:
If you can't find red quinoa, regular quinoa will work just as well.

Nutrition Info per Serving:
Calories: 401; Total Fat: 1.8 g; Carbohydrates: 64.5 g; Protein: 16.7 g; Fiber: 6.7 g

Mashed Potato Bowl with Green Peas

Prep Time: 15 minutes, Cook Time: 1 minute, Serves: 1

INGREDIENTS:
- 2 tbsps. almond milk
- 1 cup cooked baby potatoes
- ½ tsp. sea salt
- ½ cup green peas
- ½ cup great gravy

DIRECTIONS:
1. Combine the almond milk, potatoes and salt in a medium bowl. Use a fork to mash to the desired consistency.
2. Place the peas and the gravy on the top of the potatoes. Warm the bowl in the microwave on high for 1 minute, and eat.

VARIATIONS TIP:
Depending on whether you like peas, you may not find them comforting. If not, then substitute an alkaline-friendly vegetable that does comfort you, like maybe spinach or lima beans.

Nutrition Info per Serving:
Calories: 205; Total Fat: 2.4 g; Carbohydrates: 41.3 g; Protein: 8.1 g; Fiber: 7.3 g

Berry Smoothie Bowl with Mango

Prep Time: 5 minutes, Cook Time: 0, Serves: 2

INGREDIENTS:
- 1 burro banana, peeled
- 1 ½ cup mixed berries
- 1 tbsp. walnut butter, homemade
- 2 tbsps. walnut milk, homemade
- 1 mango, peeled, destoned, chopped

Extra:
- 2 tbsps. agave syrup

DIRECTIONS:
1. Plug in a high-speed food processor or blender, add the berries and burro banana, then pulse at low speed until small pieces of fruits remain in the jar.
2. Combine the butter, milk, and agave syrup in the jar, pulse until combined, and then evenly pour the mixture into two bowls.
3. Place the mango slices and some more berries(if using) on the top, and serve immediately.

Nutrition Info per Serving:
Calories: 338; Fats: 9.6 g; Carb: 64.3 g; Protein: 8.6 g; Fiber: 12.1 g

Hearty Tomato Quinoa Bowl

Prep Time: 5 minutes, Cook Time: 3 minutes, Serves: 2

INGREDIENTS:
- 1 tbsp. grapeseed oil
- ½ of green bell pepper, chopped
- ¼ cup cherry tomatoes, quartered
- ⅓ cup quinoa, cooked
- ⅓ cup basil leaves
- ⅛ tsp. cayenne pepper
- ¼ tsp. salt

DIRECTIONS:
1. Heat the oil in a pan over medium heat, when hot, add the bell pepper and cherry tomatoes, cook for 2 to 3 minutes until tender-crisp.
2. Place the cooked quinoa in a medium bowl, add the bell pepper and tomatoes mixture, then add the basil leaves.
3. Season with the cayenne pepper and salt, stir until mixed, and serve.

Nutrition Info per Serving:
Calories: 141; Fats: 6.2 g; Carb: 32 g; Protein: 6.5 g; Fiber: 4.1 g

Super Kale Quinoa Bowl

Prep Time: 10 minutes, Cook Time: 0, Serves: 1

INGREDIENTS:
- 1 cup kale, raw, steamed, or sautéed
- 1 cup cooked quinoa
- 1 tbsp. coconut oil
- ¼ cup açaí berries
- 1 tbsp. apple cider vinegar
- ¼ tsp. sea salt
- ¼ tsp. mustard powder
- Dash onion powder
- Dash garlic powder

DIRECTIONS:
1. Layer the kale and quinoa in a single-serving bowl.
2. Combine the remaining ingredients in a blender, blend until the ingredients emulsify.
3. Pour the dressing over the kale-quinoa mixture. Toss well and serve.

VARIATIONS TIP:
Remember that the stems are the part of the kale that is bitter. If you really hate kale, you can substitute spinach.

Nutrition Info per Serving:
Calories: 424; Total Fat: 18.7 g; Carbohydrates: 52.3 g; Protein: 11.6 g; Fiber: 5.1 g

The Hollywood Fruit Bowl

Prep Time: 5 minutes, Cook Time: 0, Serves: 1

INGREDIENTS:
- 1 star fruit
- ¼ watermelon, cut into slices
- ¼ cup coconut whipped cream

DIRECTIONS:
1. Slice the star fruit into star-shaped pieces.
2. In order to create star-shaped pieces, press the cookie cutter into the watermelon slices.
3. In a single-serving bowl, add the star fruit and watermelon pieces. Pour the coconut whipped cream on the top.
4. Serve immediately.

VARIATIONS TIP:
Even if you don't cut the watermelon into star shapes, this is a delicious bowl. After all, Hollywood stars make their own rules!

Nutrition Info per Serving:
Calories: 125; Total Fat: 9.6 g; Carbohydrates: 9.3 g; Protein: 1.8 g; Fiber: 2.7 g

Apple Potato Rice Bowl

Prep Time: 10 minutes, Cook Time: 2 minutes, Serves: 1

INGREDIENTS:
1 cup cooked brown rice
¼ cup cooked wild rice
1 apple, peeled, cored, and diced
½ cup mashed sweet potato
¼ cup great gravy

DIRECTIONS:
1. Layer the brown rice, wild rice, apple, sweet potato, and gravy in a medium bowl.
2. Microwave the bowl on high for about 2 minutes, or until warm. Serve.

VARIATIONS TIP:
Add some green beans or mushrooms, for extra nutrition and flavor. Maybe both!

Nutrition Info per Serving:
Calories: 579; Total Fat: 3.1 g; Carbohydrates: 45.7 g; Protein: 8.9 g; Fiber: 3.6 g

Mexican Style Black Bean Avocado Bowl

Prep Time: 10 minutes, Cook Time: 2 minutes, Serves: 1

INGREDIENTS:
1 tsp. ground cumin
1 cup sprouted black beans
1 medium sweet potato, cooked and diced
½ avocado, diced
½ cup chopped cilantro
3 tbsps. salsa fresca
Pinch sea salt

DIRECTIONS:
1. Combine the cumin and beans in a small bowl.
2. Layer the sweet potatoes in a medium microwaveable bowl, and top with the beans. Warm the vegetables in the microwave on high for 2 minutes, or until heated through.
3. Take out from the microwave and layer on the avocado and cilantro, and place the salsa fresca on the top.
4. Season with the salt and serve immediately.

VARIATIONS TIP:
To make this thyroid friendly, omit the salsa.

Nutrition Info per Serving:
Calories: 436; Total Fat: 11.4 g; Carbohydrates: 69.5 g; Protein: 17.8 g; Fiber: 17.4 g

Chapter 12: Drinks

Avocado and Apple Juice Mix

Prep Time: 5 minutes, Cook Time: 0, Serves: 2

INGREDIENTS:
½ of avocado, peeled, pitted, diced
1 apple, peeled, cored, diced
2 cups kale leaves
1 ½ cups apple juice

DIRECTIONS:
1. Plug in a high-speed food processor or blender, and add the avocado, apple, kale leaves and apple juice in its jar.
2. Use its lid to cover the blender jar and then pulse for 40 to 60 seconds until smooth.
3. After pulsing, pour the drink into two glasses and serve immediately.

Nutrition Info per Serving:
Calories: 152; Fats: 8.2 g; Carb: 16.7 g; Protein: 2.7 g; Fiber: 7.7 g

Berry Mix Sea Moss Milk

Prep Time: 5 minutes, Cook Time: 0, Serves: 2

INGREDIENTS:
½ mason jar sea moss gel
1 cup berry mix
½ cup hemp milk (optional)

DIRECTIONS:
1. Take out a jar of prepared sea moss gel.
2. Plug in a high-speed food processor or blender, place all of the ingredients in the jar.
3. Use its lid to cover the blender jar and then pulse for 40 to 60 seconds until smooth.
4. Pour the drink into two glasses and serve immediately.

Nutrition Info per Serving:
Calories: 93; Fats: 2.76 g; Carb: 12.97 g; Protein: 4.36 g; Fiber: 1.3 g

Avocado, Raspberry and Dates Moss Drink

Prep Time: 5 minutes, Cook Time: 0, Serves: 2

INGREDIENTS:
1 mason jar sea moss gel
1 avocado, pitted and peeled
½ cup raspberries
Handful dates
½ cup walnut milk, homemade

DIRECTIONS:
1. Take out a jar of prepared sea moss gel.
2. Plug in a high-speed food processor or blender, place all of the ingredients in its jar.
3. Use its lid to cover the blender jar and then pulse for 40 to 60 seconds until smooth.
4. Pour the drink into two glasses and serve immediately.

Nutrition Info per Serving:
Calories: 29.5; Total Fat: 2.71 g; Carbohydrates: 1.33 g; Protein: 0.42 g; Fiber: 0.55 g

Breakfast Tamarind, Arugula and Cucumber Drink

Prep Time: 5 minutes, Cook Time: 0, Serves: 2

INGREDIENTS:
1 cucumber, deseeded
2 ounces (57 g) arugula
2 cups Dr. Sebi's herbal tea
1 tbsp. tamarind pulp
1 key lime, juiced
Extra:
⅛ tsp. cayenne pepper
¼ tsp. salt

DIRECTIONS:
1. Plug in a high-speed food processor or blender, then place all of the ingredients in its jar.
2. Use its lid to cover the blender jar and then pulse for 40 to 60 seconds until smooth.
3. After pulsing, evenly pour the drink into two glasses and serve immediately.

Nutrition Info per Serving:
Calories: 110; Fats: 0.5 g; Carb: 30.5 g; Protein: 2 g; Fiber: 6.5 g

Dandelion Liver Cleansing Tea

Prep Time: 5 minutes, Cook Time: 10 minutes, Serves: 1

INGREDIENTS:

1 tsp. Prodigiosa powder
1 tsp. dandelion root powder
1 cup spring water

DIRECTIONS:
1. Place the Prodigiosa powder and dandelion root powder in a tea kettle, pour in the water.
2. Allow to boil for 10 minutes, remove from the heat, cover and leave for another 10 minutes.
3. Drain and serve.

Nutrition Info per Serving:
Calories: 1; Fats: 0.02 g; Carb: 0.28 g; Protein: 0.08 g; Fiber: 0.1 g

Gallbladder Rhubarb Cleansing Tea

Prep Time: 5 minutes, Cook Time: 10 minutes, Serves: 1

INGREDIENTS:

1 tsp. rhubarb root powder
1 tsp. cascara powder
1 cup spring water

DIRECTIONS:
1. Place the rhubarb root powder and cascara powder in a tea kettle, pour in the water.
2. Allow to boil for 10 minutes, remove from the heat, cover and leave for 10 minutes.
3. Drain and serve.

Nutrition Info per Serving:
Calories: 85; Fats: 0.12 g; Carb: 19.82 g; Protein: 2.99 g; Fiber: 5.6 g

Dandelion and Bromide Plus Cleansing Drink

Prep Time: 5 minutes, Cook Time: 10 minutes, Serves: 1

INGREDIENTS:

1 tsp. dandelion root powder
1 tsp. bromide plus powder
1 cup spring water

DIRECTIONS:
1. Add the dandelion root powder and bromide into a tea kettle, pour in the water.
2. Allow to boil for 10 minutes, remove from the heat, cover and leave for 10 minutes.
3. Drain and serve.

Nutrition Info per Serving:
Calories: 17; Fats: 0.8 g; Carb: 1.99 g; Protein: 0.42 g; Fiber: 0.1 g

Date and Banana Moss Drink

Prep Time: 5 minutes, Cook Time: 0, Serves: 2

INGREDIENTS:

1 mason jar sea moss gel
1 cup dates
1 burro banana, peeled
½ cup hemp milk, homemade

DIRECTIONS:
1. Take out a jar of prepared sea moss gel.
2. Plug in a high-speed food processor or blender, and add the dates, banana and milk into its jar.
3. Use its lid to cover the blender jar and then pulse for 40 to 60 seconds until smooth.
4. Pour the drink into two glasses and then serve.

Nutrition Info per Serving:
Calories: 306; Fats: 1.8 g; Carb: 74.93 g; Protein: 5.41 g; Fiber: 7.75 g

Healthy Walnut Milk

Prep Time: 10 minutes, Cook Time: 0 (soak minimum 8 hours), Serves: 4

INGREDIENTS:

1 cup of raw walnuts
3 cups of spring water + extra for soaking
⅛ tsp. pure sea salt

DIRECTIONS:
1. In a small pot, add the raw walnuts, pour in the water to cover by three inches.
2. Soak the walnuts for at least 8 hours.
3. Drain and use the cold water to rinse the walnuts.
4. In a blender, add the soaked walnuts, pure sea salt, and three cups of spring water.
5. Blend until smooth.
6. Strain it if you need to and enjoy.

Nutrition Info per Serving:
Calories: 131; Fats: 13.04 g; Carb: 2.76 g; Protein: 3.05 g; Fiber: 1.35 g

Linden Immune Boosting Tea

Prep Time: 5 minutes, Cook Time: 10 minutes, Serves: 1

INGREDIENTS:
1 tsp. linden powder
1 cup spring water

DIRECTIONS:
1. Place the linden powder in a tea kettle, pour in the water.
2. Allow to boil for 5 minutes, remove from the heat, cover and leave for 10 minutes.
3. Drain and serve.

Nutrition Info per Serving:
Calories: 0; Fats: 0; Carb: 0.01 g; Protein: 0; Fiber: 0

Key Lime Dill Tea

Prep Time: 5 minutes, Cook Time: 10 minutes, Serves: 2

INGREDIENTS:
1 sprig of dill weed
2 cups spring water
1 tbsp. key lime juice
1/16 tsp. cayenne pepper

DIRECTIONS:
1. Place a medium saucepan over medium-high heat, fill in the water, and bring it to a boil.
2. Boil for 5 minutes, then strain the dill weed tea into a bowl.
3. Stir in the lime juice until mixed, then add the cayenne pepper and stir well.
4. Pour the tea into two mugs and serve immediately.

Nutrition Info per Serving:
Calories: 2.4; Fats: 0 g; Carb: 0.5 g; Protein: 0 g; Fiber: 0.5 g

Liver-Kidney Dandelion Cleansing Tea

Prep Time: 5 minutes, Cook Time: 10 minutes, Serves: 1

INGREDIENTS:
1 tsp. burdock root powder
1 tsp. dandelion root powder
1 cup spring water

DIRECTIONS:
1. Add the burdock root powder and dandelion root powder into a tea kettle, pour in the water.
2. Allow to boil for 10 minutes, remove from the heat, cover and leave for another 10 minutes.
3. Drain and serve.

Nutrition Info per Serving:
Calories: 112; Fats: 0.23 g; Carb: 27.07 g; Protein: 2.39 g; Fiber: 5.1 g

Sweet Hempseed Milk

Prep Time: 10 minutes, Cook Time: 0, Serves: 2

INGREDIENTS:
2 tbsps. of agave syrup
2 tbsps. of hemp seeds
1/8 tsp. of pure sea salt
2 cups of spring water
1 cup blueberries (optional)

DIRECTIONS:
1. In the blender, add all of the ingredients except the fruits.
2. Blend them for 2 minutes.
3. Add the berries and blend for 30 to 50 seconds again.
4. Place the milk in a refrigerator and chill until cold.
5. Enjoy.

Nutrition Info per Serving:
Calories: 199; Fats: 4.59 g; Carb: 40.72 g; Protein: 2.3 g; Fiber: 2 g

Strawberry Sea Moss Drink

Prep Time: 5 minutes, Cook Time: 0, Serves: 2

INGREDIENTS:
1 mason jar sea moss gel
½ cup strawberries
½ cup hemp milk, homemade
1 tbsp. date sugar

DIRECTIONS:
1. Take out a jar of prepared sea moss gel.
2. Plug in a high-speed food processor or blender, place all of the ingredients in the jar.
3. Use its lid to cover the blender jar and then pulse for 40 to 60 seconds until smooth.
4. After pulsing, pour the drink into two glasses and serve immediately.

Nutrition Info per Serving:
Calories: 73; Fats: 1.42 g; Carb: 13.06 g; Protein: 3.2 g; Fiber: 1.05 g

Chapter 12: Drinks

Fragrant Chamomile Tea

Prep Time: 5 minutes, Cook Time: 10 minutes, Serves: 1

INGREDIENTS:

Handful chamomile flowers

1 cup spring water

DIRECTIONS:

1. Add the flowers into a tea kettle, pour in the water.
2. Allow to boil for 5 minutes, then remove from the heat, cover and leave for 10 minutes.
3. Drain and serve.

Nutrition Info per Serving:
Calories: 1; Fats: 0; Carb: 0.2 g; Protein: 0.04 g; Fiber: 0

Gallbladder Cleansing Tea

Prep Time: 5 minutes, Cook Time: 10 minutes, Serves: 1

INGREDIENTS:

1 tsp. Cahparral
1 tsp. Cascara powder

1 cup spring water

DIRECTIONS:

1. Place the Cahparral and Cascara powder in a tea kettle, pour in the water.
2. Allow to boil for 10 minutes, remove from the heat, cover and leave for 10 minutes. 3. Drain and serve.

Nutrition Info per Serving:
Calories: 0; Fats: 0; Carb: 0.02 g; Protein: 0; Fiber: 0

Orange and Banana Bromide Drink

Prep Time: 5 minutes, Cook Time: 0, Serves: 2

INGREDIENTS:

3 oranges, peeled
½ of a burro banana, peeled
½ tsp. bromide plus

Powder
1 ½ tbsps. date sugar
1 cup of soft-jelly coconut water

DIRECTIONS:

1. Plug in a high-speed food processor or blender, and combine the oranges, banana, bromide, sugar and coconut water in its jar.
2. Use its lid to cover the blender jar and then pulse for 40 to 60 seconds until smooth.
3. After pulsing, pour the drink into two glasses and serve immediately.

Nutrition Info per Serving:
Calories: 138.5; Fats: 0.6 g; Carb: 35.1 g; Protein: 1.5 g; Fiber: 4.7 g;

Fruity Banana Sea Moss Milk

Prep Time: 5 minutes, Cook Time: 0, Serves: 2

INGREDIENTS:

1 mason jar sea moss gel
⅓ pack dried fruit of choice

1 burro banana, peeled
½ cup walnut milk, homemade

DIRECTIONS:

1. Take out a jar of prepared sea moss gel.
2. Plug in a high-speed food processor or blender, combine all of the ingredients in its jar.
3. Use its lid to cover the blender jar and then pulse for 40 to 60 seconds until smooth.
4. After pulsing, pour the drink into two glasses and serve immediately.

Nutrition Info per Serving:
Calories: 153; Fats: 1.52 g; Carb: 33.83 g; Protein: 4.16 g; Fiber: 3.05 g

Mango Banana Sea Moss Drink

Prep Time: 5 minutes, Cook Time: 0, Serves: 2

INGREDIENTS:

1 mason jar sea moss gel
½ mango, peeled
1 burro banana, peeled

½ cup hemp milk, homemade
1 tbsp. green coconut water

DIRECTIONS:

1. Take out a jar of prepared sea moss gel.
2. Plug in a high-speed food processor or blender, combine all of the ingredients in its jar.
3. Use its lid to cover the blender jar and then pulse for 40 to 60 seconds until smooth.
4. Pour the drink into two glasses and serve immediately.

Nutrition Info per Serving:
Calories: 125; Fats: 1.68 g; Carb: 26.24 g; Protein: 4 g; Fiber: 2.6 g

Banana Herbal Drink, page 161

Chamomile and Bromide Plus Revitalizing Tea, page 161

Liver-Kidney Dandelion Cleansing Tea, page 157

Prodigiosa Kidney Cleansing Tea, page 160

Respiratory and Elderberry Syrup

Prep Time: 5 minutes, Cook Time: 5 minutes, Serves: 1

INGREDIENTS:
1 tsp. elderberry fruit
1 cup spring water

DIRECTIONS:
1. Place the fruit in a tea kettle, pour in the water.
2. Allow to boil for 5 minutes, remove from the heat, cover and let leave for 10 minutes.
3. Drain and serve.

Nutrition Info per Serving:
Calories: 2; Fats: 0.02 g; Carb: 0.55 g; Protein: 0.02 g; Fiber: 0.2 g

Prodigiosa Kidney Cleansing Tea

Prep Time: 5 minutes, Cook Time: 10 minutes, Serves: 1

INGREDIENTS:
1 tsp. burdock root powder
1 tsp. prodigiosa powder
1 cup spring water

DIRECTIONS:
1. Add the burdock root powder and prodigiosa powder in a tea kettle, pour in the water.
2. Boil for 10 minutes, remove from the heat, cover and allow to leave for another 10 minutes.
3. Drain and serve.

Nutrition Info per Serving:
Calories: 112; Fats: 0.23 g; Carb: 27.06 g; Protein: 2.39 g; Fiber: 5.1 g

Peach and Raspberry Moss Drink

Prep Time: 5 minutes, Cook Time: 0, Serves: 2

INGREDIENTS:
1 mason jar sea moss gel
1 peach, peeled
1 burro banana, peeled
½ cup raspberries
½ cup hemp milk, homemade
1 tbsp. date sugar

DIRECTIONS:
1. Take out a jar of prepared sea moss gel.
2. Plug in a high-speed food processor or blender and add the peach, banana, raspberries, milk and sugar into its jar.
3. Use its lid to cover the blender jar and then pulse for 40 to 60 seconds until smooth.
4. Pour the drink into two glasses and then serve.

Nutrition Info per Serving:
Calories: 159; Fats: 1.9 g; Carb: 34.6 g; Protein: 4.66 g; Fiber: 5 g

Respiratory Mullein and Guaco Cleansing Tea

Prep Time: 5 minutes, Cook Time: 10 minutes, Serves: 1

INGREDIENTS:
1 tsp. guaco herb
1 tsp. mullein
1 cup spring water

DIRECTIONS:
1. Place the guaco herb and mullein in a tea kettle, pour in the water.
2. Allow to boil for 10 minutes, remove from the heat, cover and let leave for 10 minutes.
3. Drain and serve.

Nutrition Info per Serving:
Calories: 0; Fats: 0.01 g; Carb: 0.01 g; Protein: 0; Fiber: 0

Irish Sea Moss Gel

Prep Time: 5 minutes, Cook Time: 0, Serves: 2

INGREDIENTS:
1 pack organic Irish sea moss
½ cup spring water

DIRECTIONS:
1. Take out a pack of sea moss, cut into chunks.
2. Wash and place in a bowl, pour in the spring water, and allow to soak for 6 hours.
3. Drain from the water.
4. Plug in a high-speed food processor or blender, add the drained sea moss and water in its jar.
5. Use its lid to cover the blender jar and then pulse for 40 to 60 seconds until smooth.
6. Pour the gel into mason jars and store in the refrigerator, or serve immediately.

Nutrition Info per Serving:
Calories: 15; Fats: 0.11 g; Carb: 3.37 g; Protein: 0.95 g; Fiber: 0.3 g

Banana Herbal Drink

Prep Time: 5 minutes, Cook Time: 0, Serves: 2

INGREDIENTS:
1 cup herbal tea
2 burro bananas, peeled
1 tbsp. agave syrup

DIRECTIONS:
1. Plug in a high-speed food processor or blender, and place the herbal tea, bananas and syrup in its jar.
2. Use its lid to cover the blender jar and then pulse for 40 to 60 seconds until smooth.
3. After pulsing, pour the drink into two glasses and serve immediately.

Nutrition Info per Serving:
Calories: 177; Fats: 1 g; Carb: 40 g; Protein: 2 g; Fiber: 4 g

Banana Sea Moss Green Drink

Prep Time: 5 minutes, Cook Time: 0, Serves: 2

INGREDIENTS:
4 tbsps. of sea moss gel
2 burro banana, peeled
4 cups mixed greens

DIRECTIONS:
1. Plug in a high-speed food processor or blender, add the gel, banana and greens in its jar.
2. Use its lid to cover the blender jar and then pulse for 40 to 60 seconds until smooth.
3. After pulsing, pour the drink into two glasses, and serve immediately.

Nutrition Info per Serving:
Calories: 120; Fats: 0.1 g; Carb: 26 g; Protein: 3.4 g; Fiber: 3.4 g

Sweet Dates Green Drink

Prep Time: 5 minutes, Cook Time: 0, Serves: 2

INGREDIENTS:
1 cucumber, peeled, deseeded
1 key lime, peeled
1 cup greens
2 dates, pitted
Extra:
2 cups of soft-jelly coconut water

DIRECTIONS:
1. Plug in a high-speed food processor or blender, then place all of the ingredients in its jar.
2. Use its lid to cover the blender jar and then pulse for 40 to 60 seconds until smooth.
3. After pulsing, pour the drink into two glasses and serve immediately.

Nutrition Info per Serving:
Calories: 112; Fats: 0.1 g; Carb: 27 g; Protein: 0.3 g; Fiber: 5 g

Chamomile and Bromide Plus Revitalizing Tea

Prep Time: 5 minutes, Cook Time: 5 minutes, Serves: 1

INGREDIENTS:
Handful chamomile flowers
1 cup spring water
1 tsp. bromide plus powder

DIRECTIONS:
1. In a kettle, add the flowers and water.
2. Allow to boil for 5 minutes, then remove from the heat, cover and leave for 10 minutes.
3. Drain and add the bromide powder.
4. Serve.

Nutrition Info per Serving:
Calories: 1; Fats: 0; Carb: 0.21 g; Protein: 0.04 g; Fiber: 0

Watermelon Lime Refresher

Prep Time: 5 minutes, Cook Time: 0, Serves: 2

INGREDIENTS:
1 watermelon, peeled, deseeded, cubed
½ of key lime, juiced, zest
1 tbsp. date sugar
2 cups soft-jelly coconut water

DIRECTIONS:
1. In a high-speed food processor or blender, add the watermelon pieces, and then add the lime zest and juice, the date sugar, pulse them until smooth.
2. Fill the watermelon mixture into two tall glasses until two-thirds full, then pour in the coconut water.
3. Stir well and serve immediately.

Nutrition Info per Serving:
Calories: 55; Fats: 1.3 g; Carb: 9.9 g; Protein: 0.9 g; Fiber: 7 g

Date Sea Moss Drink

Prep Time: 5 minutes, Cook Time: 0, Serves: 2

INGREDIENTS:

- 1 mason jar sea moss gel
- 1 tbsp. date sugar
- ½ cup spring water

DIRECTIONS:

1. Take out a jar of prepared sea moss gel.
2. Plug in a high-speed food processor or blender, place all of the ingredients in the jar.
3. Use its lid to cover the blender jar and then pulse for 40 to 60 seconds until smooth.
4. Pour the drink into two glasses and serve immediately.

Nutrition Info per Serving:
Calories: 31; Fats: 0.1 g; Carb: 7.37 g; Protein: 0.95 g; Fiber: 0.3 g

Easy Almond and Coconut Milks

Prep Time: 10 minutes, Cook Time: 0, Serves: ½ cup

INGREDIENTS:

FOR THE ALMOND MILK
- 1 cup raw almonds
- 4 cups water

FOR THE COCONUT MILK
- 2 cups unsweetened large coconut flakes
- 3 cups hot (not boiling) water

DIRECTIONS:

FOR THE ALMOND MILK
1. Combine the almonds and water in a high-speed blender, blend for 2 to 3 minutes.
2. Set a nut-milk bag over a medium bowl, pour in the almond mixture to strain. Squeeze or wring out any remaining milk with your hands.
3. Place the milk in an airtight container and store in the refrigerator.

FOR THE COCONUT MILK
4. Add the coconut flakes and hot water in a blender, blend for 2 to 3 minutes.

TO MIX THE MILK
5. Set a nut-milk bag over a medium bowl, pour in the coconut mixture to strain. Squeeze or wring out any remaining milk with your hands (depending on how hot the water is, you may have to let it cool before touching the nut-milk bag).
6. Place the milk in an airtight container and store in the refrigerator.

VARIATIONS TIP:
The milks will separate some in the refrigerator, but just give them a quick stir before using.

Nutrition Info per Serving:
Calories: 782; Fats: 48.18 g; Carb: 88.4 g; Protein: 5.57 g; Fiber: 17 g

Kale Apple Green Sea Moss Drink

Prep Time: 5 minutes, Cook Time: 0, Serves: 2

INGREDIENTS:

- 2 cups kale
- 1 cup cucumber chunks
- 1 apple, cored, diced
- 2 cups of coconut water

Extra:
- 1 tbsp. of sea moss gel
- 1 key lime, juiced

DIRECTIONS:

1. Plug in a high-speed food processor or blender, and then combine all of the ingredients in its jar.
2. Use its lid to cover the blender jar and then pulse for 40 to 60 seconds until smooth.
3. After pulsing, pour the drink into two glasses and serve immediately.

Nutrition Info per Serving:
Calories: 156; Fats: 1.8 g; Carb: 32.8 g; Protein: 9.4 g; Fiber: 10.2 g

Watermelon, Strawberries and Coconut Drink

Prep Time: 5 minutes, Cook Time: 0, Serves: 2

INGREDIENTS:

- 1 cup watermelon, chunks
- 1 cup strawberries
- 1 cup soft jelly coconut water
- 1 tsp date sugar

DIRECTIONS:

1. Plug in a high-speed food processor or blender, then place the watermelon, strawberries, coconut water and sugar in its jar.
2. Use its lid to cover the blender jar and then pulse for 40 to 60 seconds until smooth.
3. After pulsing, pour the drink into two glasses and serve immediately.

Nutrition Info per Serving:
Calories: 110; Fats: 0 g; Carb: 28 g; Protein: 0 g; Fiber: 6 g

Raspberry Sea Moss Coconut Drink

Prep Time: 5 minutes, Cook Time: 0, Serves: 2

INGREDIENTS:
- 1 mason jar sea moss gel
- ½ cup raspberries
- ½ cup green coconut
- water
- 1 tbsp. date sugar (optional)

DIRECTIONS:
1. Take out a jar of prepared sea moss gel.
2. Plug in a high-speed food processor or blender, place all of the ingredients in the jar.
3. Use its lid to cover the blender jar and then pulse for 40 to 60 seconds until smooth.
4. Pour the drink into two glasses and serve immediately.

Nutrition Info per Serving:
Calories: 85; Fats: 0.2 g; Carb: 21.17 g; Protein: 0.97 g; Fiber: 2.75 g

Creamy Strawberry and Date Jar

Prep Time: 5 minutes, Cook Time: 0, Serves: 2

INGREDIENTS:
- ½ mason jar sea moss gel
- 1 cup strawberries
- 1 burro banana, peeled
- 1 tbsp. date sugar
- 1 cup hemp milk, homemade

DIRECTIONS:
1. Take out a jar of prepared sea moss gel.
2. Plug in a high-speed food processor or blender, and place all of the ingredients in its jar.
3. Use its lid to cover the blender jar and then pulse for 40 to 60 seconds until smooth.
4. Pour the drink into two glasses and serve immediately.

Nutrition Info per Serving:
Calories: 160; Fats: 2.88g; Carb: 30.54 g; Protein: 5.63 g; Fiber: 3.15 g

Homemade Aquafaba

Prep Time: 10 minutes, Cook Time: 2 hours 30 minutes, Serves: 2-4

INGREDIENTS:
- 1 bag of garbanzo beans
- 1 tsp. of pure sea salt
- 6 cups of spring water + extra for soaking

DIRECTIONS:
1. In a large pot, add the garbanzo beans and pure sea salt, pour in the spring water. Bring to a rolling boil.
2. Remove from the heat and allow to soak for 30 to 40 minutes.
3. Strain the garbanzo beans and add 6 cups of spring water.
4. Boil for 1 hour and 30 minutes over medium heat.
5. Strain the garbanzo beans. This strained water is aquafaba.
6. Pour the aquafaba into a glass jar with a lid, place into the refrigerator to cool.
7. After cooling, the aquafaba becomes thicker. Repeatedly boil for 10-20 minutes if it is too liquid.

Nutrition Info per Serving:
Calories: 55; Fats: 0.87 g; Carb: 9.17 g; Protein: 2.95 g; Fiber: 1.8 g

Vanilla Pumpkin Banana Drink

Prep Time: 15 minutes, Cook Time: 0, Serves: 1

INGREDIENTS:
- 1 banana, frozen
- ½ cup pumpkin purée
- 1 vanilla bean, split lengthwise and seeds scraped out
- 1 cup unsweetened coconut milk
- ⅛ tsp. nutmeg
- ⅛ tsp. allspice
- ¼ tsp. cinnamon
- ½ cup ice cubes

DIRECTIONS:
1. Combine all of the ingredients in a blender.
2. Process until smooth.
3. Pour in a tall glass and serve immediately.

VARIATIONS TIP:
Make sure you use pumpkin purée (pure pumpkin) and not "pumpkin pie filling." The pie filling is filled with sugar and dairy.

Nutrition Info per Serving:
Calories: 240; Total Fat: 5.5 g; Carbohydrates: 47.6 g; Protein: 3.6 g; Fiber: 7.6 g

Chapter 13: Sauce and Dressing

Enchilada Sauce

Prep Time: 15 minutes, Cook Time: 26 minutes, Serves: 8

INGREDIENTS:
- 2 tbsps. coconut oil
- 2 tbsps. chili powder
- 2 tbsps. coconut flour
- 1 (8-ounce, 227 g) can tomato paste
- 2 cups water
- ½ tsp. cumin
- ½ tsp. onion powder
- 1 tsp. garlic powder
- ½ tsp. sea salt
- ¼ tsp. red pepper flakes

DIRECTIONS:
1. Heat the coconut oil, chili powder and coconut flour in a medium pot over medium heat. Cook for 1 minute so the flour doesn't taste raw.
2. Stir in the tomato paste, water, cumin, onion powder, garlic powder, salt, and red pepper flakes. Bring the mixture to a simmer and cook for 25 minutes, stirring occasionally.
3. Serve warm.

VARIATIONS TIP:
Add a tablespoon of Dutch-processed cocoa powder before cooking to add a depth of flavor reminiscent of a mole sauce.

Nutrition Info per Serving:
Calories: 68; Total Fat: 3.6 g; Carbohydrates: 8.3 g; Protein: 1.8 g; Fiber: 1.6 g

Coconut White Sauce

Prep Time: 15 minutes, Cook Time: 10 minutes, Serves: 6

INGREDIENTS:
- 1 tbsp. coconut oil
- 3 tbsps. coconut flour
- 2¼ cups almond milk
- 1 tsp. onion powder
- 1 tsp. garlic powder
- 1 tsp. sea salt

DIRECTIONS:
1. Gently heat the coconut oil in a saucepan over medium heat, Don't let it get too hot or the flour will instantly burn.
2. Whisk in the coconut flour to make a thick paste.
3. Add the almond milk and bring to a boil. Boil for 2 minutes, then reduce the heat.
4. Add the onion powder, garlic powder and salt. Simmer until thickened.
5. Serve warm.

VARIATIONS TIP:
Once you've mastered the sauce base, you can add all kinds of seasonings to it to change it up. Try adding basil or fresh rosemary, or use it to make a mushroom soup. The options are almost endless.

Nutrition Info per Serving:
Calories: 83; Total Fat: 4.1 g; Carbohydrates: 8.1 g; Protein: 3.5 g; Fiber: 0.5 g

Easy Bean Chili

Prep Time: 5 minutes, Cook Time: 25 minutes, Serves: 4

INGREDIENTS:
- Cooking spray
- 1 small onion, chopped
- 2 garlic cloves, finely chopped
- 1 cup diced red bell pepper
- 1 (14.5-ounce, 411 g) can diced tomatoes
- 2 cups sprouted beans, black, kidney, or pinto
- 1 (8-ounce, 227 g) jar organic pasta sauce
- 2 tbsps. homemade barbecue sauce
- ¼ cup organic salsa, mild, medium, or hot
- ¼ cup organic fresh cilantro
- Dash ground cumin
- Dash chili powder

DIRECTIONS:
1. Use the cooking spray to spray a medium-size pot. Add the onions and sauté over medium heat for 5 minutes, or until they're soft and slightly caramelized.
2. Add all of the remaining ingredients to the pot. Stir to combine. Simmer for 20 minutes.
3. Serve immediately.

VARIATIONS TIP:
Fresh cilantro and dried cilantro have vastly different flavors. If you don't have fresh on hand, omit it altogether from the recipe.

Nutrition Info per Serving:
Calories: 101; Total Fat: 2.7 g; Carbohydrates: 18.5 g; Protein: 3.9 g; Fiber: 5.3 g

Curried Eggplant Sauce

Prep Time: 15 minutes, Cook Time: 5 minutes, Serves: 2

INGREDIENTS:

1 tsp. sesame oil
Juice of 1 lemon
1 roasted eggplant, cooled, with contents removed from the shell and reserved
1 tsp. sea salt
1 tsp. curry powder
Water, as needed
Cooked quinoa, for serving (optional)

DIRECTIONS:

1. Add the sesame oil, lemon juice, eggplant, salt and curry powder into a food processor, blend until smooth.
2. Transfer the eggplant mixture to a small saucepan, warm it over medium heat for about 5 minutes. Add some water to thin, if needed.
3. Serve as is, or over quinoa if using.

VARIATIONS TIP:
To roast eggplant, simply slice it, add a little sea salt, and bake in a 300°F(150°C) oven for about 30 minutes, or until it's soft. Or, you can roast it whole as called for here, but it will need to cook a bit longer depending on the size, until it's easily pierced with a sharp knife. Refrigerate until ready to use.

Nutrition Info per Serving:
Calories: 81; Total Fat: 2.8 g; Carbohydrates: 14.1 g; Protein: 2.4 g; Fiber: 8.4 g

Vinaigrette Dressing with Variations

Prep Time: 15 minutes, Cook Time: 0, Serves: ½ to 1 cup

INGREDIENTS:

FOR THE BASIC VINAIGRETTE
1½ tbsps. apple cider vinegar
1 tbsp. diced shallot
¾ cup avocado oil
Pinch sea salt
Pinch ground black pepper
FOR THE STRAWBERRY AND LIME VARIATION
¼ cup avocado oil
¼ cup strawberries
1 tbsp. brown rice syrup
¼ cup freshly squeezed lime juice
Pinch sea salt
Pinch ground black pepper
FOR THE LEMON AND THYME VARIATION
¾ cup avocado oil
Juice and zest of 1 large lemon
1½ tbsps. apple cider vinegar
1 tbsp. chopped fresh thyme leaves
1 tbsp. diced shallot
Pinch sea salt
Pinch ground black pepper

DIRECTIONS:

1. Add all ingredients for the vinaigrette dressing of your choice in a small bowl, whisk together until well combined. Adjust seasonings to your preference.
2. Place in an airtight container and store in the refrigerator.

VARIATIONS TIP:
To get the maximum flavor from the ingredients, make sure you use fresh herbs, seasonings, and fruit.

Nutrition Info per Serving:
Calories: 741; Fat: 81.82 g; Carbohydrates: 4.28 g; Protein: 0.59 g; Fiber: 0.5 g

Easy Homemade Sweet Barbecue Sauce

Prep Time: 20 minutes, Cook Time: 40 minutes, Serves: 1 cup

INGREDIENTS:

6 quartered plum tomatoes
¼ cup of chopped white onions
2 tsps. of onion powder
½ tsp. of ground ginger
2 tsps. pure sea salt
2 tbsps. of agave syrup
¼ tsp. of cayenne
⅛ tsp. of cloves
¼ cup of date sugar

DIRECTIONS:

1. In a blender, add all of the ingredients except the date sugar, and blend them thoroughly.
2. Pour the mixture into a saucepan and add the date sugar.
3. Cook the mixture over medium heat, stirring occasionally to prevent sticking until boiling.
4. Reduce the heat to a simmer. Use a lid to cover the saucepan and cook for 15 minutes, stirring often.
5. Blend the sauce with an immersion blender until it is smooth.
6. Continue to cook at low heat for about 10 minutes, until the sauce thickens.
7. After cooking, allow the mixture to cool before using.
8. Serve and enjoy!

Nutrition Info per Serving:
Calories: 490; Total Fat: 0.48 g; Carbohydrates: 127.67 g; Protein: 1.98 g; Fiber: 4 g

Lemon Cilantro Salad Dressing

Prep Time: 15 minutes, Cook Time: 0, Serves: 12

INGREDIENTS:
- 1 tsp. freshly squeezed lemon juice
- ½ cup coconut oil
- ½ cup chopped fresh cilantro
- ¼ cup apple cider vinegar
- ½ packet stevia
- ¼ tsp. sea salt

DIRECTIONS:
1. Add all of the ingredients into a blender.
2. Blend until the oil and vinegar emulsify and the cilantro is fully incorporated.

VARIATIONS TIP:
Don't use dried cilantro or coriander in this recipe. It doesn't taste remotely the same. Pick the freshest cilantro you can find and rinse it well. Cut off the stems if you prefer.

Nutrition Info per Serving:
Calories: 80; Total Fat: 9.1 g; Carbohydrates: 0.1 g; Protein: 0.3 g; Fiber: 0.4 g

Lime Papaya Seed and Mango Dressing

Prep Time: 10 minutes, Cook Time: 0, Serves: ½ cup

INGREDIENTS:
- ¼ cup of grape seed oil
- 1 cup of chopped mango
- 1 tsp. of ground papaya seeds
- 1 tsp. of basil
- 1 tsp. of agave syrup
- 2 tbsps. of lime juice
- 1 tsp. of onion powder
- ¼ tsp. of pure sea salt

DIRECTIONS:
1. In a blender, add all of the ingredients.
2. Blend for 1 minute until smooth.
3. Add it to a salad and enjoy!

VARIATIONS TIP:
According to your liking, you can alter the seasonings. Use this dressing within two days. Store it in a sealed glass jar in the refrigerator.

Nutrition Info per Serving:
Calories: 662; Total Fat: 57.67 g; Carbohydrates: 40.94 g; Protein: 3.03 g; Fiber: 4.1 g

Cashew Almond Cheese Sauce

Prep Time: 25 minutes, Cook Time: 0, Serves: 1 ½ cups

INGREDIENTS:
- 1 cup raw cashews
- ½ cup nutritional yeast
- 1 cup almond milk
- ½ tsp. sea salt

DIRECTIONS:
1. Place the cashews in a medium bowl, pour in enough room-temperature water to cover, allow to soak for 15 to 20 minutes. Drain and rinse.
2. Add the soaked cashews, nutritional yeast, almond milk and salt into a high-speed blender, blend them together until creamy and smooth.
3. Place in an airtight glass container and store in the refrigerator.

VARIATIONS TIP:
If you want to give your cheese sauce a yellow/orange color like traditional cheese, just add 1 to 2 pinches of ground turmeric.

Nutrition Info per Serving:
Calories: 272; Total Fat: 8.37 g; Carbohydrates: 30.25 g; Protein: 20.54 g; Fiber: 5.6 g

Simple Homemade Ketchup

Prep Time: 15 minutes, Cook Time: 25 minutes, Serves: 12

INGREDIENTS:
- 1 (6-ounce, 170 g) can unsweetened tomato paste
- ½ cup apple cider vinegar
- 1 packet stevia
- ½ cup brown rice syrup
- ⅛ tsp. garlic powder
- ¼ tsp. onion powder

DIRECTIONS:
1. Combine all of the ingredients in a saucepan, whisk them over medium heat until smooth.
2. Bring the mixture to a boil. Reduce the heat and simmer for 25 minutes, stirring frequently.
3. Place in the refrigerator to chill and serve cold.

VARIATIONS TIP:
If you freeze this, you might want to run it through a blender after defrosting to remix all the ingredients to the desired consistency, as it will separate.

Nutrition Info per Serving:
Calories: 51; Total Fat: 0.1 g; Carbohydrates: 13.4 g; Protein: 1 g; Fiber: 0.7 g

Chapter 13: Sauce and Dressing

Ginger Onion Sauce

Prep Time: 10 minutes, Cook Time: 0 (chill 1 hour), Serves: 1

INGREDIENTS:
¼ cup of diced Shallots
1 cup of grape seed oil
1 tbsp. of onion powder
½ tsp. of ginger
¼ tsp. of dill
½ tsp. of pure sea salt

DIRECTIONS:
1. Add all of the ingredients in a glass jar with a lid, and shake them well.
2. Place in the refrigerator and chill for at least 1 hour.
3. Serve and enjoy!

VARIATIONS TIP:
Use it within 2 weeks. Store in a glass jar with a lid in the refrigerator.
If you have a hand blender, mix all ingredients together. The sauce is prepared and you can use it immediately.

Nutrition Info per Serving:
Calories: 1966; Total Fat: 218.13 g; Carbohydrates: 9.05 g; Protein: 1.54 g; Fiber: 1.8 g

Lime Avocado Dressing

Prep Time: 15 minutes, Cook Time: 0, Serves: 12

INGREDIENTS:
1 avocado, peeled and pitted
½ cup coconut oil
¼ cup apple cider vinegar
1 tsp. freshly squeezed lime juice
¼ cup chopped fresh cilantro
1 tsp. cumin
1 tsp. garlic powder
1 tsp. onion powder
½ packet stevia
¼ tsp. sea salt

DIRECTIONS:
1. Combine all of the ingredients in a blender.
2. Blend until well mixed and the oil and vinegar emulsify.

VARIATIONS TIP:
If you like it spicy, add a jalapeño while blending.

Nutrition Info per Serving:
Calories: 101; Total Fat: 10.8 g; Carbohydrates: 1.2 g; Protein: 0.2 g; Fiber: 0.9 g

Easy Spiced Tomato Sauce

Prep Time: 10 minutes, Cook Time: 0, Serves: 1 cup

INGREDIENTS:
5 roma tomatoes
2 tbsps. of grape seed oil
1 pinch of basil
1 tsp. of oregano
1 tsp. of onion powder
2 tbsps. of agave syrup
2 tbsps. of minced onion
1 tsp. of pure sea salt

DIRECTIONS:
1. On the bottom of the roma tomatoes, make an X cut and place them into a pot of boiling water for just 1 minute.
2. Use a spoon to remove the tomatoes from the water and shock them, transfer them into cold water for 30 seconds.
3. Take them out and use your fingers or a knife to peel them immediately.
4. In a blender or a food processor, add all the ingredients and blend for 1 minute until smooth.
5. Serve and enjoy!

Nutrition Info per Serving:
Calories: 223; Total Fat: 1.15 g; Carbohydrates: 53.53 g; Protein: 6.93 g; Fiber: 5.9 g

Sesame Orange Dressing

Prep Time: 15 minutes, Cook Time: 0, Serves: 12

INGREDIENTS:
¼ cup apple cider vinegar
½ cup coconut oil
1 tbsp. dark sesame oil
3 tbsps. chopped scallions
2 tsps. toasted sesame seeds
1 tbsp. freshly squeezed orange juice
½ tsp. garlic powder
½ tsp. ground ginger
½ packet stevia
¼ tsp. sea salt

DIRECTIONS:
1. Add all of the ingredients into a blender.
2. Blend until the ingredients are well mixed and the vinegar and oil emulsify.

VARIATIONS TIP:
If you prefer the sharp taste of fresh ginger and garlic then, by all means, use fresh. Just grate them into the blender.

Nutrition Info per Serving:
Calories: 90; Total Fat: 1.1 g; Carbohydrates: 1.1 g; Protein: 0.9 g; Fiber: 1.4 g

Avocado Onion Sauce, page 172

Cucumber Dill and Lime Dressing, page 170

Easy Homemade Sweet Barbecue Sauce, page 166

Enchilada Sauce, page 165

Chapter 13: Sauce and Dressing

Cucumber Dill and Lime Dressing

Prep Time: 10 minutes, Cook Time: 0, Serves: ½ cup

INGREDIENTS:
- ¼ cup of avocado oil
- 1 cup of quartered cucumbers
- 1 tsp. of fresh dill
- 2 tsps. of agave syrup
- ½ tsp. of onion powder
- 1 tbsp. of lime juice

DIRECTIONS:
1. In a blender, combine all of the ingredients.
2. Blend for 1 minute until smooth.
3. Add it to a salad and enjoy!

VARIATIONS TIP:
Use the fresh dill.
Seasonings can be adjusted according to your liking. Use this dressing within two days. Store it in a glass jar in the refrigerator.

Nutrition Info per Serving:
Calories: 550; Total Fat: 55.02 g; Carbohydrates: 16.58 g; Protein: 1.23 g; Fiber: 1.5 g

Ginger Tomato Onion Dressing

Prep Time: 10 minutes, Cook Time: 0, Serves: ½ cup

INGREDIENTS:
- 1 tsp. of minced ginger
- 1 tbsp. of agave syrup
- 2 chopped plum tomatoes
- 2 tbsps. of sesame seeds
- 2 tbsps. of chopped onion
- 1 tbsp. of lime juice

DIRECTIONS:
1. In a blender, add all of the ingredients.
2. Blend for 1 minute until smooth.
3. Add it to a salad and enjoy!

VARIATIONS TIP:
Use fresh ginger.
Seasonings can be adjusted according to your liking. Use this dressing within two days. Store it in a glass jar in the refrigerator.

Nutrition Info per Serving:
Calories: 443; Total Fat: 10.5 g; Carbohydrates: 85.4 g; Protein: 9.01 g; Fiber: 8.8 g

Garlic Chimichurri Sauce

Prep Time: 10 minutes, Cook Time: 0, Serves: ½ cup

INGREDIENTS:
- ¼ cup avocado oil
- 1 handful fresh cilantro leaves
- 2 handfuls fresh parsley leaves
- 3 garlic cloves
- 1 tsp. red pepper flakes
- ¼ tsp. sea salt
- 2 tbsps. apple cider vinegar
- ½ tsp. freshly ground black pepper

DIRECTIONS:
1. Combine all of the ingredients in a blender, blend them together until well combined. Adjust seasonings, if needed.
2. Place in an airtight container and store in the refrigerator.

VARIATIONS TIP:
If you don't make it to use right away, the sauce will marinate in the refrigerator for up to 2 days.

Nutrition Info per Serving:
Calories: 532; Total Fat: 54.75 g; Carbohydrates: 11.9 g; Protein: 1.77 g; Fiber: 1.4 g

Quick Barbecue Sauce

Prep Time: 15 minutes, Cook Time: 25 minutes, Serves: 6

INGREDIENTS:
- 1 (8-ounce, 227 g) can tomato sauce
- 2 cups water
- 1 onion, chopped
- 2 tsps. paprika
- 2 tsps. chili powder
- ¼ cup apple cider vinegar
- 1 packet stevia

DIRECTIONS:
1. Combine all of the ingredients in a medium saucepan, bring them to a full boil.
2. Lower the heat and simmer for 20 minutes.
3. Serve immediately, or cool and place in an airtight container and chill in the refrigerator.

VARIATIONS TIP:
This is particularly good when made with peaches or mango. Just add ¼ cup when cooking for a sweet, fruity flavor.

Nutrition Info per Serving:
Calories: 36; Total Fat: 0.8 g; Carbohydrates: 7 g; Protein: 1.3 g; Fiber: 2.3 g

Italian Infused Grape Seed Oil

Prep Time: 5 minutes, Cook Time: 0 (infuse 30 minutes), Serves: 1

INGREDIENTS:

¾ cup of grape seed oil
1 tsp. of basil
1 tsp. of oregano
1 pinch of pure sea salt

DIRECTIONS:
1. Fill the grape seed oil in a glass jar with a lid or a squeeze bottle.
2. In a small bowl, mix the basil, oregano and salt together and add them to the jar or bottle.
3. Shake it and allow the oil to infuse for at least 24 hours.
4. Add it to a dish and enjoy.

Nutrition Info per Serving:
Calories: 1450; Total Fat: 163.54 g; Carbohydrates: 1.02 g; Protein: 0.43 g; Fiber: 0.7 g

Sweet Whipped Coconut Cream Topping

Prep Time: 10 minutes, plus overnight to chill, Cook Time: 0, Serves: ¾ cup

INGREDIENTS:

1 (13.5-ounce, 383 g) can full-fat coconut milk
2 tbsps. unrefined whole cane sugar, such as Sucanat

DIRECTIONS:
1. Place the coconut milk in the refrigerator to chill overnight, and up to 24 hours.
2. Open the can. The top half will be solid (coconut fat) and the bottom half will be liquid. In a mixing bowl, add the fat solids (save the liquid for another use). Mix on high speed until peaks form, about 2 to 3 minutes.
3. Add the sugar and use your hand to stir it gently until well blended, but not to overstir, softening the mixture.

VARIATIONS TIP:
Always keep 1 to 2 cans of coconut milk in the back of your refrigerator so you can make this at a moment's notice.

Nutrition Info per Serving:
Calories: 101; Total Fat: 0.41 g; Carbohydrates: 23.61 g; Protein: 1.48 g; Fiber: 2.3 g

Garlicky Sun-Dried Tomato Sauce

Prep Time: 10 minutes, Cook Time: 0, Serves: 4

INGREDIENTS:

3 tbsps. coconut oil
1 cup cherry tomatoes, halved
½ cup tightly packed sun-dried tomatoes
1 tbsp. tomato paste
1 tsp. sea salt
1 tsp. garlic powder
⅓ cup fresh basil

DIRECTIONS:
1. Combine all of the ingredients in a food processor.
2. Pulse to combine until it reaches your desired consistency.

VARIATIONS TIP:
The tomato paste is the key to the intense tomato flavor here. Don't leave it out.

Nutrition Info per Serving:
Calories: 132; Total Fat: 12.2 g; Carbohydrates: 6.1 g; Protein: 1.4 g; Fiber: 1.5 g

Almond Milk Coconut Sauce

Prep Time: 5 minutes, Cook Time: 10 minutes, Serves: 6

INGREDIENTS:

1 tbsp. coconut oil, melted
2 tbsps. coconut flour
½ cup vegetable broth
½ tsp. sea salt
2 tbsps. almond milk

DIRECTIONS:
1. Gently heat the coconut oil in a saucepan over medium heat. Don't let it get too hot or the flour will instantly burn.
2. Place the coconut flour in the pan and whisk to make a thick paste.
3. Whisk in the vegetable broth slowly. Bring to a boil and allow it to boil for 4 minutes, or until thickened.
4. Reduce the heat to low. Add the salt and almond milk. Continue to cook until the desired consistency.
5. Serve warm.

VARIATIONS TIP:
If you do burn the flour, throw it out and start over. There's no rescuing it. Live and learn!

Nutrition Info per Serving:
Calories: 35; Total Fat: 2.5 g; Carbohydrates: 2.8 g; Protein: 1.8 g; Fiber: 0.8 g

Easy Spicy Infused Oil

Prep Time: 5 minutes, Cook Time: 0 (soak 24 hours), Serves: 1

INGREDIENTS:

1 tbsp. of crushed cayenne pepper

¾ cup of grape seed oil

DIRECTIONS:

1. Fill the grape seed oil in a glass jar with a lid or a squeeze bottle.
2. Add the crushed cayenne pepper to the jar or bottle.
3. Shake it well and allow the oil to infuse for at least 24 hours.
4. Add it to a dish and enjoy!

Nutrition Info per Serving:
Calories: 95; Total Fat: 1.1 g; Carbohydrates: 23.51 g; Protein: 1.45 g; Fiber: 2.5 g

Avocado Onion Sauce

Prep Time: 10 minutes, Cook Time: 0, Serves: 1 cup

INGREDIENTS:

1 ripe avocado
2 tbsps. of minced onion
1 pinch of basil
½ tsp. of oregano
½ tsp. of onion powder
½ tsp. of pure sea salt

DIRECTIONS:

1. Cut the Avocado in half, peel it and remove the seed.
2. Chop it into small pieces and place into a food processor.
3. Place all the remaining ingredients in the processor and blend for 2 to 3 minutes until smooth.
4. Serve and enjoy!

Nutrition Info per Serving:
Calories: 329; Total Fat: 29.51 g; Carbohydrates: 18.92 g; Protein: 4.27 g; Fiber: 13.9 g

Quick Ranch Dressing

Prep Time: 2 hours, 10 minutes, Cook Time: 0, Serves: 12

INGREDIENTS:

1 cup raw cashews, soaked for 2 hours and drained
¼ cup apple cider vinegar
¼ cup freshly squeezed lemon juice
1 tbsp. finely chopped scallions
1 tsp. garlic powder
2 tbsps. diced red onion
½ packet stevia
½ tsp. sea salt
1 tbsp. chopped fresh parsley
½ tsp. finely chopped fresh dill

DIRECTIONS:

1. Add all of the ingredients except the parsley and dill into a blender, purée until smooth and creamy.
2. Add the parsley and dill. Pulse quickly just to combine.
3. Place in an airtight container. Chill in the refrigerator for 1 hour before serving.

VARIATIONS TIP:
If you want to make a chipotle-ranch dressing, add one-half of a chipotle pepper while blending, or to taste.

Nutrition Info per Serving:
Calories: 70; Total Fat: 5.3 g; Carbohydrates: 4.3 g; Protein: 1.9 g; Fiber: 3.3 g

Nondairy Tzatziki Dill Sauce

Prep Time: 15 minutes, Cook Time: 0, Serves: 2 cups

INGREDIENTS:

1 cucumber, peeled and sliced
2 garlic cloves
1 cup raw cashews
½ cup water
2 tbsps. tahini
3 tbsps. chopped fresh dill, divided
4 tbsps. freshly squeezed lemon juice
1 tbsp. chopped fresh parsley leaves
½ to ¾ tsp. sea salt
⅛ tsp. freshly ground black pepper

DIRECTIONS:

1. Combine all of the ingredients in a high-speed blender, blend them together until creamy and smooth. Adjust the seasonings, if needed.
2. Pour into a small bowl, and stir in the remaining 2 tablespoons of the dill.
3. Place in an airtight container and store in the refrigerator.

VARIATIONS TIP:
Fresh dill will give you the optimum flavor, but you could also substitute dried dill.

Nutrition Info per Serving:
Calories: 197; Total Fat: 14.61 g; Carbohydrates: 15.69 g; Protein: 5.9 g; Fiber: 2.4 g

Creamy Brazil Nut Sauce

Prep Time: 15 minutes, Cook Time: 0 (soak 3 hours), Serves: 6 cups

INGREDIENTS:

2 cups of raw brazil nuts
1 tsp. of onion powder
2 tsps. of pure sea salt
½ tsp. of cayenne powder
1 ½ cups of homemade hempseed milk
2 tbsps. of grape seed oil
Juice from a half of Lime
1 ½ cups of spring water

DIRECTIONS:

1. Add the Brazil Nuts in a pot, pour in the water and soak for at least 3 hours or overnight. Pour out the water and rinse them.
2. In a blender or food processor, add all of the ingredients and ½ cup of the spring water.
3. Blend them together for about 2 minutes.
4. Pour in ½ cup of the spring water and blend it again.
5. Continue to add more water and blend the mixture until it achieves a creamy consistency.
6. Cool it before serving.

Nutrition Info per Serving:
Calories: 327; Total Fat: 30.99 g; Carbohydrates: 9.1 g; Protein: 8.45 g; Fiber: 3.4 g

Vanilla Coconut Whipped Cream

Prep Time: 15 minutes, Cook Time: 0, Serves: 8

INGREDIENTS:

1 (13-ounce, 369 g) can full-fat unsweetened coconut milk, chilled
1 vanilla bean, split lengthwise and seeds scraped out
1 packet stevia

DIRECTIONS:

1. Open the coconut milk can. Scoop out the thick layer of coconut milk fat with a spoon. Pour it into a large bowl. Beat with a whisk or hand mixer just as you would regular whipping cream, until fluffy.
2. Add the vanilla bean seeds and stevia, whip for another minute or so.
3. Use immediately or keep covered in the refrigerator for one to two days.

VARIATIONS TIP:
Coconut milk takes longer to whip than whipping cream. Just be patient! Also, if you want to make it sweeter, use coconut sugar instead of stevia.

Nutrition Info per Serving:
Calories: 197; Total Fat: 21.2 g; Carbohydrates: 2.8 g; Protein: 2 g; Fiber: 0.1 g

Appendix 1: Measurement Conversion Chart

Volume Equivalents (Dry)

US STANDARD	METRIC (APPROXIMATE)
1/8 teaspoon	0.5 mL
1/4 teaspoon	1 mL
1/2 teaspoon	2 mL
3/4 teaspoon	4 mL
1 teaspoon	5 mL
1 tablespoon	15 mL
1/4 cup	59 mL
1/2 cup	118 mL
3/4 cup	177 mL
1 cup	235 mL
2 cups	475 mL
3 cups	700 mL
4 cups	1 L

Temperatures Equivalents

FAHRENHEIT (F)	CELSIUS(C) (APPROXIMATE)
225 °F	107 °C
250 °F	120 °C
275 °F	135 °C
300 °F	150 °C
325 °F	160 °C
350 °F	180 °C
375 °F	190 °C
400 °F	205 °C
425 °F	220 °C
450 °F	235 °C
475 °F	245 °C
500 °F	260 °C

Volume Equivalents (Liquid)

US STANDARD	US STANDARD (OUNCES)	METRIC (APPROXIMATE)
2 tablespoons	1 fl.oz.	30 mL
1/4 cup	2 fl.oz.	60 mL
1/2 cup	4 fl.oz.	120 mL
1 cup	8 fl.oz.	240 mL
1 1/2 cup	12 fl.oz.	355 mL
2 cups or 1 pint	16 fl.oz.	475 mL
4 cups or 1 quart	32 fl.oz.	1 L
1 gallon	128 fl.oz.	4 L

Weight Equivalents

US STANDARD	METRIC (APPROXIMATE)
1 ounce	28 g
2 ounces	57 g
5 ounces	142 g
10 ounces	284 g
15 ounces	425 g
16 ounces (1 pound)	455 g
1.5 pounds	680 g
2 pounds	907 g

Appendix 2: Recipes Index

A

Alkaline Chickpeas Hot Dogs 53
Alkaline Veggies Fried Rice 45
Alkaline Zucchini Green Soup 95
Almond and Coconut Stuffed Dates 135
Almond and Sweet Potato Waffles 98
Almond Milk Coconut Sauce 171
Almond Spiced Baked Onion Rings 26
Almond Tarragon Crackers 110
Amaranth and Black Quinoa Porridge 20
Amaranth and Chickpea Pancakes 106
Amaranth Bowl with Butternut Squash and Collard Greens 70
Amaranth Chickpea Salad 79
Amaranth Porridge with Walnuts 20
Amaranth Walnut Polenta 20
Apple and Berries Smoothie 128
Apple and Dandelion Green Smoothie 118
Apple Banana Sea Moss Delight 130
Apple Grape Dates Waldorf Salad 61
Apple Pie Sea Moss Smoothie 128
Apple Potato Rice Bowl 153
Apple Slices with Peanut Butter and Granola 132
Apple, Avocado and Pear Smoothie 123
Artichoke, Potato and Asparagus Soup 85
Arugula, Zucchini and Pesto Grain Bowl 145
Asian-Style Vegetable Salad 68
Avocado and Apple Juice Mix 155
Avocado and Orange Salad 65
Avocado Blueberry Green Smoothie 121
Avocado Cucumber Smoothie 122
Avocado Lime and Tomato Toast 112
Avocado Onion Sauce 172
Avocado Toast with Spinach Basil Walnut Pesto 26
Avocado Tomato and Basil Pasta 45
Avocado Tomato Guacamole 42
Avocado, Banana and Strawberry Ice Cream 143
Avocado, Cucumber and Quinoa Salad 67
Avocado, Kale and Sprouts Salad 80
Avocado, Raspberry and Dates Moss Drink 155
Avocado, Zucchini and Basil Soup with Pumpkin Seeds 83

B

Baby Potato Fries with Mushroom 26
Baby Tomato and Kale Salad 72
Baked Apples with Walnuts 15
Baked Buffalo Cauliflowers 37
Baked Cheesy Potato and Onion 24
Baked Garlicky Almond Avocado Fries 132
Baked Grapefruit and Coconut 136
Baked Nutty Macaroni 45
Baked Oatmeal Stuffed Apple Crumble 135
Baked Onion Rings 105
Baked Peach Coconut Cobbler 133
Baked Raisins Stuffed Apples 133
Baked Spelt Biscuits 103
Baked Squash and Apples 11
Baked Sweet Potato Fries 39
Baked Vanilla Bean and Cinnamon Granola 47
Baked Vanilla Fruit Granola 133
Banana Alkaline Breakfast Bars 14
Banana Almond Spilts with Cherry 140
Banana Date Muffins 15
Banana Herbal Drink 161
Banana Mango Smoothie 128
Banana Sea Moss Green Drink 161
Banana Veggies Fries 141
Banana Walnut Muffins 137
Banana, Raspberry and Lime Smoothie 125
Barbecued Broccoli Rice and Pineapple Bowl 145
Barbecued Mango Zucchini Stuffed Mushroom Sliders 23

Basic Pie Crust   111
Bell Pepper, Zucchini and Mushroom Bowl   146
Berry Mix Sea Moss Milk   155
Berry Peach Sea Moss Smoothie   126
Berry Smoothie Bowl with Mango   152
Black Bean Pumpkin Chili   52
Black Bean Quinoa and Vegetable Bowl   146
Black Bean Vegetable Tostada with Avocado   54
Black Sapote and Nuts Pudding   111
Blackberry Banana Bars   142
Blackberry Lime Jam   139
Blackberry, Banana and Avocado Smoothie   120
Blueberry Banana Sea Moss Pudding   113
Blueberry Coconut Spelt Pancakes   113
Blueberry Flax Oats Muffins   17
Breakfast Mixed Vegetable Fajitas   13
Breakfast Quinoa Melon Smoothie   128
Breakfast Tamarind, Arugula and Cucumber Drink   155
Broccoli, Asparagus and Quinoa Salad   74
Broccolini, Bok Choy and Rice Soup   96
Broiled Chinese-Style Green Beans   53
Brown Rice Stevia Porridge   50
Brussels Sprouts with Ginger Sauce   23
Burro Banana Walnut Muffin   109
Butternut Squash Pie   102

C

Cabbage Almond Slaw   78
Carrot Fennel Slaw with Dijon Vinaigrette   25
Carrot Fruit Breakfast Porridge   15
Carrot, Hemp Seed and Oat Muffins   17
Cashew Almond Cheese Sauce   167
Cauliflower Popcorn   34
Cauliflower, Almond and Date Porridge   34
Chamomile and Bromide Plus Revitalizing Tea   161
Chayote Mushroom Chickpea Stew   87
Cheesy Baked Kale Chips   35
Cherry and Watermelon Smoothie   118
Chia Seed – Cashew Cookies   106
Chia Seed and Strawberry Overnight Oats Parfait   136

Chickpea Falafel   52
Chickpea Flour Vegetable Quiche   116
Chickpea Mushroom Loaf   55
Chickpea Rainbow Salad with Mango-Lemon Salsa   63
Chickpea Salad Burritos   17
Chickpea Sloppy Joe   58
Chickpea, Mushroom and Zucchini Bowl   145
Chilled Berry Lemon and Mint Soup   87
Chilled Mango Lime Pepper Slaw   140
Chilled Pumpkin Seed-Protein Oats Balls   13
Chilled Vanilla Granola Bars   13
Chilled Zucchini Cucumber and Lime Soup   85
Chopped Veggie Salad with Garlic-Avocado Dressing   63
Cinnamon Mango Quinoa Porridge   49
Coconut and Date Energy Balls with Walnuts   114
Coconut Banana Candy Coins   141
Coconut Cashew Almond and Date Bars   110
Coconut Chocolate and Date Cookies   113
Coconut White Sauce   165
Coconut, Raspberry and Avocado Smoothie Bowl   147
Cranberry, Brussel Sprouts and Quinoa Salad   76
Cream Berry Peach Parfait   143
Creamy Banana Bowl with Strawberry and Almond   147
Creamy Brazil Nut Sauce   173
Creamy Coconut Squash Soup   86
Creamy Cucumber Avocado Gazpacho   94
Creamy Mushroom Clams Chowder   86
Creamy Mushroom Coconut Soup   85
Creamy Onion Mushroom Soup   93
Creamy Roasted Carrot and Tomato Soup   83
Creamy Spinach Zucchini Soup   87
Creamy Strawberry and Date Jar   163
Creamy Vegan Mayonnaise Deviled Eggs   14
Cucumber Arugula Detox Salad   80
Cucumber Asparagus Hummus Sandwiches   23
Cucumber Avocado Gazpacho   94
Cucumber Dill and Lime Dressing   170
Curried Almond and Raisin Tofu Salad with Greens   61
Curried Eggplant Sauce   166

D

Dandelion and Bromide Plus Cleansing Drink 156
Dandelion Liver Cleansing Tea 156
Date Almond Raspberry Smoothie 120
Date and Banana Moss Drink 156
Date and Watermelon Tofu "Feta" Salad 62
Date Carrot Cake Cookies with Cashew Cream Frosting 112
Date Cashew Oat Bites with Raisins 46
Date Sea Moss Drink 162
Dates, Spelt and Raisin Cookies 98
Delicious Onion Chickpea Nuggets 59

E

Easy Almond and Coconut Milks 162
Easy Baked Sweet Potato and Apple 32
Easy Bean Chili 165
Easy Healthy Hummus 58
Easy Homemade Cashew and Almond Butters 103
Easy Homemade PB Frosting 57
Easy Homemade Sweet Barbecue Sauce 166
Easy Homemade Tortillas 101
Easy Roasted Garlic Cauliflower Soup 91
Easy Roasted Okra Bites 105
Easy Spelt Pasta 46
Easy Spiced Tomato Sauce 168
Easy Spicy Infused Oil 172
Enchilada Sauce 165

F

Flourless Cashew and Pumpkin Seed Cookies 109
Fonio and Mixed Veggies Salad 79
Fragrant Chamomile Tea 158
Fresh Fruit with Vanilla Cashew and Lemon Cream 139
Fresh Herb Potato Salad with Lime Garlic Dressing 73
Fresh Salsa Fresca 61
Fresh Vegetable Pizza with Garlic Tahini-Beet Spread 41
Frozen Cashew Butter Fudge 102
Fruit and Veggie Smoothie 118
Fruity Banana Sea Moss Milk 158

G

Gallbladder Cleansing Tea 158
Gallbladder Rhubarb Cleansing Tea 156
Garlic Almond Breadsticks 30
Garlic Bell Pepper-Stuffed Portobello Mushrooms 32
Garlic Broccoli Bites 27
Garlic Broccoli Carrot Bake 42
Garlic Cashew Cream–Stuffed Mushrooms 38
Garlic Chimichurri Sauce 170
Garlic Coconut and Jalapeño Soup 84
Garlic Ginger and Pear Soup 84
Garlic Lentil and Sweet Potato Taco Wraps 34
Garlic Mushroom and Lentil Salad with Lime Tahini Dressing 68
Garlic Mushroom Pâté 32
Garlic Onion and Kale Soup 84
Garlic Parsnip Leek Soup 88
Garlic-Jicama Fries with Scallion Cashew Dip 101
Garlicky Broccoli and Potato Soup 88
Garlicky Green Olive Pasta Salad 62
Garlicky Orange Broccoli Salad 68
Garlicky Parsley and Tahini Hummus 55
Garlicky Spaghetti Squash Hash Browns 11
Garlicky Sun-Dried Tomato Sauce 171
Ginger Date Spice Pudding 98
Ginger Green Beans Almondine 52
Ginger Kale and Lemon Green Smoothie 119
Ginger Onion Sauce 168
Ginger Pear Green Sparkling Smoothie 121
Ginger Rhubarb Pumpkin Pie 105
Ginger Tomato Onion Dressing 170
Grilled Romaine Lettuce with Lime Dressing 81
Grilled Vegetable Stuffed Mushrooms 38

H

Hawaiian Fruit Veggie Salsa 63
Healthy Blueberry Muffins 102
Healthy Crackers with Sesame Seeds 116
Healthy Eggplant Hummus 57

Healthy Kamut Porridge with Dates   19
Healthy Orange Banana Smoothie   125
Healthy Spiced Mushroom Bowl   150
Healthy Stir-Fry Mixed Vegetables   29
Healthy Walnut Milk   156
Healthy Watercress Cucumber Salad   80
Hearty Tomato Quinoa Bowl   152
Hemp Seed and Banana Chard Smoothie   126
Herbed Almond Crackers   110
Herbed Breakfast Bean Sausage   18
Homemade Apple Butter   134
Homemade Aquafaba   163
Homemade Chocolate Cherry Smoothie   121
Homemade Easy Chickpea Quinoa Burgers   53
Homemade Easy Roasted Vegetables   42
Homemade Gazpacho Smoothie   122
Homemade Nutty Amaranth   18
Homemade Ravioli   115
Homemade Roated Garlic Cabbage   30
Hummus, Carrots and Pesto Lettuce Wraps   42

I

Indian Curried Quinoa Vegetable Bowl   146
Irish Sea Moss Gel   160
Irish Walnuts Moss Milkshake   129
Italian Infused Grape Seed Oil   171

J

Jalapeño, Cilantro and Lentil "Burgers"   25
Jamaican Jerk Vegetable Patties   41

K

Kale and Almond Stuffed Avocados   142
Kale Apple Green Sea Moss Drink   162
Kale Detox Smoothie   126
Kale Sweet Potato and Onion Breakfast Hash   11
Kale Tomato and Avocado Salad   78
Kale, Avocado and Banana Smoothie   119
Kamut Squash and Chickpeas Soup   92

Key Lime Dill Tea   157
Kiwi, Blueberry and Hemp Seed Smoothie   126

L

Lemon and Red Lentil Pasta Salad with Sautéed Vegetables   65
Lemon Blueberry and Banana Soft Serve   143
Lemon Cashew Tarragon Soup   93
Lemon Cilantro Salad Dressing   167
Lentil and Pasta Bowl with Basil Cider Dressing   147
Lentil Tacos with Onions and Bell Peppers   39
Lentil, Carrot and Potato Stew   88
Lettuce, Kale and Peach Protein Smoothie   120
Lettuce, Zucchini and Hummus Wrap   37
Lime Avocado Dressing   168
Lime Dandelion and Strawberry Salad   72
Lime Papaya Seed and Mango Dressing   167
Lime Summer Fruit Salad   62
Linden Immune Boosting Tea   157
Liver-Kidney Dandelion Cleansing Tea   157

M

Mango and Mixed Veggies Salad   75
Mango Banana Sea Moss Drink   158
Mango Kiwi and Cashew Smoothie   121
Maple Oat Coconut Flax Granola   12
Margherita Pizza with Veggies   12
Mashed Chickpeas   59
Mashed Potato Bowl with Green Peas   151
Mexican Style Black Bean Avocado Bowl   153
Mixed Berry Banana Smoothie   123
Mixed Berry Chia Seed Coconut Pudding   137
Mixed Melon Salad   66
Mixed Vegetable Fried Rice   49
Mixed Vegetable Pancakes   38
Mixed Vegetable Potpie   39
Morning Mixed Vegetables   43
Mushroom Gravy with Walnuts   91
Mushroom Pepper Fajitas   18

N

No Baking Fig Almond Balls 108
Nondairy Sour Cashew Cream 99
Nondairy Tzatziki Dill Sauce 172
Nori Avocado Zucchini Burritos 19
Nori Vegetable Rolls with Avocado-Jalapeño Spread 35
Nut Cheesecake with Strawberry and Mango 108
Nutty Banana Berry Chia Pudding 132
Nutty Coconut Sea Moss Smoothie 120
Nutty Mixed Berry Smoothie 127
Nutty Spinach, Artichoke and Tomato Dip 36
Nutty Strawberry Shake 130
Nutty Vanilla Banana Smoothie 129

O

Olive and Mixed Vegetable Salad 79
Onion and Butternut Squash Soup 94
Onion Rye Crackers 100
Onion Sautéed Kale 40
Orange and Banana Bromide Drink 158
Orange Arugula Salad 80
Overnight Mango Banana Oats 12
Over-Night Marinated Beans Carrot Salad 74

P

Papaya, Mango and Raspberry Smoothie 125
Pasta with Alkaline Sauce and Veggies 43
Peach and Raspberry Moss Drink 160
Peach Banana Muffin with Walnuts 104
Peach Basil Salad with Sweet Orange Dressing 64
Peach Cilantro Salsa Salad with Sweet Lemon Tahini Dressing 64
Peach, Orange and Kale Smoothie 125
Pear Nachos and Almond Butter Drizzle with Almond 137
Pineapple and Coconut Oatmeal Bowl with Pumpkin Seeds 150
Pineapple Banana and Kale Smoothie 119
Pineapple Cabbage Salad with Garlic-Lime Vinaigrette 65
Pineapple Spinach Smoothie 118
Potato, Cauliflower and Broccoli Mash 31
Prodigiosa Kidney Cleansing Tea 160
Pumpkin Apple and Date Soup with Raisins 89

Q

Quick Barbecue Sauce 170
Quick Blueberry-Banana Ice Cream 141
Quick Frozen Banana and Protein Breakfast Bowl 148
Quick Ranch Dressing 172
Quinoa and Wild Rice with Cherries 50
Quinoa Eggplant and Tomato Bowl 148
Quinoa Vegetable Casserole 54
Quinoa Vegetable Stuffed Peppers 37

R

Raspberry Sea Moss Coconut Drink 163
Recovery Strawberry and Watermelon Smoothie 127
Red Pepper Tapenade Eggplant Rollups 28
Red Quinoa Cherry Bowl 151
Respiratory and Elderberry Syrup 160
Respiratory Mullein and Guaco Cleansing Tea 160
Revitalizing Onion and Chickpea Dish 59
Roasted Artichoke Salad with Sesame Seed Dressing 69
Roasted Beet and Kale Salad with Lemon-Garlic Dressing 75
Roasted Broccoli Salad with Spicy Cashew Dressing 72
Roasted Carrot and Onion Salad with Cashew-Miso Dressing 70
Roasted Carrot Soup 96
Roasted Chickpea and Avocado Salad 75
Roasted Chickpea and Kale 57
Roasted Garlic 27
Roasted Vegetable Salad 69
Roasted Zucchini Lasagna 35
Romaine Lettuce and Onion Salad 77
Root Vegetable Chips 30
Rosemary, Carrot and Sweet Potato Medallions 31
Russian Style Beet Salad 69

S

Santa's Ginger Coconut Snaps 100

Sautéed Broccoli Carrot Bowl　　151
Sautéed Eggplant and Spinach with Quinoa　24
Sautéed Onion and Strawberry Dandelion Salad　　73
Sea Vegetables Salad　　78
Self-Frosting Pineapple Carrot Cake　108
Sesame and Hemp Seed Oatmeal Cookies　　99
Sesame Orange Dressing　　168
Shredded Squash Tomato Bowl　　151
Simple Homemade Ketchup　　167
South of the Border Chopped Salad 79
Southern Collard Green and Okra Bowl　　148
Spelt Banana Walnut Bread　　19
Spelt Banana Walnut Pancakes　　111
Spiced Chickpea French Fries　　100
Spiced Flatbread 99
Spiced Mixed Vegetable Soup　　92
Spiced Party Mix 142
Spiced Tomato Bean and Bell Pepper Soup　　91
Spiced Tomato Okra Curry 29
Spiced Zucchini Dish　　43
Spicy Eggplant and Bell Pepper Stir-Fry　　24
Spicy Garlic Almonds　　112
Spicy Soursop and Kale Squash Soup　　94
Spicy Vegetable and Squash "Noodle" Salad　81
Spicy Wakame Pepper Salad with Sesame Seeds　　77
Spinach and Strawberry Avocado Salad　　77
Spinach Cucumber Liquid Guacamole　　119
Spinach Peach Green Smoothie　　127
Spinach, Blueberry and Mango Smoothie　　123
Spring Salad with Walnuts 77
Squash "Noodles" with Tomato Spaghetti Sauce　　40
Squash and Mushroom Soup　　89
Squash and Onion Soup　　83
Stick Salad　　76
Stir Fried Kale Mushroom Wild Rice 49
Stir Fried Mushroom Wild Rice　　49
Strawberry Sea Moss Drink 157
Strawberry Spelt Sorbet　　101
Strawberry Spinach Salad with Mustard Dressing　　67
Stuffed Mushroom Mini-Pizzas　　25

Stuffed Sweet Potato with Broccoli-Almond Pesto　　27
Summer Fruit Vanilla Pops 141
Summer Veggies Salad　　76
Sunshine Fruit Smoothie　　127
Super Kale Quinoa Bowl　　152
Sushi Avocado Hand Roll　　14
Sweet Blueberry and Chia Seed Vanilla Cobbler　　134
Sweet Chia Seed Fruit Jam 140
Sweet Dates Green Drink　　161
Sweet Hempseed Milk　　157
Sweet Oatmeal Porridge with Mango-Chia Fruit Jam　　20
Sweet Peach Smoothie　　128
Sweet Potato "Toast" with Spicy Garlic Avocado Topping 28
Sweet Potato Slices with Garlic Artichoke Spread　　40
Sweet Thumbprint Cookies with Blueberry–Chia Seed Jam　135
Sweet Whipped Coconut Cream Topping　　171

T

Tahini Fennel-Seasoned Falafel with Hummus Dressing 55
Tahini Hummus with Crudités　　57
Teff Chickpea Sausage　　58
Thai-Style Vegetable Salad 74
Thanksgiving Pumpkin Pudding　　106
The Hollywood Fruit Bowl 152
Tofu Salad　　64
Tomato Mushroom Stuffed Eggplant　　36
Tomato Zoodles with Avocado Sauce　　28
Triple Berry Protein Coconut Smoothie　　127
Tropical Piña Smoothie　　122

V

Vanilla Almond and Quinoa Muffins 104
Vanilla Apple Pie Crumble 136
Vanilla Banana and Cashew Cream 140
Vanilla Bean, Coconut and Cashew Truffles　　104
Vanilla Coconut Ice Cream Sundae with Fruit 122
Vanilla Coconut Whipped Cream　　173

Vanilla Orange Apple Pie   114

Vanilla Pumpkin Banana Drink   163

Vanilla Rice Treats 46

Vanilla Snickerdoodle Cookies   103

Vanilla Spiced Quinoa Pumpkin Casserole   36

Vegan "Beef" Stew   92

Vegan Baked Portobello with Avocado   21

Vegan Dandelion Detox Smoothie   123

Vegan Mushroom Chickpea Fritters 109

Vegan Mushroom Chowder   93

Vegetable and Blueberry Salad with Roasted Garlic and Miso Dressing   66

Vegetable and Garbanzo Bean Burger   54

Vegetable Salad Lettuce Wrap   76

Vegetable Spelt Noodles Soup   95

Vegetarian Chickpea Mushroom Sausage Links   114

Vinaigrette Dressing with Variations 166

W

Wakame Lime Salad   78

Walnut Date Balls with Sesame Seeds   111

Walnut Kamut Porridge   19

Walnut, Spinach and Basil Pesto with Pasta   47

Warm Garlic Asparagus Salad with Lemon-Cashew Dressing 66

Warm Garlic Ginger and Lemon Smoothie   130

Warm Garlic Sweet Potato Salad with Spicy Cashew Cilantro Dressing 67

Warm Spinach Mushroom Salad   73

Watercress Avocado and Onion Salad   81

Watermelon Greens Salad with Basil Vinaigrette   134

Watermelon Jalapeño Gazpacho   89

Watermelon Lime Refresher   161

Watermelon, Strawberries and Coconut Drink   162

Whipped Aquafaba Cream 58

Wild Rice and Broccoli Bowl with Roasted Garlic Cashew Sauce   150

Wild Rice, Mushroom Leek and Miso Soup   47

Winter Warm Fruit Compote   139

Z

Zucchini and Kale Pesto with Spaghetti Squash   29

Zucchini Banana Bread Pancakes with Walnuts   114

Zucchini Chickpea and Kale Soup   86

Zucchini Hummus and Lettuce Wrap   21

Zucchini Kale and Amaranth Patties 115

Zucchini Linguine with Avocado Sauce   31

Zucchini, Avocado and Dandelion Green Smoothie   129

Zucchini, Radish and Spring Greens Salad   70

lentil
Stevia, Kiwi,
natural flavor,

Most
Poly unsaturated
fats/oils.

orange, grapefruit,
Pineapple, milk, cheese
Sugar, Calcium chloride,
erythritol, Wheat, tomatoe,
Chicken, Beef, Pecan, Walnut,
Sunflour oil, vegatable oil/
Canola oil,

Made in the USA
Monee, IL
14 August 2023